WEST
EUROPEAN
POLITICS

Volume 21   Number 3

July 1998

A FRANK CASS JOURNAL

WEST EUROPEAN POLITICS

Editors: **Gordon Smith,** London School of Economics and Political Science
Vincent Wright, Nuffield College, Oxford
Reviews Editor: **Mark Donovan,** University of Wales, Cardiff

Editorial Board

Articles appearing in this journal are abstracted and indexed in *Social Science Index, Social Science Abstracts, Political Science Abstracts, International Political Science Abstracts, ABC Pol Sci, Sociological Abstracts* and *British Humanities Index* among others.

Manuscripts, editorial communications, books for review and advertisement enquiries should be directed to The Administrative Editor, *West European Politics*, at the address given below.

Annual subscription: (Vol.21 1998)
Institutions £170.00/$245.00 postage included
Individuals £40.00/$65.00 postage included
Single issue and back issue prices available from the publisher.

West European Politics is a refereed journal. Authors should consult the Notes for Contributors at the back of the journal before submitting their final draft. The editors cannot accept responsibility for any damage to or loss of manuscripts. Statements of fact or opinion appearing in *West European Politics* are solely those of the authors and do not imply endorsement by the editors or publisher.

Published in January, April, July and October

© Frank Cass & Co. Ltd., 1998

900 Eastern Avenue, Ilford, Essex IG2 7HH, UK
Tel: + 44 (0)181 599 8866; Fax: +44 (0)181 599 0984; E-mail: info@frankcass.com
Website: http://www.frankcass.com

Printed in Great Britain by Antony Rowe Ltd., Chippenham, Wilts.

Contents

**For details of past and future contents of this and our other journals
please visit our website at *http://www.frankcass.com/jnls***

Book Reviews

About the Contributors

Alexander Warleigh is a Lecturer in Politics of the European Union at the University of Reading, where he also holds a Research Fellowship. Formerly a researcher in the European Parliament, he has published work both on that institution and the Committee of the Regions.

Simon Hix is a Lecturer in EU Politics and Policy in the Government Department and European Institute, at the London School of Economics and Political Science. His recent publications include *Political Parties in the European Union* (Macmillan 1997), with Chris Lord, and *Reconsidering European Migration Policies* (Migration Policy Group, 1996). He is completing a book on *The Political System of the European Union* (Macmillan). His current research focuses on developing a party-political model of the EU legislative process and testing it on the operation of the co-decision procedure before and after the Amsterdam Treaty.

Robert Elgie is a Lecturer in Politics at the University of Limerick. He has published in the areas of French politics and political leadership, and has just co-authored a study of government and central bank relations with Helen Thompson.

Robert Geyer is a Lecturer in the Department of Politics at the University of Liverpool. His recent and forthcoming publications include: *The Uncertain Union: British and Norwegian Social Democrats in an Integrating Europe* (1997); *Globalization, Europeanization, and the End of Scandinavian Social Democracy?* (1998); and *EU Social Policy: An Introduction and Exploration* (1998/99). He is currently engaged in projects on EU social inclusion/exclusion policy, the impact of the EU on Norwegian citizenship, and the relevance of complexity theory to social science.

Jonas Hinnfors, PhD, is a *Docent* (Reader) in political science at the Department of Political Science, Göteborg University, Sweden. His field of expertise is public policy and political economy.

Jon Pierre, PhD, is a Professor in the Department of Government, University of Strathclyde, Scotland and Adjunct Professor in Political Science at the University of Pittsburgh. He specialises in comparative analyses in public policy, public administration, political economy and urban politics.

Patrick Le Galès is CNRS Senior Research Fellow at CEVIPOF (Sciences-Po/CNRS) and Associate Professor of Sociology and Politics at Sciences-Po Paris. His most recent books are: *Regions in Europe* (1998) edited with Christian Lequesne and *Villes en Europe, acteurs et sociétés locales* (1997) edited with Arnaldo Bagnasco.

Alan Harding is Professor of Urban Policy and Politics at the European Institute for Urban Affairs, at the John Moores University of Liverpool. His books include *European Cities towards 2000* (1994) (with J. Dawson, R. Evans and M. Parkinson) and *Regional Government, an economic solution?* (1996).

Hervé Michel is currently conducting research into British local government at St Antony's College, University of Oxford, having completed a doctorate in 1997, at the University of Rennes I, entitled 'Intercommunalities and Local Governments', which will be published by L'Harmattan in 1998.

Sarah Waters is a Lecturer in the Department of French, University of Leeds and has published numerous articles on French and Italian politics.

Moshe Maor is a Senior Lecturer at the Hebrew University of Jerusalem. His publications include *Barriers to Entry into the Israeli Political System* (with G. Doron) (1989, in Hebrew), *Political Parties and Party Systems: Comparative Approaches and the British Experience* (Routledge 1997), and *Parties, Conflicts and Coalitions in Western Europe: Organisational Determinants of Coalition Bargaining* (Routledge 1998). His current research relates to an ESRC project on the 'Convergence of West European Administrative Systems: Training, Recruitment and Role Perceptions'.

Better the Devil You Know? Synthetic and Confederal Understandings of European Unification

ALEXANDER WARLEIGH

In the wake of the Single European Act and the Maastricht Treaty there has been much work undertaken to improve the theorisation of both the politics of the European Union and the unification process under way in Western Europe. This article argues that the confederal account of the two proposed by Murray Forsyth has been mistakenly neglected, and that it is of greater relevance than the waning orthodox international relations-derived theories of neo-functionalism and neo-realism. The current vogue for attempting a synthesis of the latter is evidence of their enfeebled condition, and has proved to be fruitless because the theories are united only in their increasingly evident redundancy. The emergence of a recognisable, if incomplete, Europolity after the ratification of the Maastricht Treaty must refocus attention on the confederal analysis; the price for theoretical rigour is the rejection of the familiar but unhelpful traditional frame of enquiry.

This article seeks to explore the viability of continued recourse to theories of European unification derived from international relations (IR) at a stage in the development of the European Union (EU) where a distinct Europolity has emerged. This is a question which is being asked with increasing frequency.[1] However, the present article seeks to focus on an underexplored aspect of the issue, namely the attempts of certain theorists to fuse concepts from the two principal orthodox approaches, neo-functionalism and neo-realism, and thereby develop 'synthetic' theory.

The synthetic approach reflects the recognition of EU scholars from within the IR paradigm that the variable accuracy of neo-functionalism and neo-realism precludes their individual use as devices for use in explaining EU politics. It must be established whether such 'rescue-through-marriage' of these theories yields an increased ability to understand the workings of the EU system, or whether it is in fact the swansong of an obsolete form of conceptualisation.

West European Politics, Vol.21, No.3 (July 1998), pp.1–18
PUBLISHED BY FRANK CASS, LONDON

Initially adopting a broad focus, the article uses the relative neglect of Forsyth's confederal understanding of the EU as an example of the exclusionary effects of IR domination of EU study for much of the 40 years since the signing of the Treaty of Rome. It then proceeds to discuss the problems of neo-functionalist and neo-realist EU theory, paying particular attention to the idea and impact of synthesis. This approach is contrasted with the nascent political systems, or comparative politics school, before attention is returned to confederal theory and conclusions are drawn about the most friutful means of theorising the EU beyond this double dichotomy (neo-functionalism versus neo-realism; IR versus comparative politics).

CONFEDERAL THEORY: SO NEAR AND YET SO FAR?

In 1981, Murray Forsyth published *Unions of States: The Theory and Practice of Confederation*. His hypothesis was that integration theory (as opposed to study of the EU[2]) as a specialised field was superfluous, a misleading attempt by academic analysts to portray the EU as a new form of political organisation which required a whole new theory to explain it. His radical argument was, in essence, that: 'the political theory of economic union is ... the classical or traditional theory of confederations transposed and adjusted to the particular area of economics';[3] the EU is merely another example of a process regularly found in European history.

Forsyth traces confederation theory back to the seventeenth century and the advent of theories of sovereignty and the state in the work of such thinkers as Pufendorf, Hamilton, Rousseau and Kant.[4] He defines confederation as a voluntary and contractual union of states, and not peoples, which falls short of the creation of a federal superstate.[5] Economic union became the primary goal of confederalists (replacing defence and security concerns) after the industrial revolution, as small states needed to create larger markets in order to compete with their bigger rivals. This is a particularly telling argument when applied to the western Europe of the post-World War II period, during which state rejuvenation and coping with the loss of empire were pressing issues.

Confederations are distinguished from international organisations in that they entail the creation of supranational institutions such as an assembly or court by the contracting states in order to ensure the smooth functioning of the new system; these institutions are then imbued with permanence and legitimacy, if not always vast powers.

For Forsyth, the EU is best understood as an economic confederation with a noble ancestry (the Dutch United Provinces, the US Confederation of 1789, the Swiss Confederation, the 1834 Zollverein and the Benelux 1948).

Further, confederation should be seen as one of three classic strategies states may adopt to shape their relations with others in the international arena, along with hegemony and manipulating the balance of power. Hegemony, the ability of a state to dominate others, is well known and can take diverse forms such as empire or the imposition of economic dependence; the balance of power tactic, which involves careful diplomacy and manipulation of other states with the aim of preserving a status quo favourable to the main power, is similarly familiar. It was, for example, the mainstay of British policy on Europe throughout the nineteenth century. Confederation is typically the choice of geographically close states which seek collective security against military or economic threat, but which do not want to submerge themselves in a new centralised structure. Confederations rest on the formal equality of member states, but in fact may mask power differences which both stronger and weaker states wish to contain for the sake of collective, and greater, advantage. The EU, then, is emphatically not an entity without precedent, even if its particular institutional arrangements are unique.

This view contradicted the tenets of the dominant paradigm, itself divided internally into two schools of thought, neo-functionalism and neo-realism.[6] The former school held that European unification was a completely novel process, which was termed 'integration', and required a new theory. These scholars also maintained that the process had its own dynamic, identified as *spillover*, which acted as an inexorable centripetal logic. Neo-functionalists adapted and developed the work of the earlier functionalist school of international relations theorists (in particular David Mitrany). They expected the integration process to be élite-led, with significant roles being played by both the Commission and domestic interest groups as actors began to pursue individual and group interests rather than those of the nation states.[7]

The neo-realist perspective developed as a critique of neo-functionalist theory which, simply put, began to unravel when de Gaulle demonstrated the ability and will of a member state to frustrate the march towards the 'ever closer union' which remains the goal of the Treaty of Rome. Neo-functionalists had assumed, as a core belief, that development towards a federal state would be both automatic and unidirectional. Revised and eventually rejected even by its principal exponents,[8] neo-functionalism appeared to be discordant with the period of seeming stagnation in the EU of the 1970s and early 1980s.

Neo-realism was held to reflect this period, commonly referred to as Eurosclerosis, much more accurately. The Union was seen to be just one international organisation among many. For orthodox neo-realists, all international politics is essentially and necessarily a question of preserving as much of the status quo as possible in order to avoid a slide into the likely chaos of an international system without the anchor of the nation state order.[9] The EU was thus to be considered a policy tool of the member governments, which controlled it absolutely and would never allow its evolution into a system in its own right.

To support their case, neo-realists pointed to the dominance of the EU Council within Union decision making. It was clear that a federal outcome to the unification process undertaken by the member states was far from inevitable. The declaration of the primacy of EU law weakened the neo-realist case, however, since it clearly revealed that the unilateral exercise of national sovereignty within the EU was far less easily managed than in a typical international organisation.

The subsequent signing of the Single European Act (SEA), and creation of the internal market, took neo-realist scholars as much by surprise as the Commission's inability to surmount de Gaulle's intransigence did the neo-functionalists in the 1960s because, viewed through the neo-realist lens, it was virtually impossible to move beyond the impasse of Eurosclerosis. Enlargement of the EU had occurred, but at the price of budget overstretch; the Franco-German alliance, the traditional bedrock of integration, was weakened by the new diversity within the Union, meaning that support for deepening integration was likely to be more difficult to generate and sustain; and the emphasis on a common approach to integration, in which all member states had to move at the same speed towards the same goal, would frustrate the process, since without the ability to opt out governments would only agree to policy objectives which they could wholeheartedly support. This would necessarily reduce the scope for policy making.[10] Taken together, these developments were held to signal that the member states had failed to build a real sense of political community; the pluralistic stance adopted by national governments would necessarily impose a clear limit on European integration.

The 'recasting [of] the European bargain'[11] in the form of the SEA resusscitated European unification just as neo-realists were pronouncing its last rites. The need to respond to the economic challenge of Japan and the USA, mounting concern about dependence on an increasingly protectionist American approach to trade and security, and the demonstrable inability of even the larger member states to adapt to the rigours of globalisation on their own since the *volte face* of French policy under Mitterrand, compelled the member states to tap into the underutilised resource of the unfinished single-market project.

Moreover, the SEA caused significant institutional change (such as qualified majority voting and the co-operation procedure, which increased the influence of the European Parliament over policy making) and expansion of policy competences (such as the formalisation of Community environment policy). Completing the single market could not be achieved in a vacuum; the link between economic and political integration, explicit in the Treaty of Rome, was reaffirmed.[12]

However, despite the weaknesses of both neo-functionalism and neo-realism, *Unions of States* did not become a classic text in EU studies during this volatile period. Forsyth's work did not reflect the accepted realities of Cold War international-relations theory; it did not speak the language of neo-functionalism and neo-realism, of integration and interdependence, and was, therefore, largely peripheralised.

Nevertheless, at a moment when neo-realist revision is prevalent,[13] and synthesis of the two international relations-derived theories is also popular,[14] it is worth investigating Forsyth's work anew. The Union is a treaty-created body politic with increasingly close resemblance to the regulatory state;[15] in keeping with classic confederal stategy, we have witnessed the transformation by the single-market programme of external trade into internal commerce. Forsyth's view of a confederation (a union of states with progressive capacity and supranational institutions which are created to help make and deliver policy) may serve as a means of generating both useful research and a more thorough understanding of the EU system than the traditional approaches.

THE INADEQUACY OF INTEGRATION THEORY

Integration theory was born in the 1950s of the signing of the Rome Treaty and 'the flowering in the United States of systematic social science'.[16] It was to be an empirically based process theory which could stand comparison with those of natural science for academic rigour and verifiability. In fact, as outlined above, it has never been robust: after the demise of first generation neo-functionalism followed the minimalist outlook (and for long periods also interest) of the neo-realists. Theories such as concordance and interdependence were advanced, but can safely be included in the neo-realist camp as their basic assumptions fit those of the school. Neo-realists remained principally concerned with refining their grand theory of international politics, paying relatively little attention to the EU, as is recognised by Keohane and Hoffmann.

Interestingly, scholars have been moved to echo Forsyth by questioning that a new phenomenon called integration is to be observed in Western Europe. Neo-realists have preferred to think in terms of *interdependence*, a far narrower concept which is essentially applicable to all participants in the global economy. More recently, it has been argued that the EU represents not integration but *consociation*, a kind of integration-interdependence hybrid.[17] Additionally, the recent surge of interest in the EU among scholars of comparative politics has reintroduced the language of federalism.[18] Whatever the accuracy of such terminology, its use is a significant departure from the traditional perspective. It also implies an end to the old neo-functionalist dilemma of whether 'integration' is a process or an outcome, since analysis of the former is given explicit centrality.

In this light, it is clear that any attempt to reinstate neo-functionalism in the wake of the neo-realist collapse is problematic. Despite its apparent resonances with the 'new' EU, neo-functionalism remains a deterministic would-be grand theory seeking to impose normative understandings of a process it has regularly proved unable to explain or predict. This fact must be borne in mind when assessing the impact on EU conceptualisation of work such as Ross's study of Jacques Delors' role in developing the SEA and Maastricht Treaty (which shows that neo-functionalist views of the Commission's ability to shape policy were in many ways accurate),[19] or Wistrich's convincing argument that in the light of the SEA, the Luxembourg Compromise, which solved the de Gaulle crisis by acknowledging the right of a member state to use its veto in matters it deemed of vital national importance, did not mark a definitive victory for the minimalist approach to unification.[20]

The habit of working within the neo-realist/neo-functionalist dichotomy threatens to lead scholars down a blind alley. Neither theory has proved valid, and yet within the IR-derived paradigm there are no other commonly used conceptual tools for EU study. This rather narrow focus has induced some scholars to attempt the marriage of ideas from both schools of thought in an attempt to transcend what Kuhn would refer to as their essential tension,[21] thereby providing a workable synthetic theory of the Union and its policy making.

SYNTHETIC INTEGRATION THEORY: MISSION IMPOSSIBLE?

It is commonplace to observe that the vicissitudinous path of European unification has been reflected in the fortunes of neo-functionalism and neo-realism. These polarised perspectives have waxed and waned along with the perceived success of the EU itself. Each approach has been much criticised, but each claims partial accuracy: the premise of synthetic theory is that the best way to conceptualise the Union is to combine elements of each approach. Such reasoning has a beautiful simplicity; however, it is entirely mistaken, as an analysis of some key synthetic texts will demonstrate.

The work of Jeppe Tranholm-Mikkelsen[22] is instructive. Tranholm-Mikkelsen calls for synthesis as a means of reinstating neo-functionalism. In order to compensate for the uneven progress of the European unification process, he views integration as a dialectical process involving 'twin forces, a "logic of integration" and a "logic of disintegration"',[23] a model which seeks at once to accommodate the perceived strengths of the neo-realist approach (namely its insistence on the ultimate power of national governments and their pursuit of their own interests) *and* rehabilitate the concepts of spillover and *engrenage* (bureaucratic interpenetration).

Tranholm-Mikkelsen's dialectic has much to recommend it if it is used differently from the way he suggests. It is entirely possible that the EU is witnessing a transfer of powers from national authorities both upwards to the European level and downwards to subnational government. In that case, member states may be integrating and disintegrating simultaneously. However, this would not be a novel observation: it is a mainstay of federalist theory. A more robust (because not vested with theoretical significance) expression of the twin forces idea is developed by Helen and William Wallace with their pendulum metaphor.[24]

For Tranholm-Mikkelsen, neo-functionalists had been wrong to reject their own work simply because its revision was problematic; the enactment of the SEA produced evidence of both spillover and the influence of Union actors other than the EU Council. Unable completely to reinstate the theory because its revision was never completed, Tranholm-Mikkelsen urges its reappraisal. This judgement is not without merit; the minimalist line adopted by many scholars in the 1980s was clearly outdated. Relocating neo-functionalism and neo-realism towards the midpoint of the continuum they had established might be a successful means of shedding the troublesome deterministic aspects of each. If so, synthesis would provide an opportunity to remodel the entire IR paradigm as it has been applied to EU study: synthesists might argue that 20 years, and little else, separate the *preference convergence* hypothesis of Keohane and Hoffmann (analysed below) from Nye's concept of *élite value complementarity*.[25]

However, nothing in Tranholm-Mikkelsen's work indicates that it is possible to fuse concepts from neo-functionalism and neo-realism in a single theoretical model. His explicit objective is to reinstate neo-functionalism,[26] a fact which must inform his conceptualisation process. The dialectic he proposes owes far more to neo-functionalism than neo-realism (the emphasis on spillover, the stress placed on impersonal dynamics rather than the decisions of national governments), meaning that behind the wish for synthesis the original perspective is dominant.

The difficulty of overcoming paradigmatic assumptions is revealed even more clearly in the work of Keohane and Hoffmann. Their *preference convergence* hypothesis, whilst making overtures to neo-functionalism, is steeped in the neo-realist perspective they had previously advocated. Despite a laudable intention to adjust their theory to the post-cold war

European context, Keohane and Hoffmann are unable to shed their neo-realist skins.

The reappraisal of Ernst Haas' work undertaken by Keohane and Hoffmann is positive, but limited. For example, the spillover concept (that key neo-functionalist idea of a centripetal dynamic inherent in the integration process) is allowed to exist, but only in a truncated fashion. This is because 'spillover was not automatic. Policy change and institutional change also required a convergence of interests between states'.[27] This is a contradiction in terms; the spillover dynamic, whilst acknowledged by revisionist neo-functionalists to be less than automatic, is supposed to operate in such a way as to facilitate, or even cause, such 'preference convergence'. We are left to make the choice between chicken and egg: which came first, spillover or preference convergence?

The impossibility of synthesis across the IR divide is demonstrated throughout the text. Compromise on spillover is possible only because Keohane and Hoffmann claim the almost exclusive ability to understand it as Haas had intended.[28] Moreover, Keohane's expertise in regime theory (which sees any international organisation as predominantly a tool for national governments to employ in pursuit of their policy objectives) is used as the primary device even for the study of the post-SEA Union. This is despite the institutionalisation of qualified majority voting (QMV) in the Council on single market issues, the expansion of the powers of the European Parliament and the significant proactive contribution of the Commission in realising the 1992 project (completing the single market). All these developments are very difficult to reconcile with a neo-realist-derived understanding of international politics[29] because they signal the existence of a system beyond the hegemony not only of one member state, but all of them as a collective. It is necessary to recall that even after the creation of Coreper and the European Council, national governments depend on the input of other actors and institutions for the optimal functioning of the EU policy-making process.

The problem of competing truths thus remains. Placing the emphasis on preference convergence renders spillover meaningless because what counts is not an impersonal dynamic which pushes the integration process onwards, but governmental will. The neo-functionalist, whilst accepting the power of the European/EU Council, could feasibly object that the SEA embodies spillover. After all, in the absence of an integrationist dynamic, Eurosclerosis did not have to be overcome; could not the creation of the single market and the subsequent Treaty on European Union (TEU) reveal both the inevitability of deepening an initiated integration project and the power of non-nation state actors (the Commission) to encourage this? The fact that member states currently, and *collectively*, hold most power in the

Union does not of itself justify a neo-realist account of European unification.

A further example of the persistence of the widely differing views of the neo-functionalists and neo-realists is provided by their reactions to the TEU. A neo-realist might accept its advance on the SEA but point out that the actual treaty is far weaker than the original proposal, viewing this as continued proof of both the power of national governments and their minimalist approach to integration.[30] A neo-functionalist reading of the EU, on the other hand, would note *inter alia* the extension of QMV, the co-decision powers of the Parliament, the creation of European citizenship, the establishment of the Committee of the Regions, and the commitment to monetary union, thereby considering the TEU a significant step on the path to the elusive ever closer union, a necessary consequence of the need to protect the gains made by the establishment of the single market (SEM).

Over 20 years ago, Donald Puchala signalled that a synthetic approach to EU theory would be problematic because both major schools of thought 'partially straightjacket' the scholar by imposing their respective world views on him or her.[31] These understandings of the world and, more particularly, politics, are in opposition to each other. It should not be forgotten that neo-functionalism descends via functionalism from the idealist school of thought in international relations, whereas neo-realism's parentage is, obviously, Realist.

Since without them theory is but an amorphous collection of hypotheses with no unifying thread, however, normative assumptions are essential for successful conceptualisation. We cannot make synthetic theory without an explicit new set of common norms. The *preference convergence* hypothesis, for all its advances on earlier neo-realism, demonstrates the impossibility of making such an intra-IR paradigm agreement because each school of thought proposes a different and opposing view of any given event. As a result, attempts to conceptualise the EU synthetically are frustrated by the fact that *rapprochement* of neo-functionalism and neo-realism would effectively deprive both theories of their respective *raisons d'être* and guiding principles, a step which neither set of scholars can take without emasculating their theory. Synthetic theory is, therefore, reducible to the dominant perspective which informs any scholar attempting to make it.

RECENT INTEGRATION THEORY: THE DOUBLE DICHOTOMY

Traditional integration theories have, however, quietly become less hegemonic in recent years, efforts to create a synthesis notwithstanding. Much current thinking in the area of EU politics is the work of specialists in other fields who, enthused by the dynamism of the post-SEA era, apply their theories to the EU and find important similarities between the Union and other policy making systems. Bueno de Mesquita and Stokman, for example, apply rational choice theories to the Union's decision-making process;[32] Andersen and Eliassen use sociological organisation theory in a bid to understand the EU system.[33] Alan Milward has developed a sophisticated understanding of European unification extrapolated from historical analysis of the EU, according to which integration becomes *Realpolitik* adopted by pragmatic politicians whose primary aim was to 'rescue the nation state' in Europe after the Second World War.[34] John Peterson uses a public policy approach as part of a triple-headed model of EU decision making.[35]

This mixture of macro and micro theories is a very interesting development; Peterson harnesses both the IR-derived theories plus new institutionalism and policy networks concepts to build his model, thereby mixing iconoclasm and orthodoxy. His approach offers little comfort for advocates of the traditional approaches, however, as it drastically reduces the role allocated to neo-functionalism and neo-realism in the theorising process. Moreover, it is subject to its own problems (mixing approaches from different academic traditions, difficulties in combining macro and micro theories).[36] None the less, Peterson's work deserves to be examined very carefully as it represents something of a watershed in EU theory, being located at the interface of IR and comparative politics approaches.

Increasingly, political systems experts have become interested in the EU, detecting after the adoption of the TEU the beginnings of a European polity, and thus the possibility of making illuminating comparisons with other systems.[37] Indeed, Scharpf[38] has argued that the present EU system is one of cooperative federalism in which the primary decision making process requires the agreement of the constituent governments, and is in this way rather like that pertaining in Germany, a view shared by Kirchner.[39]

Sbragia also sees the possibility of making illuminating comparisons between the EU and federal political structures; for Sbragia, the Union is developing into an uncommon type of federation based on integration of constitutent states rather than the decentralisation of a unitary state (as was recently the case in Belgium).[40] The Union's relatively novel evolution may explain the reluctance of many observers, used to the US federal model, to apply the same label to an EU which none the less is felt by Sbragia to have many of the features of a federal polity.[41]

The multi-level governance (MLG) theorists represent an emerging school of thought which signals that the EU now constitutes a polity in its own right, albeit one whose final shape is as yet indeterminate.[42] Their focus is on the involvement of subnational actors in the policy making of the Union, both by lobbying and institutionally via national mechanisms and the Committee of the Regions. They posit a system wherein various actors from the different tiers of government (state, substate and EU) interact with varying influence according to policy area; no actor is monolithic, and the Commission performs a key role in policy development.[43] A key difference between MLG and federal theories which is worth recalling here is that federalism relies on clear, legally binding separation or sharing of powers whereas a system of MLG is characterised by constant change and variation in power and competence distribution across the range of policy areas. Such work poses a clear challenge to the established integration theories, which is investigated below.

First, let us turn to neo-functionalism. It has not enjoyed a second halcyon period despite the flourishing of ideas compatible with it in British academic circles during the 1980s and early 1990s, such as William Wallace's concept of informal integration (which analyses the impact of business and personal life on the integration process without explicitly invoking neo-functionalism).[44] This is only partially because the range of theorists in the field has expanded; despite the efforts of Tranholm-Mikkelsen, neo-functionalism has never recovered from its abandonment by its principal creator, Ernst Haas. It remains possible for many scholars – not only neo-realists – to neglect to endorse it because its shortcomings remain.

The work of Paul Taylor is here very instructive. A long-standing sceptic of neo-functionalism, Taylor is none the less unable to accept the standard neo-realist case despite his essential affinities for that world view as revealed in his 1983 book *The Limits of European Integration*. At that moment, Taylor was convinced that the unification of Western Europe was destined to go no further than it already had; ten years later, the SEA and TEU forced a reassessment. Akin to Keohane and Hoffmann, Taylor attempts to fit facts more favourable to neo-functionalism than neo-realism to his theory by pointing out that even if the EU is used more and more frequently as a means of pursuing an ever broader range of policy objectives, it is still national governments which ultimately make most decisions.

Taylor introduces to EU study the concept of consociationalism.[45] This approach holds that integration is pursued by national élites anxious to secure policy objectives. It is continued because, once established, the system yields too many benefits to justify its dismantling. Consociation seeks to explain how stability is preserved in a political context which contains great potential for conflict between actors. It sees the present systemic arrangements of the Union as indicative of the final product of the integration process: a symbiosis of EU and national actors, run by national élites that wish to consolidate their power.

Consociation theory also sugests that as the EU develops, national governments become more rather than less keen to preserve their powers in order to control the potential Frankenstein's monster they have collectively created. National governments thus remain the key actors; the Commission is seen as neutral, the Union as the arena in which member states fight their diplomatic battles on the basis of interests which diverge rather than converge as the Union becomes more powerful and each state seeks to reinforce its own identity. Nothing in this, of course, represents a concession to neo-functionalism.

The SEA (and presumably also the TEU) are explained by consociationalists as unrepresentative of the general situation, concessions made by the more reluctant states to the need to preserve the Union structures (it now being part of the status quo) in order to prevent the slide into anarchy so feared by neo-realist scholars. Such thinking is untenable. Whilst it is obviously incorrect to make theory with treaty change as one's sole reference point – the classic approach of macrotheorists – it is equally pointless virtually to ignore such major developments.[46]

Taylor calls his theory 'a dynamic view of intergovernmentalism',[48] thus placing himself squarely in the neo-realist camp. None the less, it could be argued that the existence of a self-perpetuating European system is a clear vindication of the spillover concept, and when Taylor describes the EU as a symbiosis of member states and Union institutions, he approaches Scharpf's model of co-operative federalism. Later, Taylor echoes Tranholm-Mikkelsen's view of integration as a dialectical process; attempting to reform neo-realism whilst unable truly to jettison its core concepts, Taylor ends up with just such an 'artificial, untidy result' as Puchala[48] predicted.

Other consociationalists have found similar problems in theorising the EU. Chryssochoou[49] maintains that European unification cannot be achieved at the expense of national sovereignty as the prime directive of the nation state is to preserve its individual powers. Consociation is thus a strictly limited enterprise. Such a zero-sum understanding of the EU is a limitation in itself; theory must acknowledge that by signing the Rome Treaty, member states declare that the optimal achievement of certain objectives in many fields of policy defeats a unilateral approach. The pooling of national sovereignty can be *Realpolitik* if the challenge faced by the nation-state is sufficiently strong.

There is no reason to suppose, as consociationalists do, that the Union is an inevitably limited undertaking. It may be that the EU will never be fully democratised and made into a federation; it is quite wrong, however, to preclude this from a range of possible outcomes. The unfortunate experience of past attempts to conceptualise the Union in such deterministic fashion should give consociationalists pause for thought.[50]

The application of consociation theory to the EU, then, is replete with traps for the unwary. How can the essentially neo-realist view that the

Union is but a more than usually robust international regime be wedded to the concept of symbiotic, mutually reinforcing constituent governments and new (autonomous?) supranational institutions? How can the theory focus on élites without acknowledging the teleological behaviour of the Commission? Is there no role for informal integration or policy networks? Do national governments have a monopoly on the representation of the state to the EU? The consociational revision of neo-realism, bold though it is, avoids grappling with these questions at its cost.

One of the tensions in such work is the attempt to fuse IR and political systems perspectives (consociation being a concept used in comparative politics). This tension has not yet been solved; the trend towards pluralism indicates that both approaches may yield useful ideas, but it has not yet been demonstrated that such ideas can be combined in a single model. There are, moreover, dangers in viewing pluralism as a new orthodoxy: Peterson's model suffers from this IR-political-systems tension in the same way as Taylor's. Of course, EU politics does not take place in a vacuum; it is right to insist that the EU is not an island,[51] but this does not in itself justify recourse to IR theory to explain the workings of the EU system. There is a vast difference between acknowledging the impact of global politico-economics on the policies of member states and those of the Union itself, and using IR theories to explain European unification and EU decision making. Simply put, IR theories are not appropriate if we see the Union as a polity in its own right rather than a matter of member-state foreign policy.

The alternative to consociationalism within the neo-realist paradigm is to return to first principles. This is the approach of Andrew Moravcsik, whose work since 1991 evinces a confident acceptance of the neo-realist world view, albeit with adjustments and a new focus on the micropolitics of policy choice. It therefore contains all the school's defects as well as its insights.

Moravcsik is convinced that existing realist belief is sufficient to explain the path of European unification. Regime theory is invoked, as in Keohane and Hoffmann. Domestic policy priorities shape member state demands on the tool they have created to manage interdependence (the EU), and the more powerful member countries control the others with bribes and package deals. Moravcsik's double-headed theory, Liberal intergovernmentalism, logically relies on both rationalistic liberalism (to explain policy choice) and traditional intergovernmentalism (to explain interstate bargaining), thereby preserving the traditional neo-realist approach – and problems – in spite of the innovative two-tier focus.[52]

Moreover, Moravcsik is quite clear that neo-functionalism should not be considered in any way useful by the contemporary theorist,[53] because it has no understanding of how domestic policy priorities are set or the effect of the international political economy on member state policy preference. Whatever the accuracy of such a charge, it is further evidence that synthesis across the IR divide is unlikely: the synthetic approach is obviously untenable if neo-realists can only either rewrite neo-functionalism on their own terms (Keohane and Hoffmann) or reject it entirely (Moravcsik).

A double dichotomy thus exists simultaneously between the two macrotheories *and* between the IR and comparative politics schools. This dual cleavage cannot be transcended to make unified models of Union decision making. IR theorists do not view the EU as a polity, although neo-functionalists such as Lindberg and Scheingold can see its eventual transformation into one (a process which would require a uniform path to a federal settlement on the western European model of the nation state).[54] Neo-realism rests on the assumption that the Union is essentially a passive tool of the member states. Comparative politics scholars, however, make precisely the opposite assumption, that is, that the Union forms its own polity. As a result, EU theory is in a period of insecurity, not in its own period of convergence, but rather increasingly riven with divisions.

Moreover, there is a growing body of opinion which argues that the traditional means of orientation and research generation, the IR-derived theories, offer no useful help to scholars of the Union. EU reality as evinced in the system shaped by the Rome, Maastricht and Amsterdam treaties has links with both neo-functionalism and neo-realism, but neither theory is able to describe the decision making process in anything like its entirety.[55] The present article has sought both to support this view and to demonstrate that the last hope of the IR school, synthetic theory, has proved unable to revive the traditional conceptualisations of the EU either singly or in combination. By acknowledging the need to abandon their respective normative values, and demonstrating their inability to do so, neo-realists and neo-functionalists alike have shown that synthetic theory is the swansong of a mode of thinking as obstinate as it is obsolete.

CONCLUSIONS: THEORISING THE EUROPEAN CONFEDERATION

It remains to suggest a suitable avenue for ongoing research into the theorisation of the EU. This article began with an invocation of *Unions of States*, and will end with the suggestion that theorists look again at the confederal diagnosis of the Union.

Integration, or rather unification, is not a new phenomenon, and it does not require its own theory. Neither is it appropriate to treat the EU as one international organisation among many, the almost powerless tool of its constituent governments which has no possibility of further and radical systemic development, even if such evolution cannot be guaranteed.

After the TEU, the Union is clearly neither regime nor federation, in the terms of the usual ontological dialectic.[56] 'Confederation' may therefore be a helpful label to apply. This article argues that the Union has always been a structural confederation, that is to say a union of previously sovereign states created by Treaty, which may or may not develop into a federation – a more closely bound polity – along any model, whether currently extant or novel. The TEU, by increasing the competences of the Union institutions and enhancing QMV, may mark a significant shift towards a Eurofederation, but this has not yet changed the Union's confederal nature.

Furthermore, confederal theory can express both the dominance (and *not* the hegemony) of the EU Council and the powerful role of the other Union institutions, as well as the uneven path of unification: they are simply the result of confederal structure and policy. As a result, confederal theory can be reconciled with the reality of Union politics which the more usual methods of theorising can encapsulate only in part.

Forsyth's confederal case can thus form the basis for research into Union decision making, not as a grand theory but as an acknowledgement of the nature and existence of the Europolity.[57] This of course presents its own challenges to the researcher: it shifts EU study towards the comparative perspective, but clearly confederal theory can tell us very little about the daily decision making of the Union, nor can it tell us everything about the functioning of the system in supplying the crucial ontological diagnosis. None the less, it is an important starting point for all EU scholars; in this case at least, it is better the devil we know slightly than its IR-derived counterpart whose shortcomings are rather more familiar.

NOTES

I am grateful to the Leverhulme Trust for its financial support.

1. See, for example, T. Risse-Kappen, 'Exploring the Nature of the Beast: International Relations Theory and Comparative Analysis Meet the EU', *Journal of Common Market Studies* 34/1 (March 1996) pp.53–80; S. Hix, 'The Study of the European Community: The Challenge to Comparative Politics', *West European Politics* 17/1 (Jan. 1994) pp.1–30; S. Bulmer, 'The Governance of the EU: A New Institutionalist Approach', *Journal of Public Policy* 13/4 (1993) pp.423–44; A. Sbragia, 'Thinking About the European Future: The Uses of Comparison', in idem (ed.) *Europolitics-Institutions and Policy Making in the 'New' European Community* (Washington DC: Brookings 1992).
2. The terms 'EU' and 'the Union' are used throughout this article to denote all the incarnations of the European Union. This has been done for reasons of clarity and is not meant to imply a disregard for historical accuracy!
3. M. Forsyth, *Unions of States: The Theory and Practice of Confederation* (Leicester: Leicester UP 1981) p.6.
4. Alternative views of confederal theory are to be found. P. Kropotkin uses it as part of his anarchist manifesto *Mutual Aid* (London: Freedom Press 1987). He applies it to the Leagues of Free Cities which sprang up in Europe in the Middle Ages, such as Hansa. This usage is

also invoked by Murray Bookchin who proceeds to employ it as the basis of a blueprint for an ecologically sound society which centres on powerful municipalities bound to each other in a loose confederation. See M. Bookchin, *Urbanization Without Cities – The Rise and Decline of Citizenship* (NY: Black Rose Books 1992).

5. The path from confederation to federation is taken if the member states choose to create a closer union for purposes of stability or to ensure the successful meeting of common goals which the confederal structure has proved too weak to guarantee. At that stage, the member states would invest the majority of their powers in independent supranational institutions rather than maintain collective control.

6. The use of the term 'neo-realism' might be deemed controversial as the term 'intergovernmentalism' is currently more widespread. However the latter term more properly describes a process of decision making rather than a theory of it. Moreover, revisions of classic realism have consistently been labelled in this way even though scholars within the tradition may find the term unhelpful. Keohane, for example, prefers the term 'neo-liberal institutionalist'; Moravcsik calls himself a 'liberal intergovernmentalist'. The term 'neo-realist' is thus used here to denote members of a group of scholars who share revisionist realism as a basic philosophy; 'neo-realism' refers to their thought.

7. For a full account of neo-functionalist theory, it is necessary to delve into Ernst Haas' texts *Beyond the Nation State* (Stanford UP 1964) and *The Uniting of Europe* (ibid. 1968). L. Lindberg and S. Scheingold, *Regional Integration* (Cambridge, MA: Harvard UP 1971) is an excellent guide to the revision of the theory after the de Gaulle crisis. The best secondary source is probably still to be found in C. Pentland, *International Theory and European Integration* (London: Faber 1973), although several Readers in integration theory are due to be published soon and Michael O'Neill's *The Politics of European Integration* (London: Routledge 1996) covers much useful ground.

8. E Haas, *The Obsolescence of Regional Integration Theory* (Berkeley, CA: U. of California Press 1975).

9. S. Hoffmann, *Duties Beyond Borders* (NY: Syracuse UP 1981).

10. P. Taylor, *The Limits of European Integration* (Beckenham: Croom Helm 1983).

11. W. Sandholtz and J. Zysman, '1992: Recasting the European Bargain', *World Politics* 42/1 (1989) pp. 95–126

12. G. Ross, *Jacques Delors and European Integration* (Cambridge: Polity Press 1995).

13. See for example, P. Taylor, *International Organisation in the Modern World* (London: Pinter 1993); A. Moravcsik, 'Preferences and Power in the European Community: A Liberal Intergovernmentalist Approach', *Journal of Common Market Studies* 31/4 (Dec. 1993) pp.19–56

14. See R. Keohane and S. Hoffmann, 'Institutional Change in Europe in the 1980s', in idem. (eds.) *The New European Community: Decision Making and Institutional Change* (Oxford: Westview Press 1991); J. Tranholm-Mikkelsen, 'Neo-functionalism: Obstinate or Obsolete? A Reappraisal in the Light of the New Dynamism of the EC', *Millennium* 20/1 (1991) pp.1–22.

15. See F. McGowan and H. Wallace, 'Towards a European Regulatory State', *Journal of European Public Policy* 3/4 (1993) pp.560–76.

16. E. Haas, 'The Study of Regional Integration – The Joy and Anguish of Pre-Theorising', *International Organization* 24 (1970) pp.607–46. p.607.

17. Taylor (note 13); D. Chryssochoou, 'Democracy and Symbiosis in the EU: Towards a Confederal Consociation?', *West European Politics* 17/4 (Oct. 1994) pp.1–14.

18. See for example, Sbragia (note 1); F Scharpf, 'The Joint Decision Trap-Lessons From German Federalism and European Integration', *Public Administration* 66/3 (Autumn 1988) pp.239–78.

19. Ross (note 12).

20. E. Wistrich, *After 1992: The United States of Europe* (London: Routledge 1991).

21. T. Kuhn, *The Essential Tension: Selected Studies in Scientific Tradition and Change* (U. of Chicago Press 1977).

22. Tranholm-Mikkelsen (note 14).

23. Ibid. p.18.

24. H. Wallace and W. Wallace (eds.), *Policy Making in the European Union* (Oxford: OUP 1996).

25. J. Nye, 'Comparing Common Markets: A Revised Neo-functionalist Model', in Lindberg and Scheingold (note 7).
26. Tranholm-Mikkelsen (note 14) p.4.
27. Keohane and Hoffmann (note 14) p.22.
28. Ibid. p.18
29. J. Grieco, 'The Maastricht Treaty, Economic and Monetary Union, and the Neo-rralist Research Programme', *Review of International Studies* 21 (1995) pp.21–40.
30. A. Moravcsik, 'Idealism and Interest in the EuropeanCommunity: The Case of the French Referendum', *French Politics and Society* 11/1 (1993) pp.45–56
31. D.Puchala, 'Of Blind Men, Elephants and International Integration', *Journal of Common Market Studies* 10/3 (Sept. 1972) pp.267–84.
32. B. Bueno de Mesquita and F. Stokman (eds.) *European Community Decision Making: Models, Applications and Comparisons* (New Haven, CT: Yale UP 1994).
33. S. Andersen and K. Eliassen (eds.) *Making Policy in Europe: The Europeification of National Policy Making* (London: Sage 1993).
34. A. Milward, *The European Rescue of the Nation State* (London: Routledge 1994).
35. J. Peterson, 'Decision Making in the European Union – Towards a Framework for Analysis', *Journal of European Public Policy* 2/1 (1995) pp.69–94.
36. C. Stefanou, 'European Integration Theory: Micro-Macro Theories, Spheres of Focus and Synthetic Theories', Paper to UACES Research Conference, University of Birmingham, 18–19 Sept. 1995.
37. The use of the label 'political systems' to denote theorists of the EU from outside the IR paradigm is advocated by Michelle Cini because it has a greater inclusive capacity than 'comparative politics'. This is particularly helpful given the current diversity of thought on the Union, and I am grateful to Dr Cini for pointing this out to me.
38. Scharpf (note 18); for a later view, see F. Scharpf, 'Community and Autonomy: Multi-level Policy Making in the EU', *Journal of European Public Policy* 1/2 (1994) pp.219–42.
39. E. Kirchner, *Decision Making in the European Community – The Council Presidency and European Integration* (Manchester UP 1992).
40. Sbragia (note 1).
41. Sbragia lists these characteristics as the reconciliation of interests in the political system of various territorially defined groups as well as functional interest groups, a mixture of high and low politics within the system, the existence of powerful actors at the top level of the system, the paramountcy of federal (here, EU) law, the formal equality of component states, and the inability to achieve hegemony within the system.
42. See *inter alia* L. Hooghe and M. Keating, 'The Politics of European Union Regional Policy', *Journal of European Public Policy* 1/3 (1994) pp.367–93.
43. See G. Marks, 'Structural Policy in the EC', in Sbragia (ed. (note 1); L. Hooghe (ed.), *Cohesion Policy and European Integration* (Oxford: OUP 1996).
44. W. Wallace, *The Transformation of Western Europe* (London: Pinter 1990).
45. Taylor (note 13).
46. On this issue, see Peterson (note 35).
47. Taylor (note 13) p.93.
48. Puchala (note 31) p.276.
49. See Chryssochoou (note 17).
50. On the need for avoiding determinism in EU theory, see G. Schneider and L. Cedermann, 'Changes of Tide in European Integration', *International Organization* 48/4 (1994) pp.633–63.
51. A. Hurrell and A. Menon, 'Politics like Any Other? Comparative Politics, International relations and the Study of the EU', *West European Politics* 19/2 (April 1996) pp.386–402.
52. A. Moravcsik, 'Preferences and Power in the European Community: A Liberal Intergovernmentalist Approach', *Journal of Common Market Studies* 31/4 (Dec. 1993) pp.473–524.
53. A. Moravcsik, 'Negotiating the Single European Act: National Interests and Conventional Statecraft in the European Community', *International Organization* 45/1 (1991) pp.15–56.

54. See Pentland (note 7).
55. See Bulmer (note 1); J. Andersen, 'The State of the (European) Union: From the Single Market to Maastricht, From Singular Events to General Theories', *World Politics* 47 (April 1995) pp.441–65
56. J. Ohrgaard, 'Less than Supranational, More than Intergovernmental: European Political Cooperation and the Dynamics of Intergovernmental Integration', *Millennium* 26/1 (1997) pp.1–29.
57. See S. Bulmer, 'The European Council and The Council of the European Union-Shapers of a European Confederation', *Publius* 26/4 (1996) pp.17–42 for such an analysis. According to Bulmer, the EU is a partnership of institutions, at the apex of which are the two Councils, whose task is to build consensus and navigate the centripetal and centrifugal squalls in order to produce policy outcomes.

Elections, Parties and Institutional Design: A Comparative Perspective on European Union Democracy

SIMON HIX

The standard version of the European Union (EU) 'democratic deficit' maintains that genuine pan-European elections and parties will only come about if the EU is transformed into a classic parliamentary system: if the European Parliament (EP) is given more power in the legislative and executive-selection processes. Two influential critiques of this view are that majoritarian democracy is inappropriate in such a deeply divided society, and that European-level parties would form 'cartels' rather than compete for political office. To assess these claims and critiques, a typology of multi-level systems is developed and a series of hypotheses about the role of elections and parties within these systems are proposed. These are subsequently tested in a comparative analysis of eight cases. The key finding is that European elections and parties are unlikely to emerge if the EP is given more power. Nevertheless, real 'European' elections and competitive parties may develop if the EU becomes a (partial) presidential/interlocking system: if the institutional balance is kept, but the Commission president is directly elected.

EUROPEAN UNION DEMOCRACY IN COMPARATIVE PERSPECTIVE[1]

The alliteration 'democratic deficit' is so widely used and abused when discussing the European Union (EU) that it is now almost meaningless. To clarify the concept, nevertheless, Weiler *et al.* outline a 'standard version' (SV) of the democratic deficit.[2] This SV is not directly attributable. Rather, it is the accumulation of 'received knowledge' by political, media and academic commentary on the subject. According to the SV, the democratic deficit exists because 'increasingly important government functions [have been] transferred to "Brussels"',[3] but:

> parliamentary control [of executive power in the EU] is more an illusion than a reality ... Even after Maastricht, the powers of the

West European Politics, Vol.21, No.3 (July 1998), pp.19–52
PUBLISHED BY FRANK CASS, LONDON

European Parliament in the legislative process leave formal and formidable gaps in parliamentary control ... [And] paradoxically, one has seen a gradual increase in the formal powers of the EP, and a decrease in the turn-out in European elections ... The non-emergence of trans-European political parties is another expression of the phenomenon. Critically, there is no real sense in which the European political process allows the electorate to 'throw the scoundrels out'.[4]

By focusing on the role of parliaments, elections and parties, this SV thus assumes that the EU can be measured against the type of representative democracy that exists at the domestic level in Europe and throughout the democratic world. In this model, direct and democratic elections lead to the 'formation of government' and/or the 'formation of public policy'.[5] Moreover, the main organisations facilitating this connection between voters' choices and office-holding and/or policy-implementation are political parties. Parties present rival policy agendas (manifestos) to the electorate, voters then choose between these agendas, and the winning parties take control of executive and legislative office and act cohesively to implement these agendas. This central role of parties has hence led many to see modern democracy as 'competitive party government'.[6]

By measuring the EU according to the criteria of competitive party government, therefore, the SV prescribes that the EU will only be democratic if: European elections are fought by cohesive Euro-parties which present rival agendas for EU policy action; the winning parties in the elections form the executive; and the parties act cohesively to ensure that their office-holders implement their electoral programme. This would require that the EP is the main legislative body, that the Commission is directly and constantly accountable to a majority in the EP, that the European elections are fought on European and not national issues, and that the EP party groups can construct and maintain a majority.[7]

There are, however, three types of criticism of this prescription. The first, and most obvious, maintains that this is highly *unrealistic*. For competitive party government to exist in the EU, there would need to be a dramatic shift in the institutional design of the EU – towards a fully fledged parliamentary democracy at the European level. In the wake of the problems of ratifying the Maastricht Treaty in 1993, the presence of anti-European feelings in the 1994 European elections and the referendums on EU enlargement, and the growing antipathy towards Economic and Monetary Union in even some of the core member states (such as France and Germany), there is no widespread support for such a decisive step towards European political integration. Hence, it is almost impossible to imagine such a development any time in the next five, ten or perhaps even 20 years.

At a more theoretical level, the second and third types of criticism maintain that the SV prescription is actually *undesirable*. On the one hand, there is a growing body of academic opinion that maintains that 'majoritarian' institutions at the European level would actually undermine the legitimacy of the EU. This view argues that a majoritarian decision process would replace the slow, but highly effective, 'deliberative' style of 'governance' with a competitive 'bargaining' style that would inevitably lead to an unacceptable transfer of resources or values from 'losers' to 'winners'.[8] For example, a powerful EP majority and cohesive European political parties would most likely increase the size of the EU budget and lead to large transnational economic transfers, neither of which are supported by the public. And a politicised Commission, which could no longer be a provider of 'independent expertise', would not be capable of facilitating pareto-efficient, rather than redistributive, outcomes.[9] Although applied to the EU, these arguments are similar to the view that majoritarian democracy is impractical in deeply divided (pluralist) societies, because it would lead to subjugation of a particular societal 'segment' – or 'nation' in the case of the EU.[10] I shall hence refer to this as the *'anti-Euromajoritarianism critique'*.

On the other hand, but from a slightly different angle, many scholars of party government at the domestic level in Europe are increasingly sceptical of the centrality of parties to the democratic process.[11] From the late 1980s, a new structure of party competition has begun to take shape in many party systems in western Europe. Instead of competing for public office, parties increasingly collude to use the resources of the state to promote their collective interests. As a result, rather than representing civil society, parties are increasingly becoming 'part of the state apparatus itself'.[12] Party élites have abandoned their traditional ideological differences, and consequently present almost identical policies to the electorates and are willing to 'jump into bed' with previous enemies at the slightest promise of a place in government. The result, therefore, is that parties are actually 'undermining the legitimacy of party government'.[13] Hence, cohesive and collusive Euro-parties may in fact increase rather than reduce the EU democratic deficit. I shall refer to this as the *'anti-Europarty critique'*.

So, how can we test the validity of the claims of the advocates and critics of the SV? We could simply weigh the strengths and weaknesses of the arguments on either side of the debate at an abstract level. This, in fact, is what most recent commentators on the democratic deficit do.[14] However, these analyses need to be supplemented with empirical research. In an ideal world, we could treat the EU as a laboratory and 'test' the arguments of the SV (e.g. give more powers to the EP, introduce a uniform electoral procedure). However, this may mean waiting in vain.

There is, none the less, an alternative empirical approach. Instead of treating the EU as a *sui generis* laboratory, we can test the arguments by analysing the EU in 'comparative perspective'.[15] As Heidenheimer *et al.* point out: 'By assessing one situation against another, we gain a better perspective on our current situation as well as the options and constraints we face. In short we learn through comparing.'[16]

Ever since Plato and Aristotle compared the organisation of city-states in Ancient Greece, mankind has used this 'comparative method' to analyse whether one system of government is better than another, and connect the theoretical, empirical and normative levels of analysis (e.g. de Tocqueville,[17] J.S. Mill and Lord Bryce).

The comparative method can hence be used to analyse the current, and possible future, role of parties and elections in the EU. To narrow the scope of comparison, and to focus on the issue of institutional design, I have chosen a 'most-similar-systems-design' technique.[18] By looking at political systems with two levels of institutions, we should be able to isolate the institutional structures that facilitate 'good' modes of party behaviour. This does not require treating the EU as a formal 'federation' simply as a 'federal-type' system.[19] In such a system, there are two (or more) levels of governing institutions, which possess separate jurisdictional or functional powers.[20] In so doing, we should be able to assess which types of institutional structures would be most likely to reduce the democratic deficit in the EU. In other words, do we really need full-blown Euro-parliamentary democracy to make elections work in the EU? Or, should we do everything we can to prevent majoritarian practices from undermining EU legitimacy further?

Thus, the aim of this article is to investigate the claims and counter-claims about the EU democratic deficit by undertaking a comparative analysis of elections and parties in multi-level political systems. Next an attempt is made to develop a theoretical framework and some hypotheses about the relationship between elections/parties and the institutional structure of multi-level systems. Subsequently, these hypotheses are put to the test. Finally, the results are summarised and some conclusions are drawn.

THEORETICAL FRAMEWORK

In assessing the claims and critics of the SV of the democratic deficit, we are less concerned about which particular institutional design is 'the ideal' in any system of government than with two specific issues: the institutional options for the EU system; and, what may happen if the EU follows one or other of these options. These will be tackled separately.

Institutional Design in Multi-Level Systems

There are two different kinds of institutional structure in multi-level systems that impact on the choices of voters and party leaders. First, the design of the *vertical institutions* determines how power is divided between the central and local holders of political office. In unitary systems, the institutions at the central level have almost exclusive political control: such as the power to pass laws, make regulations, and raise taxes and spend public money. In multi-level systems, in contrast, power is divided between the central and local institutions. There are, however, two very different ways that this vertical division is organised.[21]

In 'dual federalism' there is a separation of powers between the central and local levels.[22] Policy competences are divided along jurisdictional lines: each level is exclusively responsible for adopting and implementing one or more policy areas. Moreover, the holders of political office at one level are not involved in decision making at the other level. In a dual-federal system, therefore, the two levels of political institutions are said to be '*independent*'.

In 'co-operative federalism', in contrast, there is a fusion of powers between the two levels of government. Policy competences are divided along functional rather than jurisdictional lines: most policy areas are the joint responsibility of both levels, and the central level is usually responsible for setting policy frameworks whereas the local level is responsible for policy details and implementation. Moreover, the holders of executive office at the lower level are directly involved in the making of legislation at the central level – usually in a second chamber of the legislature. This is often referred to as 'executive federalism'. However, it can also be thought of as a system of 'dual leadership', where the central and state governments share executive functions.[23] In such a system, therefore, the two levels of political institutions are '*interlocking*' rather than independent.[24]

Second, the design of the *horizontal institutions* determines the structure of political opportunities for the control of executive and legislative power at the central level. There are three main ways executive and legislative authority are organised.[25] In a *presidential* system there is a clear separation of executive and legislative power. The members of the government are not members of the legislature, and the holders of executive and legislature office are elected in independent processes. In a *parliamentary* system, in contrast, there is a fusion of executive and legislative power. The executive and the legislature derive their authority from the same set of elections, and the executive must resign if it loses the majority support of the legislature. Moreover, in most cases the members of the government are also members of the legislature. However, there is also a hybrid model of horizontal institutional design, were executive authority is held *collegially*. As in a parliamentary system, the collegial executive is nominally accountable to a legislative majority. As in a presidential system, however, the make-up of the collegial executive is fixed independently of a parliamentary majority, although the executive is not directly elected. In practice, the formula for the make-up of the collegial-executive ensures the representation of all the major groups in society, and hence a permanent 'oversized majority' in any parliament.

FIGURE 1
A TYPOLOGY OF MULTI-LEVEL POLITICAL SYSTEMS

| | | *Vertical Institutions* | |
		Independent	Interlocking
	Parliamentary	1 Australia Austria Belgium Canada	2 Germany
Horizontal Institutions	Presidential	3 USA	4 (no cases)
	Collegial Executive	5 Switzerland	6 European Union

Consequently, taking these two dimensions of institutional design, we have six possible types of multi-level political systems, as Figure 1 shows.[26] The most common are the classic 'parliamentary systems' (as espoused for the European level). Of these systems, in Australia, Austria, Belgium and Canada the two levels of government are independent.[27] Germany, in contrast, is the archetypal case of interlocking federalism.[28] There is only one Western case of a multi-level presidential/independent system: the USA.[29] There are no Western cases of presidential/interlocking multi-level systems. There is, however, no inherent reason why such a system could not exist – with a president sharing executive power with a strong second chamber of Congress, where the state executives are directly represented. Switzerland is the classic collegial executive system: where a fixed formula determines the party-political make-up of the seven-member Federal Council, which guarantees an 'oversized majority' in both chambers of the Swiss Parliament. Although Switzerland has some interlocking characteristics, like Austria, the institutional design is essentially independent.[30]

The EU, however, is a case of a collegial-executive system with clearly interlocking arrangements. First, executive authority in the EU is shared between the Commission and the national governments, in the EU Council.[31] As signatories of the EU Treaty, the national governments delegate executive power to the Commission. Also, like the Canadian First Ministers' Conference, the long-term policy agenda of the EU and the institutional reform bargains (in the Intergovernmental Conferences) are worked out collectively by the heads of the executives of the EU member states (i.e. the prime ministers and the French president), in the European Council. The Commission, on the other hand, has the sole right of legislative initiative in most areas of EU social and economic policy, is responsible for supervising policy implementation, is the guardian of the EU treaties, is responsible for managing the EU budget, and has significant regulatory authority akin to the regulatory agencies at the domestic level in Europe and in the USA.[32] Moreover, political competences are divided between the EU and the national institutions along functional rather than jurisdictional lines: with legislative frameworks set at the European level in a growing number of areas of social and economic policy, but these rules subsequently requiring 'transposition' into national law and implementation by the national administrations. Nevertheless, the bulk of political competences still remain the primary authority if the member states, such as education, health and social security policies. Finally, the national governments participate directly in the EU legislative process, in the Council.

Second, the Commission is a collegial-executive body, much like the Swiss Federal Council. The formula is two Commissioners from each of the five larger member states and one from each of the ten smaller member states, and the term of office of the Commission is fixed (five years). The Commission president is nominated by the national governments, in the European Council, and under the rules of the Maastricht Treaty is now subject to an investiture vote in the EP. However, this is not like the investiture of a government in a parliamentary system, since the Commission does not require a permanent majority in the EP. Under Article 144 of the EC Treaty, the EP has a right to censure the Commission as a whole. Nevertheless, this requires a two-thirds majority vote and, despite several attempts, the EP has never used this power. In other words, this right is more similar to the power of the US Congress to impeach the American

President than to the power of a parliamentary majority to withdraw its support of the government.

In sum, the EU is likely to remain a multi-level system whatever institutional changes are made. This hence suggests that the institutional choices for the EU are limited to these six basic multi-level models.[33] There is a possibility that the EU can be reformed into any of these other models set out in Figure 1:

- the EU could be moved to box 5 (collegial-executive/independent system) if the legislative power of the EP were increased versus the Council, and the executive power of the Commission were increased versus the national governments;
- the EU could be moved to box 4 (presidential/interlocking), if the Commission president were directly elected in Europe-wide elections, but the relative power of the EP, the Commission and the Council remain unchanged;
- the EU could be moved to box 3 (presidential/independent) if the Commission president were directly elected, and the legislative power of the EP were increased versus the Council, and the executive power of the Commission were increased versus the national governments;
- the EU could be moved to box 2 (parliamentary/interlocking) if the EP were given a central role in the investiture of the Commission and the Commission were eventually dependent on a majority in the EP, but the balance of EP–Council and Commission–Council were unchanged; and
- the EU could be moved to box 1 (parliamentary/independent) if the EP were given a central role in the investiture of the Commission, and the Commission were eventually dependent on a majority in the EP, and the legislative power of the EP were increased versus the Council, and the executive power of the Commission were increased versus the national governments.

All these have been considered at different times by various academics, consultants and constitutional lawyers. However, the SV of the democratic deficit maintains that the best option would be to turn the EU into a genuine parliamentary model, in box 2 or even box 1. For example, this was the position of the EP in the 1984 Draft Treaty on European Union, and has been the general thrust of the EP's constitutional thinking in the Intergovernmental Conferences which led to the Single European Act and the Maastricht Treaty and in the 1996–97 Intergovernmental Conference on the reform of Maastricht. In all these processes the EP has argued for two main things: increasing its own power versus the Council, and increasing its role in the nomination and ratification of the Commission President – hence, the classic parliamentary/independence model.[34] However, can the democratic deficit be reduced if the EU reformers choose one of the other options? To answer this question we need to develop some hypotheses about how these institutional arrangements affect the role of parties and elections, and to test these theories against the real-world cases.

Impact of Multi-Level Institutions on Elections, Parties and Democracy: Some Hypotheses

The institutional design of a political system has a significant influence on the way elections and parties function. This can be explained in several ways. One approach is to assume that voters and party leaders are utility-maximising actors. In this framework, the institutional design determines the 'structure of political opportunities' for the main political 'agents': the options that are available, and the type of rewards that are on offer.[35] By 'constraining' these actors' behaviour, institutions produce 'structure-induced equilibria', that are different to the 'preference-induced equilibria' that result from an institution-free decision.[36] This type of approach is now widely used in the so-called 'new institutional' approaches to politics from the rational-choice school.[37] It offers a powerful analytical tool-kit to help us understand the implications of multi-level institutional structures across several political systems.

Starting with the electoral process, citizens will only bother going out to vote if they think elections are important. Rational-choice theory has always had problems coming to terms with the fact that voting seems an irrational act: the costs of voting for any individual (e.g. transport and time) far outweigh the chances of influencing the outcome of an election. However, people do vote. Hence, this is usually explained by the fact that the cost of voting is lower than the cost of not voting because of peer pressure, social responsibility or cognitive constraints (such as ideology) on individual behaviour. Nevertheless, not all elections have the same cost of not voting. If an election is deemed 'unimportant' by the peer group, by the media or by the individual, then the cost of no voting is low. From King, we can assume that the relative importance of an election is how far it can alter the 'formation of government' and/or the 'formation of public policy'.[38] Consequently, by determining how far elections can alter these two things, the institutional structure should have a significant effect on voter turnout.

Turning to the role of parties, the classic theories of party behaviour assume that party leaders either seek 'political office'[39] or 'public policy'.[40] However, most contemporary theories argue that party leaders pursue office *and* policy goals – and the key determinant of how party leaders trade-off these two goals is the structure of the institutional environment.[41] For example, if parties are unlikely to be able to achieve a monopoly position, they would rather establish a 'cartel' than suffer the costs of competing with other parties for office and policy. In many systems, parties hence tend to club together to share the spoils of government (such as public funding of their organisations) than compete for the spoils and risk losing. Consequently, by deciding how parties compete or collude in the pursuit of office and policy goals, the institutional environment is a key determinant of whether parties can reinforce or undermine democracy.

As a result, through their impact on the behaviour of voters and party leaders, the structure of opportunities in the different types of multi-level system produces different roles for elections and political parties. First, in most political systems there is a clear division between 'first-order' and 'second-order' elections. First-order elections are where the main political offices are up for grabs and the overall policy agenda is set. These are the most important elections for parties to win, and are the most relevant for the voters. However, in most systems there are other sets of elections that are not so important. These second-order elections determine who holds the lesser political offices, and do not have an impact on the overall policy-agenda. Hence, parties tend to fight these elections as 'mid-term' referendums on the party or parties that won the last first-order contest, and voters are less inclined to bother going out to vote.[42]

TABLE 1
EXPECTED ORDER OF ELECTIONS IN MULTI-LEVEL SYSTEMS

Order of Election Type of Multi-Level System	First	Second
Parliamentary/Independent	central parliament	state parliament
Parliamentary/Interlocking	central/state parliament	–
Presidential/Independent	president	congress/state executive
Presidential/Interlocking	president/state executive	congress
Collegial/Independent	–	state/central parliament
Collegial/Interlocking (EU)	state parliament	central parliament

As Table 1 shows, each type of multi-level system has a different set of first and second-order elections. Two basic principles hold. First, on the vertical institutional dimension, independent institutional structures suggest that the elections for the higher political offices (i.e. the central executive or parliament) are generally more important than those for the lower offices (i.e. the state executives and parliaments). If the system is interlocking, however, the elections for the state executives can be equally as important as those for the central offices, since policy-making power and executive authority is shared between the two levels of politics. Second, on the horizontal institutional dimension, if executive and legislative offices are fused, the main elections are the parliamentary elections. If they are separate, however, the elections for executive office (i.e. the president) are more important for parties and voters than the elections for legislative office (i.e. the congress). In a collegial-executive system, moreover, the central elections do not have an impact on the make-up of the executive or on the general policy agenda. None the less, because the EU combines an interlocking system with a collegial executive, the national elections can have a more significant impact on the exercise of executive power (through the EU Council at the European level, and in the administration of the bulk of public expenditure at the national level) than the elections to the EP. On the basis of these assumptions, the first and second order elections for the six multi-level systems can be worked out deductively, and we can test these hypotheses about the first and second order elections by looking at voter turnout in the eight cases discussed above.

TABLE 2
EXPECTED PATTERNS OF PARTY BEHAVIOUR

Level of Party Type of Multi-Level System	Cohesion	Competition
Parliamentary/Independent	high	low
Parliamentary/Interlocking	medium	low
Presidential/Independent	medium	high
Presidential/Interlocking	low	high
Collegial/Independent	medium	medium
Collegial/Interlocking (EU)	low	medium

Notes: Cohesion = level of organisational development (e.g. hierarchical leadership and decision-making structures) between legislators and executive office-holders from the same political parties in parliamentary business and in legislative–executive relations. Competition = degree to which parties compete rather than collude in elections, in the legislative process and in legislative–executive relations.

Second, the institutional design of the system alters the levels of organisational cohesion and competition between political parties, as Table 2 illustrates. On the organisational side, in an independent multi-level system, different structures of party organisation within the same party family can exist on the two separate levels of government without there being any direct political clashes (which would undermine internal party cohesion), as in the different structure of Democratic and Republican party organisation between the US Congress and the state legislatures.[43] In such a system, vertically integrated political parties are unlikely, but the cohesion of parties across the legislative and executive arenas at the central level is likely to be high.[44] However, if a system is interlocking, the two levels of party organisation come into direct competition in the central legislative process – as in Germany or the EU, where there is inherent conflict between the party organisations in the directly elected chamber (the Bundestag and the EP) and the sub-units of these parties that act in the second chamber as executives of the constituent states rather than branches of the central parties (the Bundesrat and the EU Council). Hence, we can expect higher levels of internal organisational cohesion in legislative action and legislative-executive relations in independent than in interlocking systems.[45]

Cross-cutting this, moreover, in a parliamentary system, where the executive commands a fixed majority in the lower chamber of the legislature, the level of party cohesion in the legislative process and in legislative–executive relations (i.e. the nomination and support of the executive) is likely to be high, because there is a high political price of party members not voting *en bloc*. Parties in parliamentary systems enforce cohesion through various institutional mechanisms: such as hierarchical decision structures, the delegation of policy responsibilities, and the control of committee appointments. As a result, parliamentary systems are the most conducive to 'party government', where cohesive party organisations can enforce party policy choices on their legislative and executive 'agents'.[46] In contrast, in a presidential system and in a collegial-executive system, there is little incentive against individual party members from defecting from the common position of the parliamentary faction, since this would not effect the make-up of the executive.[47] Party groups in presidential systems can use the same mechanisms to ensure internal cohesion, but the price of individual defection for the group as a whole is low, hence there is less incentive to enforce the sanctions. Consequently, taking these two sides of the institutional-structure together, the level of party cohesion in the different types of multi-level systems is likely to be as illustrated in the 'cohesion' column of Table 2.

On the competition side, as discussed above, the institutional structure affects how far parties must compete (or can collude) for political office or over the legislative agenda. Whether a system is interlocking or independent does not alter how executive office is formed at the central level, and has very little impact on the way parties interact in the legislative process. Consequently, it is the structure of the horizontal institutions that has the most impact on the level of party competition. In a presidential system, the party that wins the election for executive has a monopoly on executive authority. There is thus an incentive for parties to collude in electoral competition, to build an alliance with a real prospect of winning the required electoral majority. As a result, a common critique of the American presidential system is that unless parties act 'responsibly' there is a temptation to present identical platforms to the electorate.[48] Once in office, however, there is little possibility for parties to share the spoils of office. Hence, the choice of executive office-holder and the policy agenda is primarily made by the electorate.

In a parliamentary system, in contrast, the choice is very much in the hands of the parties. There is little incentive to cooperate in electoral competition, and a high incentive to collude in the formation of government and in legislative behaviour, to manufacture a majority (in a 'smoke-filled room') after the electorate has made its choice. This is especially true in parliamentary systems with proportional electoral laws, which tend to reduce the possibility of any one party from winning an electoral majority.[49] Finally, in a collegial-executive system, collusion in the formation of executive office is institutionalised. None the less, because of this institutionalised, oversized majority, parties can compete in legislative behaviour without bringing down the government, in setting the policy agenda and in building issue-specific coalitions on the basis of their policy promises to the electorate.[50] In other words, we should expect the levels of party competition in the different types of multi-level systems to be as illustrated in the 'competition' column of Table 2.

EMPIRICAL FINDINGS

With such a small sample (N) of states, it is difficult to draw causal inferences about the impact of the institutional structure on parties and elections. As Lijphart famously argued, 'the intensive comparative analysis of a few cases may be more promising than a more superficial statistical analysis of many cases'.[51] Lijphart also recommended that possible strategies for coping with the 'small-n problem' are: to focus on 'comparable cases'; and to reduce the number of variables.[52] Hence, by following Lijphart's advice – looking only at multi-level systems in western democracies, and focusing on the impact of institutional design on parties and elections – this research at least reduces the probability that any inferences are purely accidental.

Elections: First or Second Order?

Table 3 shows the mean levels of voter turnout in the central and state elections in the eight cases. It is impossible to draw any conclusions by comparing the level of turnouts *between* the different cases. As discussed,

TABLE 3
VOTER TURNOUT IN CENTRAL AND STATE ELECTIONS, 1974–94

Type of Multi-Level System	Case	Turnout in central elections	Turnout in state elections	Average turnout difference (1st-2nd order)
Parliament/Independent	Australia	**92.5**	88.5	4.0
	Austria	**89.3**	81.5	7.8
	Belgium	**92.5**[a]	90.1[a]	2.4
	Canada	**72.3**[b]	74.4[b]	−2.1
Paraliament/Interlocking	Germany	**84.9**	**83.7**	1.2
Presidential/Independent	USA	**52.6**/42.3[c]	45.6[c]	9.0/16.9[d]
Collegial/Independent	Switzerland	62.0[e]	69.0[e]	–
Collegial/Interlocking	European Union	63.6	**82.4**	18.8

Sources: H.H. Kerr, 'The Swiss Party System: Steadfast and Changing', in H. Daalder (ed.) *Party Systems in Denmark, Austria, Switzerland, The Netherlands and Belgium* (London: Pinter 1987); F. Mackie and R. Rose (eds.) *The International Almacac of Electoral History*, 3rd ed. (London: Macmillan 1990); *European Journal of Political Research – Political Data Yearbook* (1992, 1993, 1994, 1995); R. Dyck, *Provincial Politics in Canada,* 3rd ed. (Scarborough: Prentice Hall 1996); and election returns.

Notes: **Bold type**: expected first-order elections.
It is compulsory to vote in Australia and Belgium and in several member states of the EU.
a. The data for Belgium are for the first elections to the Regional and Community Councils, in October 1994 and the closest general election to these elections, in June 1995.
b. The data for Canada are for the six federal and provincial elections prior to 1994.
c. In the case of the USA, at the central level, the presidential elections are in bold and the congressional elections are in plain text, and at the state level, the data are for gubernatorial elections.
d. In the case of the USA, when first- and second-order elections are not held concurrently, the turnout in the first-order (i.e. presidential) elections is on average 16.9 per cent higher than in the second-order elections.
e. The data for Switzerland are for 1947–83.

voter turnout is very much a result of particular environmental factors: such as a culture of political responsibility, the level of peer pressure, or electoral laws preventing citizens from receiving state benefits if they do not vote. Nevertheless, a common variable *within* each system is the 'order' of the election, as determined by the political significance of the election. In this respect, the variation within each of the systems closely resembles the expected order of elections, as set out in Table 1 above (in Table 3, the 'first-order' elections are in bold).

In the parliamentary/independent systems, turnout in the central parliament elections (first order) is higher than in the elections for the state parliament (second order) in all cases except Canada. The average difference in the level of turnout in first-order and second-order elections for Austria, Australia and Belgium is 5 per cent. In contrast, in Germany – a parliamentary/interlocking system – the average difference in turnout in federal and Länder elections is only 1 per cent. In Canada, turnout is on average slightly higher in provincial elections than in federal elections. But, this average is offset by Quebec, where turnout is on average almost 8 per cent higher in provincial than federal elections. This suggests that Canada is on the borderline between an independent and interlocking system: where for most provinces, federal politics are more important, but for Quebec (and Prince Edward Island and Newfoundland – on the far eastern periphery), provincial politics are more important.

FIGURE 2
TURNOUT IN UNITED STATES ELECTIONS

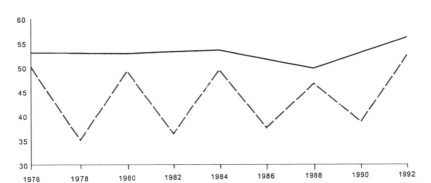

Turnout for American elections has always been low in comparison with European democracies.[53] There is, moreover, an average difference of 9 per cent in the level of participation in the first-order Presidential elections (52.6 per cent) compared to the second-order Congressional and Gubernatorial elections (42.3 and 45.6 per cent respectively). However, even these figures hide the real differences in participation rate between the first-order and second-order elections at the USA. As Figure 2 illustrates, turnout in Congressional elections in the USA is significantly dependent on whether the elections are held at the same time as presidential elections or in the 'mid-term' period. When second-order elections in the USA are held concurrently with a first-order election, the level of voter turnout is only marginally lower in the second-order election. However, when congressional elections are held when no presidential election is held, the level of voter turnout is on average 17 per cent lower, at approximately 36 per cent of the electorate.

In Switzerland, turnout is low in all elections in comparison with the other European democracies. But, turnout is on average 7 per cent higher in cantonal and communal elections than in federal elections. Although this might suggest that cantonal elections may be first-order in Swizerland, the two sets of elections can both be treated as second-order since there are higher participation rates in Swiss referendums than in either sets of elections.[54]

Finally, the levels of participation in the EU confirm the proposition that national elections are first-order elections and EP elections are second-order elections: with a staggering difference in turnout between the two types of election of almost 2 per cent. Compared with the other systems, these figures suggest that in the minds of the voters, the EU is an 'upside-down political system': where the focus of public and media attention is on national politics. This has a significant consequence for the agents of democracy, the political parties. In all the other multi-level systems, parties will either treat the electoral competition for the central political offices as the main event (as in Australia, Austria, Belgium, Canada and the United States) or will treat both levels of competition as significant arenas for battle (as in Germany, Switzerland and some parts of Canada). In the EU in contrast, there is a strong incentive for parties to fight EP elections as a collection of sub-system contests – with national manifestos (instead of European manifestos), and on the performance of the national governments (not on the performance of the EP or the Commission).

This has been pointed out ever since the first direct elections of the EP in 1979.[55] However, the context of the EP elections has rarely been compared with other multi-level systems. This analysis consequently sheds new light on the problem of creating representative democracy in the EU. The results from the other systems give some indication as to what may happen in the EU under different institutional circumstances. For example, if the EP is given more power over the European Commission (as the SV of the democratic deficit implies), EP elections will still be second-order contests if the Commission remains a collegial executive (i.e. the Swiss system). Similarly, if the Commission derives its direct political authority from a permanent majority in the EP (i.e. a parliamentary system), the EP elections may be more important in the minds of the voters, however there is every reason to suggest that national-level elections will still predominate, because the national governments will still possess greater state authority than the Commission (i.e. the German system, but with the national governments even more powerful than the Länder). This would be true as long as voters are able to think about European election choices in terms of national politics. Consequently, in such a system, for EP elections to at least parallel those for national office, the political authority of the Commission relative to national governments would have to be increased beyond anything which is feasible at present, or perhaps even in the foreseeable future.

The aim, therefore, should be to make a differentiation between the European electoral contests and the national electoral contests, without significantly increasing the power of the European Commission. This will not simply result from a uniform electoral procedure, as parties could still fight European elections as national contests (as they do in all the member states where different electoral rules are already used in European elections). However, if the EU were to move towards a presidential system, with the Commission president being elected separately from the EP, this may allow a European electoral contest to be fought along fundamentally different lines than those in national contests. In this model, the elections to the EP would remain second-order contests, and the elections for national governments *and* the Commission president would be first-order contests. Nevertheless, this conclusion would only hold if the electoral organisations and alignments were different between national/EP and Commission-president elections. Hence, this can only be confirmed by looking at the nature of party cohesion and competition across the various systems.

In sum, the levels of voter turnout *within* the various multi-level systems indicate a connection between the institutional design of the system – which determines the degree of importance of the various electoral contests – and the levels of voter participation in these contexts. This is not a novel conclusion. However, it has implications for the EU: neither the parliamentary (interlocking or independent) nor the Swiss (collegial/independent) model may be viable options for the EU, and the direct election of the Commission president may be the only way to establish genuine 'European' elections.

Party Organisational Development

Unlike the levels of voter participation, the level of party organisational development can be analysed *across* systems. Table 4 looks at five different elements of party organisational development in the various multi-level systems. In each of these elements, certain characteristics facilitate strong hierarchical organisational structures and internal party cohesion (in bold in Table 4), while others effectively prevent cohesive party organisations (in italics in Table 4). The analysis considers two different types of party organisations in the USA and the EU that exist almost completely

TABLE 4
LEVEL OF PARTY ORGANISATIONAL DEVELOPMENT

Type of System	Case	Membership structure	Main decision-making organ	Selection of party leader	Selection of election candidates	Highest sanction by party
Par/Ind	Australia	federal	**extra-parliamentary executive**	**elected by party congress**	**central & state parties**	**de-selection/ forced resignation**
	Austria	federal/ individual	**extra-parliamentary executive**	**elected by party congress**	**central & state parties**	**de-selection/ forced resignation**
	Belgium	confederal	informal parliamentary liaison	no single leader	state parties	none (but can pressure state party)
	Canada	federal	extra-parliamentart executive	elected by party congress	state parties	expulsion from parliamentary group
Par/Int	Germany	individual	**extra-parliamentary executive**	**elected by party congress**	**central & state parties**	**de-selection forced resignation**
Pre/Ind	American presidential parties	voting registration	president/ national committee	primary of registered voters	primary of registered voters	none
	American congressional parties	confederal	congressional caucus/ national committee	majority of congressional group	primary of voters/state parties	exclusion from decision making
Col/Ind	Switzerland	federal	**extra-parliamentary executive**	**elected by party congress**	state parties	**expulsion from parliamentary group**
Col/Int	EU party federations	confederal	caucus of state and EP leaders	unanimity of party leaders	–	expulsion from party
	EU EP groups	confederal	parliamentary group executive	majority of parliamentary group	state parties	expulsion (if supported by state party)

Sources:
Australia – L.D. Epstein, 'A Comparative Study of Australian Parties', *British Journal of Political Science* 7 (1997) pp.1–21; D. Jaensch, *The Australian Party System* (London: Allen & Unwin 1983).
Austria – W.C. Müller, 'Austria (1945–1990)', in R.S. Katz and P. Mair (eds.) *Party Organizations* (London: Sage 1992).
Belgium – K. Deschouwer, 'Belgium', in ibid.
Germany – R. Wildenmann, 'The Party Government of the Federal Republic of Germany: Form and Experience', in R.S. Katz (ed.) *Party Governments: European and American Experiences* (Berlin: de Gruyter 1987); T. Poguntke and B. Boll, 'Germany', in Katz and Mair *supra*.
Canada – J. Wearing, *The L-Shaped party: The Liberal Party of Canada, 1958–80* (Toronto: McGraw-Hill 1981); D.E. Smith, 'Party Government, Representation and National Integration in Canada', in P. Aucoin (ed.) *Party Government and Regional Representation in Canada* (U. of Toronto 1985).
United States – M.P. Fiorina, 'Party Government in the United States – Diagnosis and Prognosis', in Katz *supra*; R. Kolodny and R.S. Katz, 'The United States', in Katz and Mair *supra*.
Switzerland – H.H. Kerr, 'The Swiss Party System: Steadfast and Changing', in H. Daalder (ed.) *Party Systems in Denmark, Austria, Switzerland, The Netherlands and Belgium* (London: Pinter 1987); F. Lehner and B. Homann, 'Consociational Decision-Making and Party Government in Switzerland', in Katz *supra*.
European Union – L. Bardi, 'Transnational Party Federations in the European Community', in Katz and Mair *supra*; S. Hix, *Political Parties and the European Union System*, PhD Thesis (Florence: European Univ. Inst. 1995).

Notes: **Bold** type = characteristic of a strong party organisation; *italics* = characteristic of a weak party organisation. For Belgium, for the sake of comparison with the EU, the table refers to the organisations within each 'party family'.

independently of each other: the 'presidential parties' and 'congressional parties' in the USA;[56] and the 'party federations' and 'EP Groups' in the EU.[57]

In the classic 'party-government' model, parties have highly-developed organisational structures. This is the case in four of the five parliamentary systems (Australia, Austria, Canada and Germany) and in Switzerland: where party membership is either individual or federal; the extra-parliamentary executive committee (which usually comprises the leaders of the parliamentary group, members of the party in government, and representatives from state-level parties) is able to impose its will on the parties' office-holders; and the party leader is chosen by the party congress.[58] Moreover, the central party organisations are responsible for selecting (or at least overseeing the selection of) election candidates and, as a result, office-holders who defect from the official party line can be forced to resign from a government. In the party-government model, therefore, there is a 'chain' from the individual party members, via the leadership cadre and the party leader, to the execution of party policies by the party office-holders.[59]

In the USA and the EU, in contrast, party organisations are weak. Party membership is confederal in the US Congress, the EP Groups and the Europarty federations – the Party of European Socialists (PES), the European People's Party (EPP), the European Liberal, Democrat and Reform Party (ELDR), and the European Federation of Green Parties (EFGP). In US presidential elections, 'party members' do not really exist: any citizen who registers as a 'voter' for a party can participate in the election of the presidential candidate of that party. Similarly, the main decision-making organs for the Groups in the EP are the executive committees of the parliamentary groups (such as the Bureau of the PES Group), which play a more significant leadership and agenda-setting role than the 'party leaders summits' of the EU party federations (that meet at least twice a year) and the national committees/congressional caucuses of the American parties. These organs are useful fora for discussing strategy and exchanging ideas, but have few powers to impose their wishes on the party members holding legislative or executive office.

In the US Congress and the EP, the 'group leader' is chosen internally, by a majority of the members of the parliamentary 'faction'. The leader of the 'presidential party' in the USA is selected in a nation-wide primary, and the presidents of the EU party federations are chosen by a consensual-agreement of the national party and EP Group Leaders (and subsequently ratified by the Europarty congresses). Only in the case of the EPP are the offices of the leader of the Europarty federation and leader of the EP Group merged: the position is held by Wilfried Martens. In the organisational structure of the PES, the leader of the EP Group (Pauline Green) is on equal footing with the leaders of the national member parties of the PES. These later methods mean that the 'leader' is only the head of a particular hierarchy (i.e. a parliamentary group or a leadership caucus), and is not the genuine figurehead of a united and vertically-integrated party organisation.

Finally, in the EU and the USA, the parliamentary or extra-parliamentary leaderships have no say in candidate selection. In the USA, the individual party members (the registered voters) decide who stands in the elections. As a result, party office-holders cannot be removed from central decision-making structures by the central party leaderships. In the case of the US 'presidential parties', for example, once elected, the party has no possibility of de-selecting the incumbent. This is the sole choice of the electorate as a whole.

The weakness of party organisation in the EU is further illustrated in the legislative behaviour of the EP groups. A number of scholars have pointed out that in general the level of cohesion of the EP groups has risen since 1979.[60] As Brzinski states: 'Though the European Parliament does not have a government to support, and despite the fact that political groups have little ability to sanction defection, the level of voting cohesion of groups in the European Parliament is much closer to that found in European Parliamentary systems than in the US Congress.'[61]

Studies of the US Congress produce indices of agreement between 55 and 89, with an average of about 70.[62] As Table 5 shows, in contrast, in all the 'roll-call votes' between 1989 and 1994, the average index of agreement for the EP Groups was 79.8.

However, this result hides the real weakness of party organisation in the EP. Most votes in the EP have little impact on the organisational success of the sub-units of the groups: the national parties. Consequently, although national parties control candidate selection, on most occasions the sub-units have little reason to threatened de-selection of MEPs who vote against the position of the national parties. The EP groups have some sanctions against individual members but little sanction against defection by a whole national delegation. Any national delegation could easily leave the group and join another or sit with the 'non-attached' members. To prevent this, the EP groups all have a 'conscience clause', allowing any national party delegation to vote against the group line without the threat of sanctions. As a result, when national party interests are mobilised, the level of EP Group cohesion falls dramatically for those parties were the national party interests are in conflict with the position of the EP Group.

As Table 5 shows, this was the case in the July 1994 EP vote on the investiture of Jacques Santer as Commission president.[63] Because the European Council had to choose the candidate, parties in government at the

TABLE 5
PARTY COHESION IN THE EUROPEAN PARLIAMENT

Party Group (Left to Right)[a]	1989–94	Investiture of Commission President, 1994
Left Unity (Orthodox Communists)	98.6	–
European Unitaraian Left (Radical Left)	91.5	100.0
Green Group (Greens & Allies)	85.0	81.0
Party of European Socialists (Socialists/Social-Democrats)	90.4	50.0
European Radical Alliance (Left-Liberals)	–	100.0
Liberal, Democrat and Reform Party (Liberals/Centrists)	70.8	26.3
European People's party (Christian Democrats)	85.3	98.7
European Democratic Alliance (French Gaullists/ Irish FF)	74.9	84.0
European Democratic Group (British Conservatives)	84.5	–
Forza Europa Group (Forza Italia & Allies)	–	100.0
European Right (Extreme Right)	91.2	–
Rainbow Group (Regionalists & Anti-Europeans)[a]	25.9	–
Europe of Nations Group (Anti-Europeans)[a]	–	00.0
Average	79.8	71.1

Sources: 1989–1994: J. Bay Brzinski, 'Political Group Cohesion in the European Parliament, 1989–1994', in C. Rhodes and S. Mazev (eds.) *The State of the European Union, Vol.3* (London: Longman 1996). Commission Investiture: S. Hix and C. Lord, 'The Making of a President: The European Parliament and the Confirmation of Jacques Santer as President of the Commission', *Government and Opposition* 31/1 (1996) pp.63–76.

Notes: Index of Agreement = [(highest modality – sum of the other two modalities)/total number of votes cast by the group] × 100. See F. Attinà, 'The Voting Behaviour of the European Parliament Members and the Problem of Europarties', *European Journal of Political Research* 18/9 (Sept. 1990) pp.557–79.
a. The Regionalists and the Anti-Europeans are not easy to position on a left–right dimension, as they each contain parties from across the Left–Right spectrum, and are hence aligned on a different dimension of politics.

national level had a strong stake in the result of the EP vote. When it came to the EP vote, therefore, these governing parties were able to force their MEPs to support the Santer nomination (or face de-selection), where the official position of the EP Group was to vote against the nomination. For example, the Spanish, Danish and Irish social-democratic party delegations voted in favour of Santer (against the PES group line) which significantly undermined the usually high cohesion of the PES. The average index of agreement for EP Groups with internal conflicts in the Santer vote – where parties in government at the national level (who backed Santer) were opposed to the EP Group position (against Santer) – was only 48.26.

One could hence conclude that this is in fact more similar to the dynamics of party organisation in the Swiss parliament or in the US Congress than in parliamentary systems. In the US Congress, 'southern Democrats' often collaborate to vote against the caucus position if the official party line threatens their common interests, without the threat of sanctions. And, in Switzerland, research has found that the three truly 'national' parties – the Socialists, Christian Democrats and Radical Democrats (akin to the PES, EPP and ELDR in the EP) – all have relatively low levels of cohesion. Like the EP, there are few sanctions available to parties in the Swiss parliament. If members defect from the party line the government will not fall, and their Cantonal party organisation is still likely to select them for re-election. This later sanction, also like the EP, ensures that Swiss parties from a small number of Cantons are more cohesive than those that have members from all (or almost all) territorial sub-units.[64]

In sum, as expected, the strongest party organisations can be found in the parliamentary systems. However, there appears to be little difference as a result of variation between independent and interlocking vertical institutions. Parties in Switzerland also appear relatively strong, but the parties are weakened by their inability to impose their will on the party members of the collegial executive.[65] The level of development of parties in the EU is somewhere between the parallel party-organisational structure of the US system and the weak central party organisations of the Swiss system. Moreover, if the EU develops further towards a parliamentary system, where EP votes would have a significant impact on the behaviour of the Commission and the competitive position of domestic parties, there is evidence to suggest that EU party cohesion is likely to break down. With confederal organisational structures, and the selection of candidates by domestic parties, the EP Groups show high levels of organisational cohesion only when their behaviour is isolated from the exercise of executive authority in the EU system. Therefore, it may be advantageous for the EP to remain independent from the Commission: as in the existing collegial-executive system, or if the EU moves towards a presidential system.

Party Competition: Fragmentation, Polarisation and Convergence

Table 6 looks at the three standard measures of party competition: the *fragmentation* of the party system (the number of parties in the system); the *polarisation* of the party system (the distance between the most extreme parties at either end of the left–right spectrum); and the level of *convergence* in the system (the distance between the two largest parties). As the first column shows, there is some evidence to suggest a relationship between the type of multi-level system and the degree of party system fragmentation. The results do not suggest any inferences about the influence of independent/interlocking vertical institutions on the level of party system fragmentation, but they do suggest some conclusions about the impact of horizontal institutions. Duverger was the first to argue that majoritarian/ plurality elections (such as the 'winner-takes-all' contest in a presidential election) tend to produce two-party or two-bloc systems and proportional-representation elections (such as the elections of most European parliaments) tend to produce multi-party systems.[66] This seems to be partially confirmed in our results: where the Belgian and German proportional/parliamentary systems have significantly more parties than the US majoritarian/presidential system.

However, the findings also suggest something interesting about the impact of the collegial-executive system. The highest levels of fragmentation are in the Swiss and European elections. Although this is an extremely small sample, these results may reflect the fact that there is 'less at stake' in elections that do not alter the make-up of the executive, and hence less incentive against voters supporting minor parties. Similarly, Bardi argues that the nature of EP election campaigns (with their national foci) facilitates a fragmentation of the EU party system, and that the internal organisational rules of the EP are instrumental in preventing any further fragmentation of the system.[67] A note of caution, however: the level of fragmentation in Switzerland and the EU (as in Belgium) is also an indication of the existence of very heterogenous societies.[68]

Moving on to the polarisation of party systems, the only pattern that emerges from the different levels of polarisation of the party systems is that the US system is by far the least polarised. Again, this may result from the significance of socio-economic status (i.e. class) as the only major cleavage in US politics at the federal level.[69] However, class-voting has fallen dramatically in the USA since the mid-1950s. The USA is a highly fragmented multi-ethnic, multi-religious, geographically dispersed and increasingly multi-lingual society. Hence, the low level of polarisation may in fact be because the two parties are forced by the majoritarian rules to construct broad alliances in order to win a plurality in the presidential

TABLE 6
MEASURES OF PARTY COMPETITION

Type of System	Case	Effective number of parties	Party system polarisation	Distance between two main parties
Parl/Indep	Australia	2.5	5.5	2.4
	Austria	2.4	5.8	1.5
	Belgium	4.6	3.9	2.0
	Canada	2.4	6.1	2.2
Parl/Inter	Germany	3.2	7.8	2.6
Pres/Indep	United States	1.9	2.7	2.7
Coll/Indep	Switzerland	5.1	5.7	3.4
Coll/Inter	European Union	5.0	6.7[a]	2.8[a]

Sources: Column 1: D. Farrell, *Comparing Electoral Systems* (London: Prentice-Hall 1997); L. Bardi, 'Transnational Trends in European Parties and the 1994 Elections of the European Parliament', *Party Politics* 2/1 (1996) pp.99–114.
Columns 2 and 3: R. Inglehart and J. Huber, 'Expert Judgements of Party Space and Party Locations in 42 Societies', *Party Politics* 1/1 (1995) pp.73–111.

Notes: For the calculation of 'Effective Number of Parties' see M. Laakso and R. Taagepera, '"Effective" Number of Parties: A Measure with Application to Western Europe', *Comparative Political Studies* 12/1 (1979) pp.3–27.
Columns 2 and 3 are based on 'expert judgements' of party positions on a Left (1)–Right (10) scale.
a . The positions of the EU parties are calculated from the mean positions of the member parties of the European party federations – the PES, EPP, ELDR and EFGP.

contests. In other words, the presidential system suppresses the political impact of a highly polarised society, just as it seems to undermine the development of a multi-party system. In all the parliamentary and collegial systems, in contrast, the party system is relatively highly polarised, with parties on the extreme left and right being able to remain in the party system. Again, as expected, the variation between independent and interlocking systems does not appear to matter: the polarisation of the German and Canadian systems are only marginally higher than in the independent/parliamentary systems.

Finally, the horizontal institutional design of the system also seems to have an impact on the level of convergence in the party system. In all the parliamentary systems, despite high levels of fragmentation and polarisation, the distance between the two main parties is low (between 1.5 and 2.6). This cannot be explained by a Downsian model of electoral competition, where the two main parties will converge on the median voter, as this model only holds in a two-party system. In multi-party systems, if the two major parties converge on the median voter, more extreme parties can 'steal' the votes at either end of the spectrum. Consequently, the convergence in these parliamentary systems is more as a result of 'cartel' tendencies inherent in the party-government model: where there is probably little electoral cost and high financial and policy benefits from collusion in the legislative or governmental arenas.

By contrast, in the USA, despite a low level of fragmentation and polarisation, there is an important difference between the Republicans and the Democrats. For many European commentators, who have traditionally viewed the Democrats and Republicans as members of the same (or very close) party families,[70] this may be a surprising result. However, this indicates how far the major parties in the parliamentary democracies have moved since the 1960s and 1970s towards the cartel model in response to the collapse of their traditional electoral bases. In other words, the results suggest that whereas parties are forced to compete at the electoral level for presidential office in the US system, in the parliamentary democracies their competition in the electoral arena may not be matched in the legislative and governmental arenas. Hence, this confirms the hypotheses from Table 3, above, that electoral competition between parties is likely to be lower in parliamentary than presidential systems.

Moreover, the predictions from Table 3 also hold for the degree of collusion in collegial-executive systems. The results show a relatively high distance between the two major parties in the Swiss and EU party systems. As argued, this suggests that rather than the collegial arrangements precluding competition in the legislative arena, the existence of a fixed executive coalition may by a blank cheque for open competition in parliament: because the parties do not need to collude in the legislative arena to share the spoils of executive office (as they have to in parliamentary systems). Although, again, because of the small sample, this would need to be further tested.

In sum, these findings partially confirm the hypotheses: parliamentary systems tend to produce moderate multi-party systems, but with a high level of collusion between the main parties; the one example of a presidential system has a two-party system, but a clear distinction in the policy location of these parties; and collegial-executive systems have highly-fragmented multi-party systems, but with a high degree of competition between the main parties. In other words, it may again be undesirable for the EU to follow the parliamentary route. The party systems in parliamentary systems *do* seem to be more susceptible to cartelisation, as one type of the criticisms of the SV theory argues. And, moving to the direct election of the

Commission president may enable a few options to be presented to the European electorate, without undermining competition in the EP between the party groups.

CONCLUSIONS: TOWARDS AN ALTERNATIVE INSTITUTIONAL DESIGN

From this theoretical framework and these empirical findings, two tentative conclusions can be drawn about the viability of the agenda inherent in the SV of the EU democratic deficit, and about the salience of the critiques of that agenda.

First, a classic parliamentary democracy at the European level (as implied by the 'SV' of the democratic deficit) may not be the best option for the EU. The evidence suggests that making the Commission permanently accountable to a majority in the EP would *not* guarantee that EP elections become 'first-order' contests: fought on 'European' issues, by 'European' parties. For at least the foreseeable future, the EU is an 'upside-down political system': the institutions at the national level exercise greater executive authority in most areas of public policy than the European institutions, and the media and the general public are primarily concerned with who controls these national offices. Hence, the 'power' and 'prestige' rewards for party leaders are greater at the domestic level than at the European level. National political parties will consequently fight EP campaigns as mid-term referendums on the performance of the parties that 'won' the last real elections. At the electoral level, therefore, in such a system transnational parties will constantly be undermined by the competing interests of domestic parties.

Furthermore, if the Commission is made permanently accountable to a majority in the EP within this overarching structure, rather than increasing EU democracy, it would undermine party cohesion *and* undermine party competition in the legislative process. Because national party organisations (the sub-units of the EP Groups) control the selection of EP election candidates, they possess more powerful sanctions over the MEPs than do the EP Groups. In everyday EP business, a conflict of interests between the EP and national party organisations does not occur. However, if the EP Groups are able to alter the make-up of the Commission, as in a parliamentary system (and as they do in the present Commission investiture procedure), parties holding national government office (who sit in the EU Council) would have an incentive to enforce their wishes on their MEPs. In this situation, cohesive EP parties are almost impossible to maintain – as was the case in the EP vote on the investiture of the Commission president, in July 1994. This would change if the EP Groups controlled candidate selection. However, such a change is unlikely: especially when one considers the 'De Gucht Report' proposals for a uniform electoral procedure, which would still allow national parties to control the nomination of at least 90 per cent of MEP candidates. Finally, protected from electoral competition (by the 'national' character of EP elections), the EP Groups are more likely to collude (form 'cartels') in the legislative process in a parliamentary system than they do in the present collegial-executive system. At least in the present system, inter-party competition in the legislative arena can continue without the threat of undermining the stability of the executive.

In other words, if the EU follows the route of parliamentary democracy, voters will *not* be able to choose between rival European agendas, and their electoral choices will *not* be translated into legislative and executive action by cohesive and competitive parties. This may even be worse than the present system! In this respect, the critics of the SV are probably right.

Second, however, the critics of the SV may be mistaken to suggest that EU democracy is neither likely nor desirable. A full-blown parliamentary system is not the only option. The aim should be to design institutions that do facilitate genuine European elections, on the one hand, and cohesive but not collusive Europarties, on the other. From the theoretical and empirical analyses, an alternative way of doing this would be to reform the EU not into a parliamentary system but into a (partial) presidential one![71] This may initially sound subversive, but the direct election of the Commission president has been floated by various political and academic figures since the 1970s.[72] There seems to be strong evidence for this idea to be revived.

In terms of European elections, a direct election of the Commission president – or the first step towards this via an electoral college comprising all national MPs and MEPs (similar to the early American model)[73] may be the only way to allow Europe's citizens to actually 'choose' between rival agendas for European action. The problems inherent in the second-order situation for EP elections would not necessarily hold in elections for the Commission president. If candidates are required to be nominated by at least one party in a large majority (or even all) member states, parties would be responsible for fighting the election campaign on the basis of the candidates they support, and not on whether the national government is doing a good job (as they do in the present elections to the EP). Furthermore, rather than relying on cohesive party organisations to translate voters' preferences into policy actions, this system would encourage loose electoral alliances, and allow voters (not parties) to decide who exercises executive authority at the European level. The European electorate would have someone to 'throw out', and the national parties that supported the winning candidate would be accountable to the national electorates for his/her actions once in office. And, without the threat of conflicts with national party organisations and an institutional incentive to collude to support the executive, the EP Groups would maintain their present level of cohesion and structure of competition. In other words, against the *anti-Europarty critique* (as set out in the first part of this article), it *is* feasible that competitive-but-not-collusive parties could exist at the European level under a different institutional design.

As Lord Bryce warned, nonetheless: 'The student of institutions is apt to overrate the effect of mechanical contrivances in politics.'[74] Any theory of parties and elections cannot ignore the significance of societal divisions.[75] For example, in most multi-level systems 'societal federalism' (a territorially fragmented social structure) restricts the emergence of cohesive political parties as much as the design of the institutions of government.[76] But more significantly for the argument presented here, the existence of societal 'segmentation'- instead of societal homogeneity or cross-cutting cleavages – is often cited as a major reason why presidential systems fail.[77] In such societies (e.g. the EU), majoritarian presidential coalitions are invariably built between rival societal/territorial segments rather than broad cross-segmental or transterritorial alliances.[78] In applying this principle to the EU, Weiler has often used the analogy of a hypothetical *Anschluss* between Denmark and Germany, that would place the Danes in 'perpetual opposition' despite representation in the Bundestag.[79] In other words, the direct election of the Commission president would be undesirable and illegitimate because it would leave whole nations opposed to the majority-winning coalition.

However, for two reasons this *anti-Euromajoritarianism critique* may also be questioned. First, a direct election of the Commission president would not transform the EU into a completely majoritarian system. The EU legislative process would remain highly consensual: requiring 'oversized majorities' in the EP and the Council. And, executive authority would remain shared with the Council – which when acting as an executive is a collegial body (requiring a unanimity of national governments). If the interlocking structure of the vertical institutions is unchanged (i.e. the EU becomes a 'presidential/interlocking' rather than 'presidential/independent' system), therefore, the role of national governments in the legislative and executive processes would be maintained, as a counter weight against the naturally enhanced status of a directly elected Commission President, and the existing accountability links to national parliaments and electorates would be preserved. In other words, such a change to the process of selecting the Commission president would leave most of the 'consociational' elements of the EU constitution untouched,[80] particularly in the exercise of 'state power' in the areas of justice and home affairs and common foreign and security policy fields. The election of the Commission president would be a 'safety valve' in a system which is prone to policy *immobilisme* as a result of too many 'veto players' in the decision process.[81] This would be similar to the use of referendums in the Swiss system to break collegial deadlocks and drive the policy agenda forward – and is hence in the same vain as proposals for European-wide referendums.[82]

Second, the rules for electing the Commission president can be drafted in a such a way as to ensure that a majority-winning coalition is transnational and not inter-national. For example, candidates could be required to be nominated by at least one party in a *every* member state. This would most likely restrict the nominations to one from each 'party family' – Socialists, Liberals, Christian Democrats/Conservatives and maybe Greens.[83] Such a nomination rule would ensure that at least one group of élites (and supporters) in every nation would be associated with the winning candidate. In other words, a system could be constructed that guarantees cross-segmental support for executive authority, and does not leave any single territorial/national group subjugated. The majoritarianism of a presidential election could hence be moderated by non-majoritarian nomination rules.

All in all, the exercise of political authority at the European level is increasingly questioned by Europe's citizens. To address these grievances, social science must combine normative reasoning with theoretical, comparative and empirical research. In so doing, we find that democracy in the European Union is certainly desirable *and* maybe possible, but only if we are more ingenious about the design of institutional mechanisms for holding executive power accountable to Europe's voters.

NOTES

1. Earlier versions of this article were presented at the workshop on 'Regional Integration and Multi-Level Governance', at the Joint Sessions of the European Consortium for Political Research, 27 Feb.–4 March 1997, Bern, Switzerland, and at the panel on 'EU Democracy in Global Perspective', at the 5th Biennial Conference of the European Community Studies Association, 29 May–1 June 1997, Seattle, Washington. I am especially grateful to Liesbet Hooghe, Peter Leslie, Gary Marks, Mark Pollack, Philippe Schmitter, Hermann Schmitt and William Wallace for their comments on these earlier drafts.
2. J.H.H. Weiler, U.R. Haltern and F.C. Mayer, 'European Democracy and Its Critique', in J. Hayward (ed.) *The Crisis of Representation in Europe* (London: Frank Cass 1995) pp.4–39.
3. Ibid. p.6.
4. Ibid. pp.7-8.
5. A. King, 'What do Elections Decide?', in D. Butler, H.R. Penniman and A. Ranney (eds.) *Democracy at the Polls* (Washington DC: American Enterprise Inst. 1981).
6. E.g. M. Weber, 'Politics as a Vocation', in H.H. Gerth and C. Wright Mills (eds.) *From Max Weber: Essays in Sociology* (Oxford: OUP 1942); E.E. Schattschneider *Party Government* (NY: Rinehart 1942); J. Schumpeter, *Capitalism, Socialism and Democracy* (London: Allen & Unwin 1943); R. Rose, *The Problem of Party Government* (London: Macmillan 1974); and I. Budge and H. Keman, *Parties and Democracy* (Oxford: OUP 1990).

7. Cf. H. Vredeling, 'A Common Market of Politics Parties', *Government and Opposition* 6/3 (1971) pp.448–61; D. Marquand, 'Towards a Europe of Parties', *Political Quarterly* 49/3 (1978) pp.438–45; G. Pridham and P. Pridham, *Towards Transnational Parties in the European Community* (London: Policy Studies Institute 1979); S. Williams, 'Sovereignty and Accountability in the European Community', in R.O. Keohane and S. Hoffman (eds.) *The New European Community* (Boulder, CO: Westview 1991); F. Attinà, 'Parties, Party Systems and Democracy in the European Union', *International Spectator* 27/3 (1992) pp.67–86; D. Tsatsos, 'European Political Parties? Preliminary Reflections on Interpreting the Maastricht Treaty Article on Political Parties (Article 138a of the EC Treaty)', *Human Rights Law Journal* 16/1 (1995) pp.1–9; S. Hix, 'Parties at the European Level and the Legitimacy of EU Socio-Economic Policy', *Journal of Common Market Studies* 33/4 (1996) pp.527–54; J. Lodge, 'The Future of the European Parliament', in J. Lodge (ed.) *The 1994 Elections to the European Parliament* (London: Pinter 1995); M. Pederson, 'Euro-parties and European Parties: New Arenas, New Challenges and New Strategies', in S.S. Andersen and K.A. Eliassen (eds.) *The European Union: How Democratic Is It?* (London: Sage 1996); S. Hix and C. Lord, *Political Parties in the European Union* (London: Macmillan 1997).
8. D. Obradovic, 'Policy Legitimacy and the European Union', *Journal of Common Market Studies* 34/2 (1996) pp.191–221; M. Jachtenfuchs, 'Democracy and Governance in the European Union', *European Integration On-Line Papers* 1 (1997) http://eiop.or.at/eiop/texte/1997.002a.htm; C. Joerges and J. Neyer, 'Constitutionalising the European Polity through the Transformation of Intergovernmentalist Bargaining into Deliberative Political Process, unpublished mimeo (1997); F.W. Scharpf, 'Economic Integration, Democracy and the Welfare State', *Journal of European Public Policy* 4/1 (1997) pp.18–36; and J.H.H. Weiler, 'Legitimacy and Democracy of Union Governance', in G. Edwards and F. Pijpers (eds.) *The Politics of European Treaty Reform* (London: Pinter 1997).
9. R. Dehousse, 'Constitutional Reform in the European Community: Are There Alternatives to the Majority Avenue?', in Hayward (note 2); G. Majone, 'Regulatory Legitimacy', in idem *Regulating Europe* (London: Routledge 1996).
10. E.g. G.A. Almond, 'Comparing Political Systems', *Journal of Politics* 18/2 (1956) pp.391–409; A. Lijphart *The Politics of Accommodation: Pluralism and Democracy in The Netherlands* (Berkeley: U. of California 1968); and R.A. Dahl, *Democracy and Its Critics* (New Haven, CT: Yale U. Press 1989) p.19.
11. K. Lawson and P. Merkl (eds.) *When Parties Fail* (Princeton UP 1988); J.L. Reiter, 'Party Decline in the West: A Skeptic's View', *Journal of Theoretical Politics* 1/3 (1989) pp.325–48; H. Daalder, 'A Crisis of Party?', *Scandinavian Political Studies* 15/4 (1992) pp.269–88; and R.S. Katz and P. Mair, 'Changing Models of Party Organization and Party Democracy: The Emergence of the Cartel Party', *Party Politics* 1/1 (1995) pp.5–28.
12. Ibid. p.14.
13. P. Mair, 'Political Parties, Popular Legitimacy, and Public Privilege', in Hayward (note 2) p.38.
14. E.g. A. Weale, 'Democratic Legitimacy and the Constitution of Europe', in R. Bellamy, V. Bufacchi and D. Castiglione (eds.) *Democratic and Constitutional Culture in the Union of Europe* (London: Lothian 1995); J.H.H. Weiler, 'Does Europe Need a Constitution? Demos, Telos and the German Maastricht Decision', *European Law Journal* 1/3 (1995) pp.219–58; and D.N.Chryssochoou, 'Europe's Could-Be Demos: Recasting the Debate', *West European Politics* 19/4 (Oct. 1996) pp.787–801.
15. E.g. F.W. Scharpf, 'The Joint-Decision Trap: Lessons from German Federalism and European Integration', *Public Administration* 66/3 (1988) pp.239–78; G. Majone, 'Regulatory Federalism in the European Community', *Environment and Planning C: Government and Policy* 10 (1992) pp.299–316; A.M. Sbragia, 'Thinking About the European Future: The Uses of Comparisons', in idem (ed.) *Euro-Politics* (Washington DC: Brookings 1992); S. Hix, 'The Study of the European Community: The Challenge to Comparative Politics', *West European Politics* 17/1 (Jan. 1994) pp.1–30; and T. Risse-Kappen, 'Exploring the Nature of the Beast: International Relations Theory and Comparative Policy Analysis Meet the European Union', *Journal of Common Market Studies* 34/1 (1996) pp.53–80.

16. A.J. Heidenheimer, H. Heclo and C.T. Adams *Comparative Public Policy*, 3rd ed. (NY: St Martin's 1990), p.1.
17. As Tocqueville argued: 'Without comparisons to make, the mind does not know how to proceed'. A. de Tocqueville, R. Boesche (ed.) *Selected Letters on Politics and Society* (Berkeley: U. of California Press 1985), p.191.
18. A. Przeworski and H. Teune, *The Logic of Comparative Social Inquiry* (NY: Wiley 1970).
19. Scharpf (note 15) and Sbragia (note 15).
20. Cf. K.C. Wheare *Federal Government*, 3rd ed. (NY: OUP 1953); W.H. Riker *Federalism: Origin, Operation, Significance* (Boston: Little, Brown 1964); W.H. Riker, 'Federalism', in F.I. Greenstein and N.W. Polsby (eds.) *Handbook of Political Science, Vol.5* (Reading: Addison-Wesley 1975); and D.J. Elazar, 'Federalism', in S.M. Lipset (ed.) *The Encyclopaedia of Democracy* 2 (1995) pp.474–82.
21. Cf. H. Bakvis and W.M. Chandler (eds.) *Federalism and the Role of the State* (Toronto UP 1987).
22. E.S. Corwin, 'The Passing of Dual Federalism', *Virginia Law Review* 36/1 (1950) pp.1–24.
23. The concept of 'dual leadership' comes from Blondel. He uses the term to refer to dual monarchies, semi-presidential republics and the constitutional arrangements in some communist systems. However, the theoretical and normative principles of Blondel's dual leadership (e.g. the existence of two political constituencies) also exists in interlocking federal systems. See J. Blondel, 'Dual Leadership in the Contemporary World: A Step Towards Executive and Regime Stability?', in D. Kavanagh and G. Peele (eds.) *Comparative Government and Politics* (London: Heinemann 1984).
24. F.W. Scharpf , B. Reissert and F. Schnabel (eds.) *Politikverflechtung* (Kronberg: Scriptor 1976).
25. A. Lijphart, 'Introduction', in idem (ed.) *Parliamentary versus Presidential Government* (Oxford: OUP 1992); M.S. Shugart and J.M. Carey, *Presidents and Assemblies* (Cambridge: CUP 1992); and G. Sartori, *Comparative Constitutional Engineering* (London: Macmillan 1994).
26. There are numerous other multi-level systems, such as Mexico, Brazil, India, Nigeria, South Africa and Russia. However, I focus on Western systems to control for the influence of culture. By taking systems were the cultural constraints on actors' behaviour are relatively similar, we can focus on the structure of institutions as the main explanatory variable. This consequently avoids the problem of making generalisations about the performance of parliamentary and presidential systems across different cultures. Cf. S.M. Lipset, 'The Centrality of Political Culture', *Journal of Democracy* 1/4 (1990) pp.80–3.
27. In Australia, Belgium and Canada, both chambers of the central legislatures are elected independently of the state governments, and the policy competences of the central and state administrations are strictly defined. The Austrian Länder governments sit in the upper-house of the central legislature, the Bundesrat. Nevertheless, the Austrian system is still a case of independent federalism because: the upper-house is considerably weaker than the lower-house; the Länder governments are weaker than the Austrian Federal Government in the exercise of executive authority; and the representation in the Austrian Bundesrat is proportional to the whole electorate, and there is no over-representation of the smaller Länder. See A. Lijphart, *Democracies* (New Haven, CT: Yale UP 1984) pp.174–5.
28. The German Länder governments not only sit in the upper-house of the central legislature, the Bundesrat, but also have a very powerful role in central policy formulation and adoption. Moreover, under the German constitution many policy competences are shared between the Federal and Länder governments, and the Länder governments have an extensive policy implementation and administration role. Canada is not included in this category, but has an 'interlocking' characteristic in the system: where the federal-provincial First Ministers' Conference has a central role in setting the medium- and long-term political agenda, particularly in the area of institutional reform.
29. The USA is the archetypal case of an independent federal system. The legal jurisdiction of the American states are protected under the Constitution. Moreover, as Schattschneider points out: 'the Senate [has] established the principle that individual senators are not bound by the instructions of state legislature'. See E.E. Schattschneider, *Semisovereign People* (Hinsdale: Dryden Press 1960) p.14.

30. Like the German Bundestag, the Swiss Cantons are represented in the second chamber of the Swiss parliament, Ständerat. However, like the US Senate, the Ständerat is more a central parliamentary chamber than an explicit 'organ of state interests'. Tax-raising and policy competences are also clearly divided between the federal and Cantonal governments in Switzerland, with the Cantons possessing more tax-raising powers than the Federal governments.

31. Cf. K. Lenaerts, 'Some Reflections on the Separation of Powers in the European Community', *Common Market Law Review* 28/1 (1991) pp.11–35; and D. Curtin, 'The Constitutional Structure of the European Union: A Europe of Bits and Pieces', *Common Market Law Review* 30/1 (1993) pp.17–69.

32. Majone (note 9).

33. This, of course, assumes that EU institutional design will continue to be somewhat similar to the domestic political systems in the Western world. Schmitter and others argue, however, that a 'Euro-polity' cannot be based on these models because the EU is not a 'state'. Nevertheless, unless we abandon our basic democratic principles (about the relationship between executive and legislative power, for example) the institutional choices for the EU are necessarily limited. See P.C. Schmitter, 'Imagining the Future of the Euro-Polity with the Help of New Concepts', in G. Marks, F.W. Scharpf, P.C. Schmitter and W. Streek (eds.) *Governance in the European Union* (London: Sage 1996); S.S. Andersen and T. Burns, 'The European Union and the Erosion of Parliamentary Democracy,' in S.S. Andersen and K.A. Eliassen (eds.) *The European Union: How Democratic Is It?* (London: Sage 1994); Jachtenfuchs (note 8).

34. R.Corbett, F. Jacobs and M. Shackleton, *The European Parliament*, 3rd ed. (London: Catermill 1995) pp.299–306.

35. K.A. Shepsle, 'Institutional Arrangements and Equilibrium in Multidimensional Voting Models', *American Journal of Political Science* 23/1 (1979) pp.27–59; W.H. Riker, 'Implications from the Disequilibrium of Majority Rule for the Study of Institutions', *American Political Science Review* 74/2 (1980) pp.432–46; and M.J. Laver and K.A. Shepsle, 'Coalitions and Cabinet Government', ibid. 84/3 (1990) pp.873–90.

36. K.A. Shepsle, 'Institutional Equilibrium and Equilibrium Institutions', in H.F. Weinberg (ed.) *Political Science: The Science of Politics* (NY: Agathon 1986); K.A. Shepsle, 'Studying Institutions: Some Lessons from Rational Choice', *Journal of Theoretical Politics* 1/2 (1989) pp.131–47.

37. P. Dunleavy, *Democracy, Bureaucracy and Public Choice* (London: Harvester-Wheatsheaf 1990); D.C. North, *Institutions, Institutional Change and Economic Performance* (Cambridge: CUP 1990); G. Tsebelis, *Nested Games* (Berkeley: U. of California Press 1990).

38. King (note 5).

39. A. Downs, *An Economic Theory of Democracy* (NY: Harper & Row 1957); W.H. Riker, *The Theory of Political Coalitions* (New Haven, CT: Yale UP 1962).

40. R. Axelrod, *Conflict of Interests* (Chicago: Markham 1970); D.A. Wittman, 'Parties as Utility Maximisers', *American Journal of Political Science* 67/2 (1973) pp.490–8.

41. K. Strom, 'A Behavioural Theory of Competitive Political Parties', ibid. 34/2 (1990) pp.565–98.

42. The 'second-order elections theory', in its original formulation, also suggests that in second-order elections voters will tend to vote for different parties than the ones they really support – either as a protest or because there is lower risk that these parties will be elected. However, evidence from recent EP elections also suggests that if voters choose different parties this may be an indication of the elections developing some first-order characteristics (e.g. a genuine transnational element to the election, such as the anti-European votes in France and Denmark). Consequently, in testing the second-order model, I focus on the voter-turnout hypothesis rather than the voter-choice hypothesis. See K.-H. Reif and M. Schmitt, 'Nine Second-Order National Elections: A Conceptual Framework for the Analysis of European Election Results', *European Journal of Political Research* 8/1 (1980) pp.3–45; and C. van der Eijk, M. Franklin and M. Marsh, 'What Voters Teach Us About Europe-Wide Elections: What Europe-Wide Elections Teach Us About Voters', *Electoral Studies* 15/1 (1996) pp.149–66.

43. R.S. Katz and R. Kolodny, 'Party Organization as an Empty Vessel: Parties in American Politics', in R.S. Katz and P. Mair (eds.) *How Parties Organize* (London: Sage 1994).
44. W.M. Chandler and M.A. Chandler, 'Federalism and Political Parties', *European Journal of Political Economy* 3/1 (1987) pp.87–101.
45. W.M. Chandler, 'Federalism and Political Parties', in H. Bakvis and idem (eds.) *Federalism and the Role of the State* (Toronto UP 1987).
46. R.S. Katz, 'Party Government: A Rationalistic Conception', in F.G. Castles and R. Wildenmann (eds.) *Visions and Realities of Party Government* (Berlin: de Gruyter 1986).
47. Shugart and Carey (note 25) pp.175–86.
48. E.g. American Political Science Association, 'Towards a More Responsible Two-Party System', *American Political Science Review* 44/ Supplement (1950); Schattschneider (note 29); and Committee on the Constitutional System, *A Bicentennial Analysis of the American Political Structure* (Washington DC: idem 1982).
49. B. Grofman and A. Lijphart (eds.) *Electoral Laws and Their Political Consequences* (NY: Agathon 1986); D. Farrell, *Comparing Electoral Systems* (London: Prentice-Hall 1997).
50. F. Lehner and B. Homann, 'Consociational Decision-Making and Party Government in Switzerland', in R.S. Katz (ed.) *Party Government: European and American Experience* (Berlin: de Gruyter 1987).
51. A. Lijphart, 'Comparative Politics and Comparative Method', *American Political Science Review* 65/3 (1971) p.685.
52. Ibid. pp.686–8; cf. Przeworski and Teune (note 18); A. Lijphart, 'The Comparable Cases Strategy in Comparative Research', *Comparative Political Studies* 8/1 (1975) pp.158 77; D. Collier, 'The Comparative Method', in A.W. Finifter (ed.) *Political Science: The State of the Discipline II* (Washington DC: APSA 1993).
53. Esp. A. Lijphart, 'Unequal Participation: Democracy's Unresolved Dilemma', *American Political Science Review* 91/1 (1997) pp.1–14.
54. W. Linder, *Swiss Democracy: Possible Solutions to Conflict in Multicultural Societies* (London: Macmillan 1994), p.91.
55. Reif and Schmitt (note 42).
56. Katz and Kolodny (note 43).
57. L. Bardi, 'Transnational Party Federations, European Parliamentary Party Groups and the Building of Europarties', in Katz and Mair (note 43); Hix and Lor (note 7).
58. In practice, however, in many cases the choice of the party leader is really determined at the élite level and subsequently presented to the party congress as a *fait accompli* and/or the party leader (i.e. chairman/woman) is only one of several leaders (alongside the leader of the parliamentary group and/or the leading office holder/prime ministerial candidate).
59. In the case of Belgium, this party-government model only holds for the individual community parties (e.g. the Flemish and Francophone Socialists). However, the organisation structures within each Belgian 'party family' are weaker than even in the European Parliament.
60. E.g. F. Attinà, 'The Voting Behaviour of the European Parliament Members and the Problem of Europarties', *European Journal of Political Research* 18/3 (March 1990) pp.557–79; J. Bay Brzinski, 'Political Group Cohesion in the European Parliament, 1989–1994', in C. Rhodes and S. Mazey (eds.) *The State of the European Union, Vol.3* (London: Longman 1996); T. Raunio, *Party Group Behaviour in the European Parliament* (U. of Tampere 1996).
61. Brzinski (note 60).
62. E.g. M.P. Fiorina, 'Party Government in the United States – Diagnosis and Prognosis', in R.S. Katz (ed.) *Party Governments: European and American Experiences* (Berlin: de Gruyter 1987) pp.285–6.
63. S. Hix and C. Lord, 'The Making of a President: The European Parliament and the Confirmation of Jacques Santer as President of the Commission', *Government and Opposition* 31/1 (1996) pp.63–76.
64. H.-P. Hertig, 'Party Cohesion in the Swiss Parliament', *Legislative Studies Quarterly* 3/1 (1978) pp.63–81.
65. Lehner and Homann (note 30).
66. M. Duverger, *Political Parties: Their Organization and Activity in the Modern State* (NY:

Wiley 1963); D.W. Rae. *The Political Consequences of Electoral Laws*, 2nd ed. (New Haven, CT: Yale UP 1971).

67. Bardi (note 37).

68. I.e. S.M. Lipset and S. Rokkan (eds.) *Party Systems and Voter Alignments* (NY: Free Press 1967).

69. S.M. Lipset, *Political Man* (Garden City, NY: Doubleday 1959).

70. E.g. K. von Beyme, *Political Parties in Western Democracies* (London: Gower 1987).

71. To reiterate, I use the term 'partial' to emphasise that the direct election of the Commission President would not transform the EU into a full-blown Euro-presidentialism because significant executive powers would still be held by the national governments, in the EU Council. In other words, the EU would be a type of 'dual-executive' or presidential-collegial system.

72. Cf. V. Bogdanor, 'The Future of the European Community: Two Models of Democracy', *Government and Opposition* 21/2 (1986) pp.161–76; M.J. Laver, M. Gallagher, M. Marsh, R. Singh and B. Tonra, *Electing the President of the European Commission*, Trinity Blue Papers in Public Policy, No.1 (Dublin: Trinity College 1995); M. Duverger, 'Reflections: The Political System of the European Union', *European Journal of Political Research* 31/1 (Jan. 1997) pp.137–46.

73. S. Hix, 'Choosing Europe: Real Democracy in the European Union', in *EuroVisions: New Dimensions of European Integration*, Demos Collection, Issue 13 (London: Demos 1998).

74. In A.M. Schlesinger Jr, 'Leave the Constitution Alone', in D. Robinson (ed.) *Reforming American Government* (Boulder, CO: Westview 1985).

75. E.g. Lipset (note 69); Lipset and Rokkan (note 68); A. Lijphart, *Democracy in Plural Societies: A Comparative Explanation* (New Haven, CT: Yale UP 1977).

76. D. Truman, 'Federalism and Party Systems', in A. MacMahon (ed.) *Federalism* (Garden City, NY: Doubleday 1955).

77. J.J. Linz, 'Crisis, Breakdown and Reequilibrium', in idem and A. Stepan (eds) *The Breakdown of Democratic Regimes* (Baltimore, MD: Johns Hopkins UP 1978); J.J. Linz, 'The Virtues of Parliamentarism', *Journal of Democracy* 1/4 (1990) pp.84–91; S. Mainwarring, 'Presidentialism, Multipartism, and Democracy: The Difficult Combination', *Comparative Political Studies* 26/2 (1993) pp.198–228.

78. A. Lijphart and R. Rogowski, 'Separation of Powers and the Management of Political Cleavages', in K. Weaver and B. Rockman (eds.) *Political Institutions and their Consequences* (Washington, DC: Brookings 1991).

79. E.g. Weiler (note 14) p.228.

80. P. Taylor, 'The European Community and the State: Assumptions, Theories and Propositions', *Review of International Studies* 17/2 (1991) pp.109–25; and D.N. Chryssochoou, 'Democracy and Symbiosis in the European Union: Towards a Confederal Consociation', *West European Politics* 17/1 (Jan. 1994) pp.1–14.

81. G. Tsebelis, 'Decision Making in Political Systems: Veto Players in Presidentialism, Parliamentarianism, Multicameralism and Multipartyism', *British Journal of Political Science* 25 (1995) pp.283–325.

82. E.g. P.C. Schmitter, 'How to Democratize the Emerging Euro-Polity: Citizenship, Representation, Decision-Making', unpublished mimeo (1996); J.H.H. Weiler, 'Proposals for Democratising the EU', presentation at the conference on 'European Citizenship', LSE/Goethe Inst., 20–22 March 1997.

83. Cf. Laver *et al.* (note 72).

Democratic Accountability and Central Bank Independence: Historical and Contemporary, National and European Perspectives

ROBERT ELGIE

Recently there has been a general move towards greater central bank independence in Europe. Countries such as Belgium, Britain, France and Spain have all increased the autonomy of their respective central banks. In this context, some people have argued that the prospects for democratic, representative government have been weakened. In these countries, democratically elected governments can no longer control the process of monetary policy making. By constructing an index of central banks' independence, this article shows that the recent moves towards central bank independence in Britain and France have not challenged the basic foundations of indirect political accountability. However, it also shows that the proposed institutional architecture of the European Central Bank is a departure from the norms of political accountability and that, in this case, there is a distinct 'democratic deficit' which needs to be addressed.

In recent years the issue of central bank independence has become increasingly topical. Countries such as Belgium, France and Spain have all passed legislation to increase the decision-making autonomy of their respective central banks. More generally, the European Central Bank has come under close scrutiny as the deadline for the introduction of European Monetary Union has drawn nearer. In this context, one point which has been regularly discussed is the relationship between central bank independence and democratic accountability. As one commentator has stated: 'The dilemma faced in industrial democracies is how to introduce institutional reform in order to reduce the political incentives which exist for the over-zealous use of short-term discretionary action without threatening the basic principles of democratic government.'[1] For some, it appears as if European governments have been caught on the horns of this dilemma by introducing institutional reforms at the expense of democratic government. In order to

West European Politics, Vol.21, No.3 (July 1998), pp.53–76
PUBLISHED BY FRANK CASS, LONDON

eliminate the propensity towards short-term, electorally motivated business cycles, governments have ceded monetary policy-making powers to unelected central bankers. Consequently, the prospects for democratic, representative government, so it is argued, have been weakened.

This article examines the relationship between central bank independence and the principles of democratic government. It aims to show that in a national context the recent moves towards central bank independence in Britain and France have not challenged the basic foundations of indirect political accountability. There has not been a general return to a pre-democratic era of monetary policy-making procedures. At the same time, it also aims to show that the proposed institutional architecture of the European Central Bank (ECB) is, indeed, a departure from the norms of political accountability. In this case, there is a distinct 'democratic deficit' which needs to be addressed.

There are three main parts to the article. The first part establishes a methodology by which the relative independence of central banks can be measured. The second part draws upon this methodology to illustrate the changing nature of the government/central bank relationship in Britain and France since the seventeenth century in the context of arguments about democratic accountability. The third part also draws upon this methodology to show that the structures of the proposed ECB are different from those of the newly independent Bank of England and Bank of France and, moreover, that the ECB is not, contrary to the beliefs of certain commentators, simply a copy of the Bundesbank. It will also be argued that the ECB's proposed structures are largely incompatible with the basic principles of representative government. In the conclusion, the implications for reform of the ECB are briefly discussed.

MEASURING CENTRAL BANK INDEPENDENCE

In order to examine the relationship between governments and central banks, it is necessary to measure the relative degree of independence of the one from the other.[2] Over the years, many different scholars have tried to identify the most appropriate indicators by which the degree of central bank independence may be assessed. Indeed, to this end a veritable cottage industry has sprung up. However, despite (or perhaps because of) the proliferation of the various indices of central bank independence, there is still no common agreement as to which indicators of independence are the most germane. Such persistent disagreement has led one writer to conclude that, as yet, there is 'no ability to say that some institutional features are necessary or sufficient for behavioral independence'.[3] There is no agreed basis for measuring the extent to which central banks are independent from government control. In an attempt to provide such a basis, this article proposes a comprehensive list of indicators of central bank independence. These indicators can be classified under two separate headings: political independence and economic independence.

'Political independence' may be defined as the central bank's ability to make policy decisions without interference from the government. The appropriate indicators of political independence are indicated in Appendix 1 (pp.69–71). They include those elements which regulate, first, the relationship between the government and the central bank's governor (or equivalent post), the sub-governors (where appropriate) and the members of the board of governors and, second, the government's intervention in the internal decision-making process of the central bank. In terms of the first set of criteria, political independence indicators concern how the governor, sub-governors and members of the board of governors are appointed; how nominations for appointments are made; the length of the term of office; whether or not appointees need professional qualifications; whether or not they may be summarily dismissed from office, or reappointed; whether or not they may hold other posts simultaneously; plus, in the case of the sub-governors and the board of governors, whether appointments are staggered; and, in the case of the board of governors alone, whether there are government representatives on the board. In terms of the second set of criteria, political independence indicators concern whether or not the board takes decisions collectively; whether or not its members have to take instructions from the government; whether or not any government representatives have a veto; whether or not the government fixes the board members' salaries; whether or not the bank has to report periodically to the legislature and, finally, whether or not the bank's capital is privately owned. On the basis of these indicators, it may reasonably be asserted that if the level of government interference is consistently low, then the degree of central bank political independence will be high.

'Economic independence' may be defined as the central bank's ability to use the full range of monetary policy instruments without restrictions from the government.[4] The indicators of economic independence include the presence or absence of an overriding mission; the bank's ability or inability to control interest rate moves, exchange rate parities and monetary policy generally; the obligation or interdiction to lend monies to the government; the intervention or otherwise in the budgetary process; and the regulation or non-regulation of the wider banking sector (see Appendix 1). Once again, on the basis of these indicators, it may reasonably be asserted that if the central bank has a large number of monetary policy instruments at its disposal and if it may use them without restrictions, then the degree of economic independence from the government is high.

This twofold classification provides the necessary and sufficient criteria by which to judge central bank independence. A completely independent central bank would be one which was free from government intervention across the whole set of political indicators; it would have the full range of monetary policy instruments at its disposal; and it would be able to use all of these instruments without any government restriction. By contrast, a completely dependent central bank would be one which was subject to unbounded government intervention across the set of political indicators; and it would either have no monetary policy instruments at its disposal, or it would be subject to absolute government restrictions on all of those that it was able to use. Needless to say, the degree of independence is likely to lie somewhere in between these two extremes. As Goodman states: '[i]ndependence is best conceived as a continuous, not a dichotomous variable'.[5] In other words, there is a continuum of independence and no central bank is likely to occupy a position at either extreme of this continuum. Instead, the overall degree of central-bank independence will vary according to the extent of government intervention, the number of monetary instruments at the bank's disposal and the level of government restrictions on the bank's use of these instruments.

On the basis of the above indicators, it is necessary to construct a methodology by which it is possible to place any particular central bank at any time at the appropriate point on the continuum of independence. In other words, it is necessary to devise a methodology to measure the extent to which central banks are subject to governmental control. Many of the aforementioned scholars who have identified various indicators of central bank independence have also tried to measure the degree of independence on the basis of their preferred set of indicators. Once again, though, there is no common agreement as to which is the best way of measuring central bank independence. However, by far the most sophisticated methodology devised to date can be found in the article by Cukierman et al.[6] They coded each of their preferred indicators of central bank independence on a scale from 1.00 for complete independence to 0.00 for complete dependence. For example, the indicator concerning the term of office of the central bank governor was coded 1.00 if it was over eight years, 0.75 if was from six to eight years, 0.50 if it was five years, 0.25 if it was four years and 0.00 if it was below four years. Similar codings were devised for the other 15 indicators and these 16 individual indicators were then aggregated into eight separate sets. Each of these sets was given a weighted value, ranging from 0.20 for the set of four indicators concerning the governor to 0.05 for the set containing the single indicator concerning the borrowers to whom the bank may lend. On the basis of the codings of individual indicators and the weighted values of the eight sets of indicators, figures for the degree of central bank independence were calculated.

Clearly, any such figures give a false sense of precision in that they are built up from the subjective codings of essentially contestable indicators rather than objectively measurable and identifiable criteria. Nevertheless, this methodology has two particular advantages. First, it indicates that the extremes of complete independence (an overall score of 1.00) and complete dependence (an overall score of 0.00) are unlikely to be reached. This finding corresponds to the intuition that all central banks are likely to be found at some point on the continuum of independence rather than at either of the two extremes. The most independent central banks will always face some government control, while the most dependent central banks will always enjoy some degree of freedom. Second, it indicates that there are likely to be small differences in the degree of independence even between seemingly similar central banks. This finding corresponds to the further intuition that no two central banks are likely to operate identically. For example, even if the Bundesbank and the Swiss central bank are in many ways alike, they do not operate in precisely the same manner as each other. So, this approach encourages comparison, but not over-generalisation.

For both of these reasons, the methodology devised by Cukierman *et al.* will serve as the general basis of measuring central bank independence in this article. However, it will be adapted and refined in two ways so as to make it more appropriate to the purposes of this study. First, this article will use the indicators of central bank independence that are identified in Appendix 1. This means that it considers a larger number of indicators (37) than the Cukierman *et al.* study (16) and, in particular, it considers a much greater number of indicators of political independence, so making the methodology more suited to the purposes of this study. Second, this article will code the sets and sub-sets of independence indicators differently, giving greater emphasis to the indicators of political independence and so, once again, tailoring the methodology to suit the purposes of the study at hand. (See Appendix 1). In sum, this revised version of the Cukierman *et al.* methodology still provides a means by which to measure the degree of central bank independence from the government. Moreover, it does so in a way which combines the advantages of the original study, but which also increases the consideration given to the indicators of political independence. The result is a methodology which can be applied to compare the full nature of central bank independence both at a single point in time and across time and on the basis of which conclusions about the relationship between central banks and democratic accountability may be drawn.

THE INDEPENDENCE OF THE BANK OF ENGLAND AND THE BANQUE
DE FRANCE IN HISTORICAL PERSPECTIVE AND ARGUMENTS ABOUT
DEMOCRATIC ACCOUNTABILITY

Central banking in both Britain and France has a long history. Both the Bank
of England and the Banque de France were created in the pre-democratic
era. The Bank of England is the second-oldest central bank in the world. It
was established in 1694 in the middle of a war which had provoked a severe
crisis of the state's finances. The Banque de France is a much younger, but,
in comparative terms, still an extremely venerable institution. It was
established in 1800 in the period of instability following the French
Revolution and shortly after Napoleon Bonaparte's rise to power.

Since the time of their creation, the relationship between the banks and
their respective governments has been subject to reform. (See Appendix 2
and Appendix 3, pp.71–4).[7] Initially, both banks were privately-owned
institutions which enjoyed a considerable amount of autonomy. In the 1920s
and 1930s, though, both banks came under increasing political control.
Immediately following the Second World War, both banks were then
nationalised. Finally, in the mid-1990s, both banks were once again given a
large degree of independence. For this article, the most recent reform of the
two banks is the most interesting. In both countries this reform was
criticised and in both cases one of the main criticisms was that the
government was shifting the responsibility for monetary policy making
from elected representatives to unaccountable central bankers. It is this
argument which will be addressed.

The figures in Appendix 2 and Appendix 3 would seem unequivocally
to support the argument that British and French governments have divested
themselves of monetary policy-making responsibilities. In the British case,
on 6 May 1997 the newly elected Labour Chancellor, Gordon Brown,
announced that he was giving the Bank of England 'operational
responsibility' for setting interest rates and, more generally, that he was
reforming the Bank's structures and procedures.[8] This was an unexpected
announcement and one which fundamentally changed the relationship
between the Bank and the government. In terms of the indicators of central
bank independence outlined above, Brown's reform resulted in a shift on the
continuum of independence from a score of 0.20 to a score of 0.48. In other
words, it resulted in the move from an extremely dependent central bank in
comparative terms to a relatively independent central bank. Moreover, this
shift meant that the Bank nominally returned to a regime similar to the one
under which it had operated immediately prior to reform and nationalisation
in 1946 when it scored 0.46. Indeed, it meant that the Bank returned to a
situation not too dissimilar from the one under which it had operated for the

first 200 years of its existence during the period of free trade, *laissez-faire* economics and, for most of this period at least, little more than an incipient form of representative government. During this period it scored 0.59.

In the French case the Banque de France was last reformed in 1993. At this time, the French government, led by Gaullist Prime Minister Édouard Balladur, granted the Banque de France a considerable degree of policy-making autonomy. In terms of the indicators of central bank independence, Balladur's reform resulted in a shift on the continuum of independence from a score of 0.18 to a score of 0.59. As in the British case, then, it resulted in the move from an extremely dependent central bank in comparative terms to a relatively independent central bank. Furthermore, also as in the British case, this shift meant that the Banque seemed to return to an operational regime similar to the one under which it had operated prior to the sweeping reform of the Popular Front government in 1936 when it scored 0.42. Indeed, and once again as in the British case, it also meant that the Banque returned to a situation not too dissimilar from the one under which it had operated in the first few years of its existence from the time of its creation in 1800 to its first significant reform in 1808 during which period it scored 0.57.

In both Britain and France the reforms were criticised in terms of their detrimental impact on the system of democratic accountability. In Britain, even some of Chancellor Brown's own colleagues were quick to emphasise this effect of the reform. For example, Labour MP Denzil Davies is quoted as saying: 'I would oppose any legislation that makes the Bank of England independent without democratic accountability. It is extraordinary that a party committed to opening up government and reducing the powers of unelected officials should take this kind of step.'[9] Similarly, Brown's Conservative Party predecessor, Kenneth Clarke, suggested that he was against the reform precisely because it undermined the government's accountability to Parliament.[10] Indeed, this is the traditional argument which was put forward over the years by commentators who were opposed to the Bank's independence. As one academic observer has noted, central bank independence appeared to be fundamentally at odds with the principle of parliamentary sovereignty which underpins the British system.[11] The implication of this principle is that 'every political action or decision can be reversed by Parliament, and this is incompatible with the principle of an independent central bank'.[12] The 1997 reform, then, marked a major shift not just in policy-making responsibilities but also basic constitutional thought.

In France, too, some of the government's supporters were critical of the decision to reform the central bank. For example, in a newspaper article, three leading gaullist deputies wrote: 'As if democracy really had something to gain from a system in which an exorbitant amount of power is given to a clan of technocrats and notables, who cannot be dismissed what is more, and who are so independent that there is no-one from whom they can receive orders and no-one to whom they must account'.[13] In addition, certain elements on the left also voiced their opposition. For example, during the debate in the National Assembly, former Socialist Party minister and leader of the small Mouvement des Citoyens party, Jean-Pierre Chevènement, argued that: 'the denationalisation of the Banque de France has its place in the ongoing movement which is emptying the concepts of democracy and citizenship of all their substance'.[14] Unlike Britain, the French system does not operate according to the principle of parliamentary sovereignty. Nevertheless, the reform of the Banque de France was still criticised by Chevènement for being part of a tendency towards 'republican deconstruction' which weakened the link between the people and the process by which decisions that affect the people are made.[15]

It is apparent, then, that recent reforms of the Bank of England and the Banque de France fundamentally altered the relationship between the banks and their respective governments and that these reforms were criticised on the basis that they were said to reduce the level of democratic accountability in this most sensitive of policy areas. In fact, though, the precise nature of the reforms needs to be examined in more detail before over-hasty judgements are drawn as to their impact on the decision-making process. If the reforms are disaggregated and their impact on the indicators of political independence and economic independence are considered separately, then the overall picture changes somewhat.

This argument is based on the assumption that all other things being equal a low level of central bank political independence equates with a high level of indirect democratic accountability and vice versa. The indicators of political independence consist of items which are traditionally associated with the requirements for such accountability. These include the issue of whether or not the government is responsible for appointments to and dismissals from the bank, whether or not the bank must report to the legislature, whether or not the government can veto the bank's decisions, whether or not the bank's capital is publicly owned, and so on. It is these indicators which are central to arguments about democratic accountability rather than the indicators of economic independence. This is because even if a bank was operationally responsible for a great many policy instruments (and, hence, registered a high score for economic independence), if that bank was also subject to complete political control (and, hence, registered a low score for political independence), then those charged with making its operational decisions would still be politically accountable. Conversely, if a bank had few policy instruments at its disposal (and, hence, registered a low score for economic independence) and yet its decision makers were not subject to any political control (and, hence, registered a high score for political independence), then those decision makers would – still be able to use whatever powers they possessed free from the fear of political interference. Therefore, in order properly to examine arguments about central banks and democratic accountability, it is necessary first and foremost to consider not the overall level of independence, but simply the level of political independence that they enjoy.[16]

In this context, the 1997 reform of the Bank of England created the situation where the Bank had an overall score of 0.48 on the continuum of independence. This figure is the average of the sum of weighted means for political independence (0.46) and the mean score for economic independence (0.50). The overall 1997 score is, indeed, similar to the same scores in both the 1694–1931 and the 1931–46 periods (0.59 and 0.46 respectively). However, when the figures for political and economic independence are disaggregated the 1997 situation shows itself to be very different from the situations in the two previous periods. So, whereas now the bank scores 0.46 for political independence and 0.50 for economic independence, from 1694–1931 it scored 0.76 for political independence and 0.43 for economic independence and from 1931–46 it scored 0.78 for political independence and 0.14 for economic independence. In other words, the general picture from 1694–1931 was of a bank which was politically independent but economically dependent. As such, though, the high level of political independence meant that it was largely unaccountable to the government of the day which was itself, of course, also largely unaccountable for much of this time.

Now, the situation is different. The Bank is more politically dependent than during this time but more economically independent. In other words, it registers a relatively high overall score on the continuum of independence primarily because it has a relatively large number of economic policy instruments at its disposal, even though it is more politically dependent, and, hence, more politically accountable. In short, then, although the level of political independence is greater now than under the regime created by the 1946 reform (0.46 now compared with 0.26 then), there has not been a return to the pre-1931, mainly pre-democratic situation in terms of political accountability. Indeed, the current government has been sure to include procedures for indirect accountability in the newly reformed institution so as to maintain a degree of political control.

A similar situation applies in the French case. Following the 1993 reform, the Banque de France scored 0.59 overall on the continuum of independence which was the average of the score for political independence (0.53) and the score for economic independence (0.64). As in the British case, while the overall 1993 score is similar to both the 1800–08 and the 1808–1936 overall scores (0.57 and 0.42 respectively), the disaggregated figures for political and economic independence after 1993 are, again, very different from those for the first two periods. From 1800–08 the Banque scored 0.77 for political independence and 0.36 for economic independence and from 1808–1936 it scored 0.45 for political independence and 0.36 for economic independence. As with the Bank of England, then, the Banque's level of political independence was greater from 1800–1936 than the level of economic independence. Now, the situation is reversed. The level of economic independence is greater than the level of political independence. Overall, the Banque is undoubtedly much more independent now than it was immediately prior to the 1993 reform. However, it is still considerably less politically independent and, hence, more accountable than it was from 1800–08 and only slightly more politically independent now than it was from 1808–1936.

This disaggregation of political and economic independence helps to put the recent reforms of the Bank of England and the Banque de France into some perspective. It is certainly the case that in Britain and France both central banks are now less politically accountable than was the case immediately prior to the most recent reform in the two countries. However, it is wrong to suggest that because both banks are now more independent overall then the level of political accountability is low and that there has been a return to the situation in previous periods of pre-democratic governments and *laissez-faire* economics. Instead, in both Britain and France the level of economic independence is currently greater than the level of political independence, suggesting that there is still considerable sensitivity to the issue of democratic accountability. Moreover, in both countries the current level of political independence is also for the most part less than was the case in the first centuries of the two banks' existence, suggesting that methods of indirect political accountability are still built into the system.

DEMOCRATIC ACCOUNTABILITY AND THE EUROPEAN CENTRAL BANK

The European System of Central Banks (ESCB) was established in the 1992 Maastricht Treaty on European Union. The linchpin of the ESCB is the European Central Bank itself. Currently, of course, the ECB exists only on paper. It will not become operational until the beginning of Stage III of European Economic and Monetary Union which is due to commence on 1 January 1999. Nevertheless, despite the fact that, as yet, the ECB is still merely notional, it is possible to examine its organisation and procedures by referring to and extrapolating from the relevant articles and protocols of the Maastricht Treaty. In this context, it is necessary to examine the organisational architecture of the ECB and the relationship between the Bank and the principle of democratic accountability.

Superficially at least, there are similarities between the themes and issues surrounding the proposed creation of the ECB and those concerning the recent reforms of the Bank of England and the Banque de France. (See Appendix 4, pp.74–6). The first main similarity is that the ECB registers a very high overall score on the continuum of independence (0.68). This indicates that the ECB corresponds to the model of an extremely independent central bank. The second main similarity is that the ECB has been criticised for being politically unaccountable. For example, during the 1992 referendum on the Maastricht Treaty in France, the *de facto* leader of the 'no' campaign, Philippe Séguin, specifically attacked this aspect of the EMU proposals. He said: 'the choice of [ECB] independence is based on the conviction that the currency is too serious or too dangerous a matter to be left in the hands of politicians ... As for me, when it is a question of monetary choices, the economic and social consequences of which are considerable, I believe that democratic control is always a better guarantee than technocratic irresponsibility.'[17] Academics too have underlined this aspect of the ECB: 'The effect of the "independence" of the European central bank would be to allow virtually unaccountable officials to dictate economic policy, at a time when the central organs of the EU will still lack legitimacy and citizen identification'.[18]

In both ways, then, there appears to be a considerable degree of correspondence between the ECB and the newly-reformed British and French central banks. However, the similarities are only superficial. If the scores for political and economic independence are disaggregated, then the differences between the ECB, on the one hand, and the Bank of England and the Banque de France, on the other, become apparent in two main respects. First, whereas in the case of both national central banks the score for economic independence is currently greater than the score for political independence (0.50 against 0.46 and 0.64 against 0.53 respectively), the opposite is true for the ECB (0.64 for economic independence against 0.72 for political independence). In this respect, the ECB corresponds less to the situation of the British and French central banks in the twentieth century and more to the situation of these banks in the mainly pre-democratic seventeenth, eighteenth and nineteenth centuries. Second, and most significantly, the level of political independence for the ECB is simply much greater than the level of political independence for the Bank of England and the Banque de France. Here, the ECB scores 0.72, whereas the two other banks score 0.46 and 0.53 respectively. In other words, the ECB is much less politically accountable than either of the other two banks.

At this point it is useful to make a comparison between the ECB and the Bundesbank. There is a common perception that the ECB was modelled on the Bundesbank. Indeed, this is also an academic perception in some quarters. For example, Busch argues that there are 'great similarities in the institutional setup' of the two banks and states that this 'makes it clear that the ESCB was modelled along the lines of the Bundesbank'.[19] Indeed, when the banks' scores on the continuum of independence are compared, we find that the ECB's figure is virtually the same (0.68) as the figure for the Bundesbank (0.67) which would seem to back up this argument. However, when the scores for political and economic independence are disaggregated, then the differences between the two institutions become apparent. The ECB's score for political independence (0.72) is greater than the Bundesbank's score (0.63), whereas its score for economic independence (0.64) is less than the score for its German counterpart (0.71). In short, the ECB is somewhat less politically accountable than the Bundesbank, even if the German central bank has a larger number of economic policy instruments at its disposal. Consequently, as one study notes: '[u]nlike the Bundesbank, the broadly representative council of which both protects its substantial degree of independence and ensures its accountability, [the ECB] will lack legitimacy'.[20]

These findings suggest that criticisms about the democratic accountability of the ECB are more pertinent than those which have recently been made with regard to the Bank of England and the Banque de France. The institutional configuration of the ECB does not simply mirror that of either the Bundesbank or the reformed central banks in Britain and France. In fact, decision makers in these three countries have been careful to build the basic requirements for indirect democratic accountability into the structures of their respective banks, something which is missing in the case of the ECB. This means that, if anything, the ECB resembles the organisation of the Bank of England and the Banque de France not today but in the pre-democratic period when they were initially created. This suggests that, unlike even the most independent of national central banks, the ECB does indeed suffer from a 'democratic deficit'.

CONCLUSION

In recent years there has been considerable convergence in the pattern of government/central bank relations in Europe.[21] In the first place, there has been a general move towards greater central bank independence. In part, this has been necessitated by the Maastricht Treaty. Point 5 of article 109(e) of the Treaty states that '[e]ach member state shall, as appropriate, start the process leading to the independence of its central bank' during the second stage of European Monetary Union (EMU), from 1 January 1994, and article 108 notes that this process had to be completed by the start of the third stage of EMU, once due to begin as early as 1 January 1997. As a result, therefore, Belgian, French and Spanish governments (although not, of course, the British government) were obliged to reform the status of their respective central banks, and to do so quickly, in order simply to qualify for EMU. In addition, though, there has also been a degree of more specific legislative convergence. For example, article 107 of the Maastricht Treaty states that 'neither the ECB, nor a national central bank, nor any members of their decision-making bodies shall seek or take instructions from Community institutions or bodies, from any government of a member state or from any other body'. In a similar vein, article 1 of the 1993 French reform confirms that the Banque de France 'can neither request nor accept instructions from the government', while the equivalent article of the Spanish reform indicates that 'neither the government nor any other public authority may give instructions to the Banco de España regarding either the objectives or the implementation of monetary policy'. In essence, the French and Spanish governments simply copied the relevant section of the Maastricht Treaty when drafting their own legislation. For both reasons, increasingly the issues and concerns surrounding central-bank independence are no longer country specific, but affect European polities generally.

In this context, of course, even the most independent of national central banks are subject to various forms of indirect democratic accountability. For example, even though the Bundesbank is not formally obliged to report to the German legislature, appointments to the bank are generally subject to some degree of political control. The government, then, can influence the composition of the bank's decision makers and, by extension, the conduct of monetary policy. The same is true for the Banque de France, which, for its part, is also obliged to report annually to the Assemblée Nationale, the Banco de España, which is also obliged to 'regularly inform parliament and the government of its objectives and the implementation of monetary policy', and the Bank of England, which, as Chancellor Brown stated, 'will make reports to and give evidence to the House of Commons, through the Treasury select committee, on an enhanced basis'.[22] This is not say that the level of accountability in all four, and other, cases should not be increased. There is at least some justification for the argument that these banks are not subject to a sufficient number of democratic controls and that greater patterns of democratic accountability should be ensured. Neither is it to say that governments are unequivocally weakened by greater central-bank independence. Indeed, governments may be able to avoid electoral punishment if they can blame or 'scapegoat' the independent central bank for an unpopular economic performance.[23] Nor is it to say that the powerful partisan, business and banking epistemic community which is in favour of central-bank independence does not threaten to stifle pluralistic debate.[24] The merits of what the French call *la pensée unique* need to be at least debated alongside those of *l'autre politique*. Instead, it is simply to deny the argument that ostensibly 'independent' central banks are free to act with impunity. Evidence suggests that responsibility for monetary policy has not been completely ceded to unaccountable central bankers.

This point can be reinforced by examining the way in which monetary policy is made under regimes with a supposedly independent central bank. Evidence from the German case suggests that policy is the result of an iterated process of argument and counterargument between members of the political community and the central banking community. There are continuous attempts by representatives of the government to influence the thinking of the central bankers. This is why clashes between the two institutions have been commonplace. In the first 25 years of the Bundesbank's history, the bank tended to get the better of the struggles.[25] More recently, though, the 'myth' of Bundesbank power has been eroded and political influence has increased.[26] Similarly, recent evidence suggests that in the last four years the same sort of policy-making process has been at work in France. There have been no formal deals between the government and the Banque. As the legislation requires, no demands have been made and no instructions have been given. Instead, each side has simply used the usual channels of information to let the other know what it wants and what it is willing to do publicly in order to bring it about. Most notably, Chirac's announcement in October 1995 that he was committed to meeting the criteria for European Economic and Monetary Union and the Banque's subsequent declaration that the time was right for interest rate reductions should be seen in this context.[27] So, even with an 'independent' central bank, political representatives still use their albeit limited powers to influence the process of monetary policy making.

The evidence also suggests, though, that the situation with regard to the ECB may be very different. The disaggregation of political and economic indicators of independence shows that the level of indirect democratic accountability is likely to be low. It is the case that article 15.2 of the Protocol on the Statute of the European System of Central Banks and of the European Central Bank, which is part of the Maastricht Treaty, does state that 'the ECB shall address an annual report on the activities of the ESCB and on the monetary policy of both the previous and the current year to the European Parliament, the Council and the Commission, and also to the European Council'. Similarly, appointments to the Bank's decision-making institutions are made at the level of politically accountable heads of state or of government after consultation with the European Parliament. Overall, though, the figures show that the ECB enjoys a very high level of political independence. Indeed, if anything, the figures in Appendix 4 slightly underestimate the level of political independence because of the very nature of the European Union. In a national context, the indicators of independence measure the relationship between the central bank and institutions which, now at least, are directly accountable, such as the legislature, the cabinet, or a directly elected president. However, in the European context, the indicators of independence tend to measure the relationship between the ECB and institutions which themselves are only indirectly accountable, such as the European Council and the Council of Ministers, or which are scarcely accountable at all, such as the European Commission. The only directly accountable institution is the European Parliament which has very few powers with regard to the ECB. Extrapolating from this we can conclude that, whereas the process of monetary policy making in the national context consists of a constant interaction between directly accountable representatives of the government and members of the central bank, the same may not turn out to be true at the European level.

These findings suggest that reform is needed at the European level. Such reform might take one or both of two forms. First, some sort of 'economic government', such as the one recently proposed by the French authorities, might be installed. The point of such a reform would to be to construct an institution which would oversee the ECB's work and, perhaps, have the power to veto, delay, or at least discuss its decisions. As such proposals currently stand, though, it is highly unlikely that any such economic government would itself be directly accountable and so the basic problem of political independence and accountability at the European level would remain. Second, the EU's institutions themselves might be reformed. If the Commission was directly elected or if the European Parliament was given full powers to appoint people to and dismiss them from the Commission, then the general level of EU accountability would undoubtedly increase. Such a reform, though, is scarcely on the agenda and, of course, would not be introduced solely to make the ECB more accountable. Therefore, criticisms of the ECB are likely to persist and, as the process of European Monetary Union gets under way, may become yet more pertinent still.

NOTES

1. Brian Snowdon, 'Politics and the Business Cycle', *Political Quarterly* 68 (1997).
2. This section draws upon some of the information and the Appendices in Robert Elgie and Helen Thompson, *The Politics of Central Banks* (London: Routledge 1998).
3. John T. Woolley, 'The Politics of Monetary Policy: A Critical Review', *Journal of Public Policy* 14 (1994) p.63.
4. Alberto Alesina and Lawrence H. Summers, 'Central Bank Independence and Macroeconomic Performance: Some Comparative Evidence', *Journal of Money, Credit and Banking* 25 (1993) p.153.
5. John B. Goodman, *The Politics of Central Banking in Western Europe* (London: Cornell UP 1992) p. 8.
6. Alex Cukierman, Steven B. Webb and Bilin Neyapti, 'Measuring the Independence of Central Banks and Its Effect on Policy Outcomes', *World Bank Economic Review* 6 (1992) pp.353–98.
7. The years in Appendix 2 and Appendix 3 correspond to the main occasions when the banks were reformed.
8. The text of Brown's letter to the Governor of the Bank of England in which the details of the reform are outlined can be found in the *Financial Times*, 7 May 1997.
9. Ibid. p.7.
10. *The Times*, 7 May 1997, p.2.
11. Andreas Busch, 'Central Bank Independence and the Westminister Model', *West European Politics* 17 (1994) pp.53–72.
12. Ibid. p. 62.
13. *Le Monde*, 16 June 1993, p.2. All translations are by the author.
14. Ibid., 10 June 1993, p.7.
15. Ibid.
16. Needless to say, the index of independence does not indicate the degree to which the government itself is democratically accountable. It simply indicates the degree of central bank accountability to the government.
17. In the supplement to *Libération*, 31 Aug. 1992, p.9.
18. Paul Hirst and Grahame Thompson, *Globalization in Question* (Oxford: Polity Press 1996) p.162.
19. Busch (note 11) p.55.
20. Hirst and Thompson (note 18) p.162.
21. For a discussion of this issue, refer to Kenneth Dyson, Kevin Featherstone and George Michalopoulos, 'Strapped to the Mast: EC Central Bankers between Global Financial Markets and Regional Integration', in *Journal of European Public Policy* 2 (1995) pp.465–87.
22. Reported in the *Financial Times*, 7 May 1997, p. 7.
23. See, for example, the 'scapegoating' argument in the context of eastern Europe by Dwight Semler, 'Focus: The Politics of Central Banking', *East European Constitutional Review* 3 (1994) p.51, and in the context of the US by John T. Woolley, *Monetary Politics: The Federal Reserve and the Politics of Monetary Policy* (Cambridge: CUP 1984) p.11.
24. The argument that central bank independence has been pursued by a powerful epistemic community is made in Kenneth Dyson, *Elusive Union: The Process of Economic and Monetary Union in Europe* (London: Longman 1994) pp.250–2.
25. See, for example, David Marsh, *The Bundesbank: The Bank that Rules Europe* (London: Mandarin 1992) p.170.
26. Roland Sturm, 'How Independent is the Bundesbank?', *German Politics* 4 (1989) pp.39–40.
27. Elgie and Thompson (note 2) Ch.6.

Political Independence (overall weighting 0.50)

(i) *The governor* (weighting 0.30)

(a)	Appointment	1.00	Appointments made by the bank itself
		0.50	Appointments made with some bank involvement
		0.00	Appointments made by government
(b)	Nomination	1.00	Nominations made by the bank itself
		0.50	Nominations made with some bank involvement
		0.00	Nominations made by government
(c)	Qualifications	1.00	Some professional qualifications are necessary
		0.00	No professional qualifications are necessary
(d)	Term of office	1.00	Over eight years
		0.50	Between five and eight years
		0.00	Below five years
(e)	Dismissal	1.00	Complete security of tenure
		0.50	Dismissal with some bank involvement
		0.00	No security of tenure
(f)	Renewability	1.00	Not renewable
		0.50	Renewable once
		0.00	Renewable
(g)	Other posts	1.00	Other office-holding not permitted
		0.00	Other office-holding permitted

(ii) *Sub-governors* (weighting 0.20)

(a)	Appointment	1.00	Appointments made by the bank itself
		0.50	Appointments made with some bank involvement
		0.00	Appointments made by government
(b)	Nomination	1.00	Nominations made by the bank itself
		0.50	Nominations made with some bank involvement
		0.00	Nominations made by government
(c)	Qualifications	1.00	Some professional qualifications are necessary
		0.00	No professional qualifications are necessary
(d)	Term of office	1.00	Over eight years
		0.50	Between five and eight years
		0.00	Below five years
(e)	Dismissal	1.00	Complete security of tenure
		0.50	Dismissal with some bank involvement
		0.00	No security of tenure
(f)	Renewability	1.00	Not renewable
		0.50	Renewable once
		0.00	Renewable
(g)	Other posts	1.00	Other office-holding not permitted
		0.00	Other office-holding permitted
(h)	Staggering	1.00	Staggered appointments
		0.00	Appointments made simultaneously

(iii) *Board of governors* (weighting 0.20)

(a)	Govt. reps.	1.00	There are no govt. representatives on the board
		0.75	There is a minority of govt. representatives on the board
		0.25	There is a majority of govt. representatives on the board
		0.00	There are only govt. representatives on the board
(b)	Appointment	1.00	Appointments made by the bank itself
		0.50	Appointments made with some bank involvement

	0.00	Appointments made by government
(c) Nomination	1.00	Nominations made by the bank itself
	0.50	Nominations made with some bank involvement
	0.00	Nominations made by government
(d) Qualifications	1.00	Some professional qualifications are necessary
	0.00	No professional qualifications are necessary
(e) Term of office	1.00	Over eight yearas
	0.50	Between five and eight years
	0.00	Below five years
(f) dismissal	1.00	complete security of tenure
	0.50	Dismissal with some bank involvement
	0.00	No security of tenure
(g) Renewability	1.00	Not renewable
	0.50	Renewable once
	0.00	Renewable
(h) Other posts	1.00	Other office-holding not permitted
	0.00	Other office-holding permitted
(i) Staggering	1.00	Staggered appointments
	0.00	Appointments made simultaneously

(iv) *Decision-making process* (weighting 0.30)

(a) Policy making	1.00	Collective
	0.00	Not collective
(b) Instructions	1.00	The board does not accept government instructions
	0.00	The board accepts government instructions
(c) Veto	1.00	Govt. representatives do not have a veto
	0.00	Govt. representatives do have a veto
(d) Salary	1.00	The bank fixes its own salaries
	0.00	The government fixes board members' salaries
(e) Capital	1.00	100 per cent private capital
	0.50	Some private capital
	0.00	No private capital
(f) Legislature	1.00	Bank does not have to report periodically to the legislature
	0.00	Bank must report periodically to the legislature

Economic Independence (overall weighting 0.50)

(i) Mission	1.00	A single stated mission to guarantee price stability
	0.50	A plurality of missions
	0.00	No mission statement at all
(ii) Monetary policy	1.00	The bank determines monetary policy
	0.50	Some degree of bank involvement in monetary policy
	0.00	The government determines monetary olicy
(iii) Interest rates	1.00	The bank decides key interest-rate movements
	0.00	Government decides key interest-rate movements
(iv) Exchange rates	1.00	The bank determines exchange-rate parities
	0.00	The government determines exchange-rate parities
(v) Regulation	1.00	The central bank regulates the wider banking sector
	0.50	Central bank is jointly responsible for regulation
	0.00	The government is the chief regulator
(vi) Govt. lending	1.00	Bank is prohibited from lending to the government
	0.50	Some limits to bank's obligation to lend to the government
	0.00	The bank is obliged to lend to the government
(vii) Budget	1.00	The bank plays a part in the budgetary process
	0.00	The budget is the government's sole responsibility

To derive the figure for weighted political independence, the mean of each of the four sets of indicators identified above is first calculated. The weighted mean of each is then arrived at by taking this figure and multiplying it by the appropriate weighting. The sum of weighted means is then calculated to give the figure for political independence and this figure is multiplied by 0.5 to give the overall total for weighted political independence. To derive the figure for economic independence, the mean figure for the seven indicators is simply calculated. This figure is then multiplied by 0.5 to give the overall total for weighted economic independence. The sum of the totals for weighted political independence and weighted economic independence is the figure for overall central bank independence.

APPENDIX 2
BANK OF ENGLAND INDEPENDENCE, 1694–1997[a]

Political Independence	1694	1931	1946	1997
Governor (0.3)				
Appointment	1.00	1.00	0.00	0.00
Nominations	1.00	1.00	0.00	0.00
Qualifications[b]	1.00	1.00	0.00	0.00
Term[c]	0.00	1.00	0.50	0.50
Dismissal	1.00	1.00	1.00	1.00
Renewability	1.00	0.00	0.00	0.00
Other posts	0.00	0.00	1.00	1.00
Total	5.00	5.00	2.50	2.50
Mean	0.71	0.71	0.36	0.36
Weighted mean	0.21	0.21	0.11	0.11
Sub-governors (0.2)				
Appointment	1.00	1.00	0.00	0.00
Nominations	1.00	1.00	0.00	0.00
Qualifications	1.00	1.00	0.00	0.00
Term	0.00	0.50	0.50	0.50
Dismissal	1.00	1.00	1.00	1.00
Renewability	1.00	1.00	0.00	0.00
Other posts	0.00	0.00	1.00	1.00
Staggering[d]	—	—	—	1.00
Total	5.00	5.50	2.50	3.50
Mean	0.71	0.79	0.36	0.44
Weighted mean	0.14	0.16	0.07	0.09
Board of governors (0.2)[e]				
Government representatives	1.00	1.00	0.25	0.25
Appointment	1.00	1.00	0.00	0.50
Nominations	1.00	1.00	0.00	0.00
Qualifications	1.00	1.00	0.00	1.00
Term	1.00	1.00	0.00	0.00
Dismissal	1.00	1.00	0.00	1.00
Renewability	0.00	0.00	0.00	0.00
Other posts	0.00	0.00	0.00	1.00
Staggering	1.00	1.00	1.00	1.00
Total	7.00	7.00	1.25	4.75
Mean	0.78	0.78	0.14	0.53
Weighted mean	0.16	0.16	0.03	0.11

Political Independence (cont.)	1694	1931	1946	1997
Decision-making process (0.3)				
Decisions	0.00	0.00	0.00	1.00
Instructions	1.00	1.00	0.00	1.00
Government veto	1.00	1.00	0.00	1.00
Salary	1.00	1.00	0.00	0.00
Capital	1.00	1.00	0.00	0.00
Legislature	1.00	1.00	1.00	0.00
Total	5.00	5.00	1.00	3.00
Mean	0.83	0.83	0.17	0.50
Weighted mean	0.25	0.25	0.05	0.15
Political independence	0.76	0.78	0.26	0.45
Weighted political independence	0.38	0.39	0.13	0.23

Economic Independence	1694	1931	1946	1997
Mission	0.00	0.00	0.00	0.00
Monetary policy	1.00	0.00	0.00	0.50
Interest rates	1.00	0.00	0.00	1.00
Exchange rates	0.00	0.00	0.00	0.00
Bank regulation	0.50	0.50	1.00	0.00
Government lending	0.50	0.50	0.00	1.00
Budget	0.00	0.00	0.00	0.00
Total	3.00	1.00	1.00	3.50
Mean	0.43	0.14	0.14	0.50
Weighted economic independence	0.21	0.07	0.07	0.25

Overall Independence	**0.59**	**0.46**	**0.20**	**0.48**

a. Unlike the Banque de France, the Bank of England was primarily governed by precedent rather than statute until 1946. The codings reflect this situation.
b. Until 1946, the Bank's Court of Directors was composed mainly of 'merchants' of the City of London [Elizabeth Hennessy, 'The Governors, Directors and Management' in Richard Roberts and David Kynaston (eds.) *The Bank of England: Money, Power and Influence 1694–1994* (Oxford: Clarendon Press 1995) pp.185–216.]. Consequently, although formally no professional qualifications were needed to serve on the Court, in practice this was a requirement. This has implications for codings relating to the governor, deputy governor and the Court and is reflected in the calculations.
c. For all governor, sub-governors and board of governors calculations, the figure for the term of office is the average of actual terms rather than the legal term.
d. Until 1997, there was only one deputy governor. Calculations are adjusted accordingly.
e. For all figures until 1997, the board of governors is deemed to be the Court of Directors. For 1997 figures, the board of governors is deemed to be the Monetary Policy Committee.

APPENDIX 3

BANQUE DE FRANCE INDEPENDENCE, 1800–1997

Political Independence	1800	1808	1936	1945	1973	1993
Governor (0.3)[a]						
Appointment	1.00	0.00	0.00	0.00	0.00	0.00
Nominations	1.00	0.00	0.00	0.00	0.00	0.00
Qualifications	1.00	0.00	0.00	0.00	0.00	0.00
Term[b]	0.50	0.50	0.50	0.50	0.50	0.50
Dismissal	1.00	0.00	0.00	0.00	0.00	1.00
Renewability	0.00	–[c]	0.00	0.00	0.00	0.50
Other posts	0.00	0.00	1.00	1.00	1.00	1.00
Total	4.50	0.50	1.50	1.50	1.50	3.00
Mean	0.64	0.08	0.21	0.21	0.21	0.43
Weighted mean	0.19	0.03	0.06	0.06	0.06	0.14
Sub-governors (0.2)						
Appointment	1.00	0.00	0.00	0.00	0.00	0.00
Nominations	1.00	0.00	0.00	0.00	0.00	0.00
Qualifications	1.00	0.00	0.00	0.00	0.00	0.00
Term	0.50	0.50	0.50	0.50	0.50	0.50
Dismissal	1.00	0.00	0.00	0.00	0.00	1.00
Renewability	0.00	–	0.00	0.00	0.00	0.50
Other posts	0.00	0.00	1.00	1.00	1.00	1.00
Staggering	1.00	1.00	0.00	0.00	0.00	0.00
Total	5.50	1.50	1.50	1.50	1.50	3.00
Mean	0.69	0.21	0.19	0.19	0.19	0.38
Weighted mean	0.14	0.04	0.04	0.04	0.04	0.08
Board of governors (0.2)[d]						
Government representatives	1.00	0.75	0.25	0.00	0.00	0.75
Appointment	1.00	1.00	0.00	0.00	0.00	0.00
Nominations	1.00	1.00	0.00	0.00	0.00	0.50
Qualifications	1.00	1.00	0.00	0.00	1.00	1.00
Term	0.50	1.00	0.50	0.50	0.50	1.00
Dismissal	1.00	0.00	0.00	0.00	0.00	1.00
Renewability	0.00	0.00	0.00	0.00	0.00	1.00
Other posts	0.00	0.00	0.00	0.00	0.00	1.00
Staggering	1.00	1.00	1.00	0.00	1.00	1.00
Total	6.50	5.75	1.75	0.50	2.50	7.25
Mean	0.72	0.64	0.19	0.06	0.28	0.81
Weighted mean	0.14	0.13	0.04	0.01	0.06	0.16
Decision-making process (0.3)						
Decisions	1.00	1.00	0.00	0.00	1.00	1.00
Instructions	1.00	1.00	0.00	0.00	0.00	1.00
Government veto	1.00	0.00	0.00	0.00	0.00	1.00
Salary	–[e]	1.00	0.00	0.00	0.00	0.00
Capital	1.00	1.00	1.00	0.00	0.00	0.00
Legislature	1.00	1.00	0.00	0.00	0.00	0.00
Total	5.00	5.00	1.00	0.00	1.00	3.00
Mean	1.00	0.83	0.17	0.00	0.17	0.50
Weighted mean	0.30	0.25	0.05	0.00	0.05	0.15

Political Independence (cont.)	1800	1808	1936	1945	1973	1993
Political independence	0.77	0.45	0.19	0.11	0.21	0.53
Weighted political independence	0.39	0.23	0.10	0.06	0.11	0.27

Economic Independence	1800	1808	1936	1945	1973	1993
Mission	0.00	0.00	0.00	0.00	0.00	0.00
Monetary policy	1.00	1.00	0.00	0.00	0.00	1.00
Interest rates	1.00	1.00	0.00	0.00	0.00	1.00
Exchange rates	0.00	0.00	0.00	0.00	0.00	0.00
Bank regulation	0.00	0.00	0.00	0.50	0.50	0.50
Government lending	0.50	0.50	0.50	0.50	0.50	0.50
Budget	0.00	0.00	0.00	0.00	0.00	0.00
Total	2.50	2.50	0.50	1.00	1.00	4.50
Mean	0.36	0.36	0.07	0.14	0.14	0.64
Weighted economic independence	0.18	0.18	0.04	0.07	0.07	0.32

Overall independence	0.57	0.42	0.13	0.13	0.18	0.59

a. For 1800 figures, the president of the *comité central* is deemed to be the governor and the other two posts on the *comité central* are deemed to be the sub-governors.
b. For all governor, sub-governors and board of governors calculations, the figure for the term of office is the average of actual terms rather than the legal term.
c. For 1808 figures, the governor's and sub-governors' terms of office were unlimited and so the renewability figure is left blank.
d. For all figures until 1993, the board of governors is deemed to be the *Conseil général*. For 1993 figures, the board of governors is deemed to be the *Conseil de la politique monétaire*.
e. For 1800 figures, the law stated that Banque members would not be remunerated and so the salary figure is left blank.

APPENDIX 4
EUROPEAN CENTRAL BANK AND BUNDESBANK INDEPENDENCE

Political Independence	ECB	Bundesbank
Governor (0.3)[a]		
Appointment	0.00	0.50
Nominations	_b	0.00
Qualifications	1.00	1.00[c]
Term	0.50	1.00
Dismissal	1.00	1.00
Renewability	1.00	0.00
Other posts	1.00	0.00
Total	4.50	3.50
Mean	0.75	0.50
Weighted mean	0.23	0.15

Political Independence (cont.)	ECB	Bundesbank
Sub-governors (0.2)[d]		
Appointment	0.00	0.50
Nominations	–	0.00
Qualifications	1.00	1.00
Term	0.50	1.00
Dismissal	1.00	1.00
Renewability	1.00	0.00
Other posts	1.00	1.00
Staggering	1.00	1.00
Total	5.50	5.50
Mean	0.69	0.69
Weighted mean	0.14	0.14
Board of governors (0.2)[e]		
Government representatives	0.75	0.75
Appointment	0.50	0.50
Nominations	0.50	0.00
Qualifications	1.00	0.00
Term	0.50	1.00
Dismissal	1.00	1.00
Renewability	0.50	0.00
Other posts	1.00	0.00
Staggering	1.00	1.00
Total	6.75	4.25
Mean	0.75	0.47
Weighted mean	0.15	0.09
Decision-making process (0.3)		
Decisions	1.00	1.00
Instructions	1.00	1.00
Government veto	1.00	1.00
Salary	1.00	1.00
Capital	0.00	0.00
Legislature	0.00	1.00
Total	4.00	5.00
Mean	0.67	0.83
Weighted mean	0.20	0.25
Political independence	0.72	0.63
Weighted political independence	0.36	0.32

Economic Independence	ECB	Bundesbank
Mission	1.00	1.00
Monetary policy	1.00	1.00
Interest rates	1.00	1.00
Exchange rates	0.00	0.00
Bank regulation	0.50	0.00
Government lending	1.00	1.00
Budget	0.00	1.00[f]
Total	4.50	5.00
Mean	0.64	0.71
Weighted economic independence	0.32	0.36
Overall Independence	**0.68**	**0.67**

a. The governor is deemed to be the President of the ECB.
b. No reference is made to nomination procedures for either the President, the Vice-President or the members of the Executive Board of the ECB.
c. By tradition the President of the Bundesbank has experience in economics.
d. For the ECB, the sub-governors are deemed to be the Vice-President of The European Central Bank and the members of the Executive Board. For the Bundesbank, the sub-governors are deemed to be the Directorate.
e. For the ECB, the board of governors is deemed to be the Governing Council. As a result of the overall composition of the Governing Council, except where indicated national legislation is the primary source of information for each coding in this section. The coding figure is an estimated average of the appropriate national legislation.
f. The Bundesbank's advice can be ignored, but it does play a part in the budgetary process.

Globalisation and the (Non-) Defence of the Welfare State

ROBERT GEYER

This article explores the relationship between globalisation and the development of the British and Norwegian welfare states. Focusing on the welfare state policies of the British and Norwegian labour parties and their relationships to the European Union (an important indicator of the impact of globalisation on West European nation-states), it argues that despite the growing importance of global dynamics and pressures, national-level forces were the predominate factors in the development of the British and Norwegian welfare states and relations to the EU in the 1980s and 1990s. Consequently, globalisation does not lead to welfare state convergence, but to divergence, interwoven with national-level dynamics.

Since the 1970s, the welfare state in Western Europe has been in a state of crisis. Internally, the welfare state has been eroded by demographic changes, the costs of its expansion, post-materialist issues and neo-liberal political and economic challenges. Externally, the globalisation of economic activity has undercut the economic and political bases of support for the welfare state by forcing nation-states to conform to international markets forces and compete with the social systems and welfare states of other countries and regions.

Of these two broad categories of factors, the second set has recently been receiving the greater attention. Authors that represent this position argue that the constraints of globalisation have become so tight that welfare states must become more oriented towards an international market dynamic and less 'de-commodifying'[1] if they are going to survive. Following this logic, despite varying national contexts and the policies of differing political parties, the welfare states of the advanced industrial countries should become increasingly similar as the forces of globalisation squeeze them into a market-oriented welfare-state model. In essence, it does not matter whether the national institutional contexts are conservative or social democratic, if the welfare state is conservative, liberal, or social democratic,[2] or if a leftist or rightist party is in power, the international

West European Politics, Vol.21, No.3 (July 1998), pp.77–102
PUBLISHED BY FRANK CASS, LONDON

constraints have become so extreme that only market-conforming welfare-state structures will be allowed.3

In this article, I intend to add my voice to the growing chorus of those who oppose this interpretation of the overwhelming constraints of economic globalisation.[4] I will do so by comparing the development of the British Labour Party's (Labour) and the Norwegian Labour Party's (DNA, *Det Norske Arbeiderpartiet*) European Community/European Union (EC/EU)[5] policies in the 1980s and 1990s and the role of the welfare state in these policies.

How will tracing the development of these two social democratic parties'[6] EU policies demonstrate the limited impact of globalisation on their welfare states? First, for Western Europe in the 1980s and 1990s the power and influence of globalisation has been strongly linked to the rise and development of the neo-liberal elements of the EC/EU. Certainly, as will be shown in a later section, globalisation is more than just the EU. However, the rise of the EC/EU and the growth of its neo-liberal orientation have been one of the key factors behind the success of globalising economic and political forces in Western Europe. Thus, examining the development of a nation-state's EU policy should be a good indicator of its relationship to the forces of globalisation.

Second, the welfare state is more than just a set of static institutions. It takes potent political forces to create and maintain it. In the Western European context one of the major political supporters of the welfare state has been social democratic parties. In the British case, many of the main elements of the British welfare state were developed and enacted under Labour Party leadership.[7] In the Norwegian case, the DNA played the unquestioned dominant role in its welfare state formation.[8] Therefore, if the support of these parties is one of the key foundations of welfare state continuation and ability to resist the forces of globalisation, then how these parties view and respond to the EU should provide one with a deeper understanding of the current welfare state transformation and its future prospects. Obviously, the political support for the welfare state goes beyond social-democratic party, and welfare-state institutions have, to some degree, a life of their own. Nevertheless, examining the effect of globalisation on one of the main political foundations of the welfare state should be interesting in itself and provide some fascinating insights into the relationship between globalisation and the welfare state.

In this work, after a brief historical review of the development of the British and Norwegian labour parties' EC/EU policies and a short examination of globalisation, I will argue that despite the changes in globalisation it was the 'historical institutional'[9] dynamics within the national context that had the most influence on the EC/EU policy developments and the role of the welfare state in those policies. For the British Labour Party in the late 1980s and early 1990s, due to the (1) relative historical weakness of EU opposition, (2) weak social democratic nature of its national institutional context, (3) liberal nature of its welfare state, and (4) success of Labour Party 'modernisation', the EC/EU offered some opportunities and strategies that the party could not afford to miss and was not seen as a major threat to the British welfare state. On the other hand, for the Norwegian DNA, with (1) the historical and institutional strength of the anti-EC/EU movement, (2) its much stronger social-democratic institutional context, (3) a social-democratic welfare state, and (4) the contested success of DNA 'modernisation', the EC/EU offered the party few clear strategic or electoral opportunities and was a direct threat to its welfare state. This recognition of the continued importance of the national sphere forces one to recognise that globalisation is both reality (in that constraints have tightened) and perception (but not to the extent which many politicians and academics believe). As to be examined subsequently, this divergence between reality and perception carries clear implications for the future of the welfare state.

A BRIEF HISTORY OF THE BRITISH LABOUR PARTY'S EU POLICY

From the first debates over membership in the 1950s and 1960s, through the membership referendum in 1975, to the demand for withdrawal from the EC in the early 1980s, the Labour Party has had an uncertain relationship to the EU.[10] Immediately after World War II, Britain's attitude to Europe was strange and contradictory. After having spent five years fighting to free the continent from the ravages of fascism, Britain seemed to want nothing more than to distance itself from Western Europe as much as possible. Labour Party leaders, like most British élites, saw three main 'circles' of British foreign policy.[11] The Atlantic alliance with the USA was the primary circle. The Commonwealth was the secondary circle. The third and least important circle was Western Europe. Strategies towards European integration, such as the 1950 European Coal and Steel Community (ECSC) and the 1957 European Economic Community (EEC), were rejected by the Labour leadership as being disruptive to the two main circles of foreign policy.

Interestingly, at the time they saw Britain (and Scandinavia) with its emerging welfare state and policies of national planning and economic controls at the forefront of democratic socialist development. Early forms of European integration were seen as being dominated by an 'anti-socialist' bloc, overly oriented towards the free market, and threatening to limit the ability of a Labour government to pursue traditional social-democratic strategies of full employment, social justice and national economic control.[12]

However, by the late 1950s and early 1960s attitudes within the Labour leadership began to change due largely to the changing importance of the circles. The link to the USA remained strong, but Britain was no longer an equal partner in the alliance. The Kennedy administration even encouraged Britain to join the EEC in order to counterbalance the influence of de Gaulle's French nationalism. The Commonwealth had begun to splinter and spiral out of British control. Meanwhile, the Western European states began to experience a period of unprecedented economic success. Joining the EEC in order to reorient Britain within Western Europe became an increasingly popular idea within a growing segment of the Labour leadership. Despite deep divisions over the issue within the party and union movement, in 1962 the Labour Party supported joining the EEC, but with reservations regarding the terms of membership. That first application was rejected by de Gaulle who saw the British as lackeys of the Americans. A second application in 1967, sent by the Wilson Labour government, was also rejected by de Gaulle. However, following the death of de Gaulle in 1970, the British application was finally accepted.

The period from 1970 to 1975 is one of the most divisive in the Labour Party's history. As the party went into opposition in 1970, criticism of the EC grew rapidly.[13] The party began to split into three main factions: pro-Europeans (mostly on the Right), anti-Europeans (mostly on the Left), and pragmatists (Centre). These factions struggled with each other over the direction of Labour's EC policy. At this time, Labour did not see the EC as posing specific threats to the welfare state. However, the Left and Centre within the party were very critical of early forms of European monetary union and wanted guarantees upon entering the EC that it would not interfere with the British state control over the national economy.[14]

When Labour returned to power in 1974 it attempted to solve the EC issue by holding a national referendum. The result of the referendum was a major victory for the pro-Europeans as the vote was almost two to one in favour of membership (67.6 per cent 'yes' to 32.4 per cent 'no'). Nevertheless, this did not eliminate the divisions within the party. As early as 1977, a motion was tabled at the Labour Party conference for running the next election on a platform of opposition to membership. Following Labour's defeat in the 1979 election, the party became increasingly antagonistic to the EC. The party's 1980 conference voted to leave the EC as soon as a Labour government was elected. The issue of the welfare state or threats to it did not play a substantial role in these debates. Much more important was the concern with the party's ability to pursue a nationalist economic strategy, the so-called Alternative Economic Strategy.[15]

Following the formation of the Social Democratic/Liberal Party Alliance to the right of the Labour Party and the disastrous electoral results in 1983 (Labour winning only 28 per cent of the national vote), the party began to moderate its opposition to the EC. Under the leadership of Neil Kinnock, Labour began to pursue a policy of 'new realism' towards the EC. Open opposition to the EC was dropped and a more pragmatic approach to its costs and benefits was emphasised. Following Labour's improvement during the 1987 election, Kinnock instituted a general 'policy-review' process that included a re-evaluation of Labour's EC policy.[16] This process coincided with the development of the revival of the EC in the mid to late 1980s under the '1992 Project' and the creation of the 'Social Dimension'.[17] With its emphasis on basic social and workers' rights, the Social Dimension made the EC increasingly attractive to the Labour Party. After years of impotent rage over the reduction in union rights and welfare state cutbacks by the Thatcher government, the EC seemed to open up a 'second front' against Thatcherism. In a complete turnaround from its position in the 1950s, Thatcherite Britain was seen as a conservative European force and the EC as a progressive one. As the 1989 Labour Party document, *Meet the Challenge, Make the Change* argued:

> [W]e have a very different vision from the present government of what the future should be. Mrs Thatcher persists in trying to impose her free market dogmas on the rest of the EC, seeking to thwart or evade every measure for social progress. She wants Europe to be a market, with minimum regulation for big business and finance. We want it to be a community too – not just because its more desirable in human terms, but because it also is a precondition for durable economic success. We want Britain to take a lead in building social Europe.[18]

At the same time as the policy review process was increasingly uniting Labour around a pro-EC/EU position, the Conservatives became increasingly divided by the issue. During the 1992 election, Labour's united pro-European policy was much more popular than the divisive Conservative's policy.[19] Following the 1992 election, the new Conservative Prime Minister, John Major, was continually confronted with a disruptive group of Eurosceptic Conservative MPs. On several issues the government came within a few votes of losing its majority in parliament.

With Labour's improvement in the 1992 election, success in the 1994 European elections, and the election of two pro-European party leaders, John Smith (1992–94) and Tony Blair (1994 onwards), Labour's conversion from Eurosceptic to Eurobeliever seemed virtually complete. Most interestingly, the role of the welfare state became increasingly prominent as Labour adopted its more pro-EC/EU attitude. In essence, the party leadership argued that after years of Conservative rule the British welfare state was so woefully underdeveloped that even the relatively low European standards enshrined in the Social Dimension and Social Charter were an improvement over the Conservatives' vision. Furthermore, Britain had little to fear from the competition between social and welfare state regimes ('social dumping' as the Commission called it) since it was so poorly developed relative to the other EC/EU member states. Thus, despite occasional anti-European protestations (generally aimed at countering the Conservative's attempts at portraying Labour as 'soft on Europe'), acceptance of the EU had been locked into the Labour Party by the early 1990s.

Finally, the campaign and results of the 1997 election confirmed the pro-EU orientation of the Labour Party. With the Conservatives deeply divided over the EU and the Liberals strongly pro-EU, Labour could easily portray itself as the united and pragmatic pro-EU party, defending British interests at the same time as pursuing a co-operative relationship with the EU.[20] Following the election, Labour has carried out its pragmatic and constructive position. It ended the British opt-out of EU social policy and has pursued an active policy agenda during its six-month presidency of the EU Council (January – June 1998), promoting the three 'E's': enlargement, European Monetary Union (EMU) and employment. In regards to EU social policy, Labour has taken a positive, but sceptical position. It has agreed to adopt existing EU social policy, but has been reluctant to see the expansion and development of those policy areas, citing the subsidiarity rights and the need to prove that EU social policies are more effective than national level policies. It has also firmly resisted the expansion of EU labour policies.

A BRIEF HISTORY OF THE NORWEGIAN LABOUR PARTY'S EU POLICY

From the first discussions over European integration in the 1950s and 1960s, the divisive national referendum in 1972, the creation of the European Economic Area (EEA) agreement in 1991, to the second national EU referendum in 1994, Norwegian society and the Norwegian Labour Party (DNA) have been extremely divided over European integration.[21] After five years of German occupation during World War II, the Norwegians were uninterested in strategies of European integration, sceptical of continental entanglements, and tended to mirror the policies and concerns of their traditional ally, Britain. Following the British lead, the DNA government (which lasted from 1945–65) took a critical attitude towards the 1951 ECSC and the 1957 EEC. At the time, DNA élites were resistant to ceding sovereignty, concerned about the *laissez-faire* economic nature of the ECSC and EEC, afraid of European competition, and sceptical of the success of integration. As Arne Skaug (a prominent DNA politician and ambassador to the OEEC) wrote in a letter to the DNA foreign minister in July 1950:

They (the continental leaders) adhere to a *laisser-faire* policy ... They are by and large opposed to income equalisation, and frequently opposed to public investments and control of investments. They consider trade liberalisation as a goal in itself ... They are not really concerned with adhering to agreements about maintaining full employment. The Anglo-Scandinavian system is largely the opposite of the continental European.[22]

The opportunity to ignore European integration changed drastically in the 1960s. When Britain, Denmark and Ireland applied in 1961, the DNA government felt compelled to follow and submitted its first application in April 1962. However, when the British were rejected in 1963, the Norwegians immediately withdrew. Similarly, the Norwegians reapplied with the British in 1967 and were again unwilling to join when the British were rejected. As already mentioned, with the death of de Gaulle in 1970, the British and Norwegian applications were accepted.

As membership in the EC became increasingly likely, opposition to joining became widespread and highly organised. Norwegian farmers and fishermen were deeply afraid of losing their special rights and protection. Northern and rural areas of Norway were frightened of a weakening of the Norwegian 'districts' (regional) policy. These groups organised themselves under the organisation 'Nei til EF' (No to the EC). Meanwhile, the left within the DNA became increasingly critical of the liberal economic nature of the EC and the constraints it would put upon national economic controls and of the pressures it would put upon the Norwegian model and welfare state. Within the DNA, opposition to the EC organised around a group called the 'Labour Movement Information Committee'.[23]

In the prelude to the 1972 EC referendum, the DNA became increasingly divided over the issue. The right wing and leadership of the party continued to argue that Norway could not survive economically or politically outside of the EC. Key markets would be cut off. Living standards would decline. In essence, Norway needed to be in the EC to remain competitive. Moreover, it was not a threat to basic Norwegian institutions and democratic controls. The left wing of the party argued that the EC would ruin the farmers and fishermen, destroy government economic control, weaken the welfare state, flood the economy and society with larger foreign interests and demands, and most importantly, rob the society of the sovereignty and democratic control it needed to pursue its particular social-democratic concerns.[24] The 1972 referendum was a close vote, 53.5 per cent voted no, 46.5 per cent voted yes. Of DNA members, 58 per cent voted yes, 42 per cent voted no.

In the 1973 election (Norwegian elections occur every four years) the

DNA's share of the national vote dropped drastically from 46 per cent to 35 per cent as disgruntled DNA voters drifted to the Left into the anti-EC Left Socialist Party.[25] The DNA responded by banishing the EC issue from virtually all party debates and policies. For the DNA leadership, the referendum had 'solved' the issue and recovering its electoral footing was top priority. The DNA could get away with this strategy since most of the other parties had been divided over the EC issue and had no wish to revive the often bitter and acrimonious debates.[26]

This strategy of ignoring the EC continued until the mid-1980s. In 1986, the newly-elected DNA government under Prime Minister Gro Harlem Brundtland encouraged a re-evaluation of the relationship between the European Free Trade Association (EFTA, of which Norway was a member) and the EC.[27] This led to the foundation of the European Economic Area (EEA) agreement between the two organisations in 1988–89. Through the EEA, Brundtland hoped to bring Norway into the EC without directly confronting membership.

Unfortunately for Brundtland, as the DNA inched closer to Europe, the anti-EC movement within the Norwegian society and DNA quickly began to revive. These groups were quick to criticise the EEA and any moves towards eventual EC membership. As Eilef Meland, one of the Left Socialist Party's parliamentary representatives, said in a Storting debate following the announcement of the agreement:

> For SV the main question is, what is there space for in the EES (European Economic Space/Area)? Is there space for full employment, welfare and social security, a progressive environmental policy and international solidarity? Which door is open in that European room? Is there a window towards the Third World, or the East ... The EC represents an extreme market-oriented society, and overly adjusting to the EC will entail extreme changes in Norway. It will be nothing more than a formality from the EEA to direct membership [my translation].[28]

From 1990–92 Brundtland was constantly forced to backtrack and qualify her support for eventual membership in the EC/EU. The EEA agreement did not go as smoothly as planned. Groups within the major trade-union organisation, the LO (Landsorganisasjon), began to criticise the EEA, and the anti-EC organisations were beginning to re-emerge in anticipation of Brundtland's eventual push for EC membership.[29] Nevertheless, in mid-1992, following a vote by the regional divisions of the DNA which supported applying for membership 184–94, Brundtland openly supported membership.

After the submission of the Norwegian application in 1992 (along with the Austrian, Finnish and Swedish applications), the party tried unsuccessfully to hold down the EC/EU debate by arguing that the debate should wait until the application negotiations were completed.[30] In reality, from then on the EU debate became extremely repetitive and shrill. Whether it was a basic issue (such as the EC's influence on unemployment, the welfare state, regional policy, sovereignty, etc.) or a current event (such as the Maastricht deal, the whaling crisis, or the ice cream crisis)[31] each side of the EU debate had its own version of the issue/event. This version would then be repeated as often and loudly as possible. Not only was every event analysed for its pro- or anti-EU implications, but every conceivable group formed in order to express its opinion and support or oppose the EU.[32] Throughout this debate, the welfare state and the effects of EU membership on it were central issues.[33]

In April 1994 the negotiations were completed and each of the four EU applicants scheduled membership referendums. In an obvious attempt to maximise support for membership, the referendums were ordered so that the most pro-European states would vote first. Austria voted to join in June 1994 (66 per cent yes – 33 per cent no), Finland in September (63 per cent – 37 per cent), and Sweden in early November (57 per cent – 43 per cent). Norway voted in late November and up until the last minute the referendum was too close to call. However, in the end the no-side won, 52.3 per cent to 47.7 per cent. Amazingly, there was only a 1.2 per cent change from the 1972 result. Exit polls estimated that DNA voters were again split 60 per cent – 40 per cent in favour of membership.[34]

From 1994–97, the DNA remained in government and pursued a cautious 'shadowing' strategy through the EEA, indirectly following the main contours of EU policy. Interestingly, the feared collapse of the Norwegian economy, due to non-membership in the EU never occurred. In fact, the economy recovered significantly in 1995 and 1996, bringing unemployment down traditionally low levels. At the same time, the Swedish economy, newly linked to the EU, went through a period of sustained structural difficulties, spiralling social spending, and massive government debt. For many Norwegians, the benefits of staying out of Europe became increasingly obvious and the feeling of having made the right choice in 1994 was remarkably strong. The EU issue vanished during the September 1997 national election. Key issues revolved around health, education, pensions, and what to do with the massive oil fund. During the campaign, the DNA Prime Minister, Thorbjørn Jagland (who replaced Brundtland in 1995) demanded that if the DNA did not receive over 36.9 per cent of the national vote (the DNA performance in the 1993 election), it would not continue to form a minority government. In the election the DNA only recieved 35 per cent and quickly stepped down. A weak coalition government, led by the Christian People's Party and controlling only 42 out of 165 seats in the Norwegian Storting, was formed in the aftermath of the election and continues to govern at present (spring 1998). In opposition, the DNA, particularly at élite levels, remains a pro-EU party. However, opposition within its membership and Norwegian society continue to limits its EU position and constrain its policy choices.[35]

WESTERN EUROPEAN 'GLOBALISATION' IN THE 1980S AND 1990S

Following this brief history of the British and Norwegian social-democratic EU policies, one must turn to the forces of globalisation and examine what they were and how they should have affected the EU and welfare-state policies of the two parties. To begin, the forces of globalisation may be global, but their effects vary drastically from region to region. I would argue that there were three main elements of globalisation that affected both British and Norwegian Labour-Party policy towards the EU and their welfare states. These were the: (1) growth of economic internationalisation, (2) success of European integration under the EC's 1992 Project, and (3) neo-liberal development of EC/EU during the late 1980s and early 1990s. Theorists of globalisation would expect these factors to encourage both the British and Norwegian labour parties to adopt a more pro-EU policy position and to accept the greater constraints that globalisation and EU membership would place upon their respective welfare states.

The growing internationalisation in trade, production, and finance in the 1970s, 1980s, and 1990s disrupted earlier nationalist strategies for dealing with international economic disturbances.[36] As Richard Cooper pointed out in the late 1960s,[37] nation-states that are confronted with an increasingly constraining international economic context are forced to pursue one of two strategies: renationalise the economy or internationalise policy formation. As attempts at renationalising the economies failed in the 1970s and early 1980s and the costs of breaking with the international economy grew higher, joining the EC/EU in order to create some form of international policy formation seemed increasingly attractive. This internationalisation of the national economy, creating higher unemployment, poor economic performance, and greater competition with goods from countries with lower social standards and minimal welfare states, put increasing strains on the British and Norwegian welfare states and encouraged their supporters to look to some form of EU welfare state for relief.

Moreover, the success of the EC's 1992 Project created its own dynamic of attraction. Both economically and politically, the EC appeared to be an island of stability in an increasingly tumultuous international order.[38] Moreover, with the development of the EC/EU's 'social dimension' and 'social charter', the EC/EU seemed to be laying down a base for some form of Euro-welfare state that could unite the various member-state welfare states and give them the strength to resist the international forces. Thus, if one looked only at these two factors, the international context seemed to strongly encourage both British and Norwegian labour parties to move towards pro-EU positions and to see the EU as an opportunity for maintaining their advanced welfare states. Moreover, one might have expected that the international influence towards international integration would be even stronger in a small country like Norway than in Britain.

However, despite the high hopes of many European social democrats, the EC/EU as it evolved under the 1992 Project (1985–92) developed an increasingly neo-liberal character that should have exerted an increasingly repulsive influence on the two labour parties.[39] Of the six main elements of the 1992 Project (the common market strategy, decision-making reform, integration strategy reform, political union, monetary union and the social dimension), four of them had a pronounced neo-liberal character. The strategy for the creation of a genuine common market (crystallised in Lord Cockfield's 'White Paper') was based strongly on free market principles and enhancing the 'four freedoms' of the movement of capital, goods, persons and services. Decision-making reform (enshrined in the 1986 Single European Act and the 1992 Maastricht Treaty) within the EC/EU greatly strengthened the hand of market oriented policies by creating qualified majority voting within the Council for issues relating to the creation of the common market. This made it much easier for market-enhancing rules to be passed, while EC/EU social policy and market-constraining rules still had to be passed, predominately, by a unanimous vote. Further, the replacement of the harmonisation integration strategy (which required policies to be harmonised between the member-states) with mutual recognition (which stated that all member states must accept and recognise the policies of other member states) encouraged a European competition of national regulations and social standards ('social dumping' as previously referred to) that strengthened transnational market forces in relation to national regulatory forces.[40] Moreover, the EMU, with its emphasis on the independent nature of the future European central bank and strict constraints on government deficit spending and monetary policy, had a pronounced free-market and anti-inflationary character. This bias would have strongly restrained Keynesian policy at both the national and European levels. Finally, the failure of the development of the social dimension, despite some advances under the Maastricht and Amsterdam treaties,[41] demonstrated the inability of the EC/EU to counterbalance its increasing free-market orientation with some form of European level social policy or rudimentary welfare-state structure.

In general, the neo-liberal development of the EC/EU should have discouraged a pro-European policy among traditional social-democratic parties and a belief in the ability of the EU to protect national welfare state structures. If so, the various elements of globalisation were working against each other; economic internationalisation and the revival of European integration encouraging a pro-EU policy and European strategy for defending the welfare state and specific EC/EU policy developments discouraging such a policy and strategy. Possibly, the first two factors could be used to help explain the British case, while the third could explain the Norwegian case. This is obviously an insufficient explanation for both cases, since each occurred in both contexts. Thus, I would argue that it is only at the national level where one can truly begin to explain the divergent experiences of the two labour parties. We have already seen some of the historical factors which help to explain their policy divergence. Now we must turn to the national institutional factors.

DIFFERING NATIONAL 'SOCIAL DEMOCRATIC' CONTEXTS

How can one summarise and compare the national contexts for the two labour parties? The best way is through a comparison of the basic national institutional structures which electorates the degree of social democratic institutionalisation and orientation of the particular national context. For example, if a country possessed a strong corporatistic tradition and a politically dominant social-democratic party, then it could be said to posses two important institutional elements of a national social-democratic orientation. Given a variation in national social-democratic contexts, I would expect to see a substantial divergence in the labour parties relations to the EU and the role of the welfare state in that policy. For example, a country with a strong social democratic national context would be more reluctant to maintain positive relations with the free market oriented EU and more determined to resist the international influences pushing for a pro-EU policy. Contrarily, a labour party caught in a weak social democratic context may be less able to resist internationalising economic forces and see many more benefits in pursuing a pro-EU policy.

In comparing the British and Norwegian cases, I would emphasise seven main areas of institutional comparison: the strength of the social democratic movements, degree of societal corporatism, structure of the financial system, industrial relations, the party system, degree of party 'modernisation', and the structure of the welfare state. Of these various factors, the most important for the role of the welfare state in EU policy were the degree of party modernisation and welfare state structure. First, the Norwegian social-democratic movement[42] was much more powerful, organised and electorally successful than its British counterpart. The DNA was in government throughout much of the 1980s and 1990s and maintained around a 40 per cent share of the vote in national and local elections. Meanwhile, the Norwegian trade union movement organised around 65 per cent of the workforce. On the other hand, the British Labour Party was in opposition throughout the 1980s and 1990s, maintained a 30 per cent share of the vote, and the British unions organised about 40 per cent of the workforce. Second, Norwegian society maintained a much more corporatistic organisational structure than British society. Tripartite bargaining between unions, owners, and the state at a national and sub-national level played a much larger role in Norwegian incomes policy, industrial policy and overall economic planning than it ever did for the British case.[43] Third, the Norwegian financial system, despite substantial changes in the 1980s and 1990s, remained much more nationally oriented and state-directed than the internationally oriented British financial system. Despite growing international monetary constraints on the Norwegians, the dominance of the Norwegian Bank over the Norwegian credit markets and its key role in major Norwegian companies gave the Norwegian government a much larger range of options than the British government.[44] Fourth, Norwegian industrial relations maintained their highly organised, corporatistic, and centralised character throughout the period, while British industrial relations became increasingly fragmented and pluralistic under the twin forces of de-industrialisation and the legislative onslaught of the Conservative Party against traditional trade-union rights.[45]

Fifth, the structure of the Norwegian party system is much more conducive to social-democratic dominance than the British system. The DNA confronts a historically fragmented right in a proportional electoral system. Due in part to this structure, the DNA has been the largest party since the 1930s. Meanwhile, the British Labour Party confronted a united right in a plurality electoral system. Throughout the 1980s and 1990s Labour (and especially the centrist Alliance coalition) was a loser under this system, unable to form a coalition government with the Alliance or have much influence from the opposition benches. This has been radically altered by the 1997 British national election. Nevertheless, the result of that election was strongly due to the divisions within the Conservative Party. If and when they are capable of reuniting, the Labour Party will once again be faced with its traditional electoral problems.

Sixth, during the 1980s and 1990s one of the central struggles within European social-democratic parties was over party 'modernisation'. Modernisation generally meant a shift to the right within the party, distancing the party from the trade unions, downplaying traditional commitments to full employment and government control over the economy, and accepting the role of international market forces. The battle over party 'modernisation', shaped the outcome of and was linked to the development of the EU policies and the role of the welfare state in both parties. In each case, a critical element was the degree to which right-learning 'modernisers' or left-leaning 'traditionalists' dominated within the parties. Who were these modernisers and traditionalists? And, how did they affect EU policy and the role of the welfare state?

In Britain, the modernisers were an coherent faction of the Labour Party.[46] They generally represented the centre-right pragmatist wing of the party. They had middle-class origins, weak links to the trade-union movement, and tended to be party professionals. They were strongly electorally oriented with a central strategy of moving the party to the centre of the political spectrum in order to win electoral victory and recapture the power of the state. In order to do this they argued that the party must do two main things: reorient the structure of the party (centralising power in the party leadership, weakening the links to the trade unions, and broadening the membership base) and redirect party policy (weakening commitments to full employment, reflationary monetary and fiscal policy, and an expansive social-democratic welfare state).

For modernisers in the Labour Party, the pro-EU policy played a key role. The modernisers used the EU as a rhetorical strategy and as a clear policy constraint for supporting their changes in party structure and policy. For example, by arguing for a pro-EU policy, the modernisers could stress the impossibility of national economic strategies such as the ill-fated Alternative Economic Strategy, the need to accept many of the welfare-state changes (the decline of public housing) of the Thatcher years, and to recognise the limitations of the state for solving problems such as unemployment and poverty (typical tasks of the welfare state).[47] Central modernising leaders have been Neil Kinnock, John Smith and Tony Blair.

Opposed to the modernisers within the party were the so-called traditionalists. Generally, this group was less cohesive than the modernisers, composed of various leftist factions, strongly linked to the trade unions, and came from more traditional working-class backgrounds. Determined to maintain the traditional party structure and policy commitments, this party faction continued to resist the modernisers changes throughout the 1980s and 1990s. However, as the party became more and more desperate to return to government, the power and influence of the traditionalists continued to decline. At present, traditionalists only represent a small faction of the Labour leadership. One of the last strong traditionalists, Bryan Gould, resigned from the shadow cabinet in 1993 in protest against the party's support of the EMU.

In the Norwegian case, there has been a similar development of a modernisation faction within the DNA.[48] Worried about the rise of the traditional and radical right in Norwegian politics, the modernising wing of the party became very concerned that the party would not be able to maintain its electoral dominance in the Norwegian political system. The leaders of this wing within the party have been the former prime ministers Gro Harlem Brundtland (from the 1980s until 1995) and Thorbjørn Jagland (from 1995 to present). At nearly the same time as the rise of the modernisers in the British Labour Party, in the early to mid-1980s, Brundtland and the modernising wing came to power within the DNA. Slowly but steadily, this wing pushed for an increasing modernisation of the party.

From the late 1980s until present, membership of the EU played a key role in the strategies of the modernisers. As in the British case, Norwegian modernisers used the need to integrate with Europe and future membership plans in the EU to shift the burden of national economic control and responsibility away from the party. Furthermore, the EU was used as a justification and strategy for weakening the party's links to the LO (the main national trade-union organisation), to the trade unions in general, to downplay the importance of public solutions to individual and national problems, and to stress the financial and competitive constraints on the welfare state.

However, in contrast to the British experience, the power of the Norwegian modernisers was strongly contested. Some traditional strategies, such as the dominance of the state within the financial system and the importance of state solutions to social problems were successfully challenged. Some elements of the party's trade-union link were weakened, and attempts were made to shift the party to the right in order to recapture the 'centre' of the political spectrum. However, all of these strategies achieved only limited results. Despite the best efforts of Brundtland, Jagland, and other modernisers, the modernisation strategy was constantly on the defensive and forced to take very contradictory positions.

The development of the EU issue and its linkage to the modernisation strategy illustrated this defensiveness and the resulting contradictions. The modernising leadership of the DNA was forced to take a very hesitant and careful approach to the EU throughout the late 1980s and early 1990s. To both the left and the right of the DNA were two strongly anti-EU parties that were waiting to take advantage of any move by the party in a pro-EU direction. Within the party itself was a highly organised traditionalist anti-EU faction. Hence, whenever the modernists tried to isolate or eliminate a traditionalist or EU opponent, that individual had several parties to chose from where he/she could continue to voice an opinion. Furthermore, in order to minimise the resistance of the traditionalists to the EU, modernisers had to argue that the EU would substantially aid the current development of

Norwegian social democracy. During the 1994 EU referendum campaign, Brundtland was often forced to argue that the EU would actually help maintain Norway's social democracy, full employment and welfare state, despite its neo-liberal orientation. Both polls and election results indicated they had not succeeded in convincing DNA voters. The consequence was that, despite some changes, the DNA remained a strongly traditionalist party, greatly divided over the EU issue, and supportive of the existing welfare-state structure.[49]

Seventh, and most importantly, as a variety of authors have argued, the British welfare state is 'liberal', while the Norwegian is 'social democratic'.[50] The British welfare state is based predominately on a liberal model. Assistance is commonly modest, means-tested and is associated with a negative normative stigma. Universal elements are generally minimalised (the key exception is the National Health Service). Benefits are oriented mainly towards a low-income clientele. Further, the effects of the welfare state are directed towards minimising their impact on the national market environment. This type of welfare state: 'minimises de-commodification effects, effectively contains the realm of social rights, and erects an order of stratification that is a blend of a relative equality of poverty among state-welfare recipients, market-differentiated welfare among the majorities, and a class-political dualism between the two'.[51]

During the 1980s, the liberal orientation of the British welfare state was accentuated by the reforms of the Conservative Party. In general, benefits were reduced and linked more directly to means-testing requirements. Areas such as welfare-state support for housing policy were eliminated. Further, the government did everything it could to further stigmatise the welfare recipient. Even though the Conservatives did not radically reduce the size of the welfare state, and certain key elements, especially the National Health Service, continued to exist and confer universalistic benefits, the liberal nature of the British welfare state was strengthened. The Labour Party was virtually powerless to stop these changes. It never had the votes in parliament to stop welfare-state modifications despite the fact that the majority of voters opposed many of the Conservatives' welfare-state modifications.[52]

During the late 1980s and early 1990s, the Labour Party did not see the EU as either a substantial threat to, or saviour of, the British welfare state. Labour Party documents mentioned a possible link between the two, but made no clear connection. General pronouncements in support of the EU's social dimension and European social rights were made, especially by the TUC,[53] but both the party and unions focused on specific policies or rights upon which the EU had an impact. The more general argument that the British welfare state would be undermined or salvaged by the EU was never given a prominent position in the Labour Party's thinking.

There are two main reasons for this. First and foremost, the most obvious and important threat to the British welfare state was the Conservative Party. If a Labour Party member were discussing the various threats and opportunities for the British welfare state, examining how the EU would affect it would seem like a very secondary activity. Second, the basically liberal nature of the British welfare state was not obviously inconsistent with the neo-liberal nature of the EU. As already mentioned, the liberal British welfare state is strongly market oriented. Further, in many areas of welfare-state provision and benefits, the British state is one of the least generous in north-west Europe. Therefore, increasing market influence or competition from other welfare states brought about by the ability of EU citizens to shop between various welfare-state regimes posed no clear threat to the British welfare state. All in all, the effect of the EU on the British welfare state was a minor issue in the British Labour Party debate.

By contrast, the future of the welfare state was one of the central questions in the debate over the DNA's policy towards the EU. The Norwegian welfare state is known for the strength of its social-democratic orientation. The Norwegian social-democratic welfare state stresses universalistic benefits which are directed towards the vast majority of the population. Benefits are not means-tested, are substantial, and are seen as an extension of the social-citizenship rights of the individual citizen. Moreover, due to their universalistic nature, receiving welfare-state benefits does not carry with it the social stigma that is found under liberal welfare states. The social-democratic welfare state:

> translates into a mix of highly de-commodifying and universalistic programmes that, nonetheless, are tailored to differentiated expectations. Thus, manual workers come to enjoy rights identical to those of salaried white-collar employees or civil servants; all strata are incorporated under one universal insurance system, yet benefits are graduated according to accustomed earnings. This model crowds out the market, and consequently constructs an essentially universal solidarity in favour of the welfare state. All benefit; and all will presumably feel obliged to pay.[54]

The key weakness of this type of welfare state lies in the need to maintain full employment in order to minimise the cost of the welfare state's social guarantees. So long as full employment is maintained, extensive guarantees can be sustained. However, if full employment is lost, the costs of the welfare state drastically expand and political pressure to reduce it is significantly increased.[55]

In the debate over the DNA's EU policy, the expected effect of the EU on the Norwegian welfare state played a significant role. The pro-EU modernisers argued that within the EU, the welfare state was a predominately national question. If Norway decided to pursue a significantly larger and social-democratic welfare state, then there was nothing within the EU system that would alter this decision.[56] In fact, argued the pro-EU modernisers, by joining the EU Norway would increase its ability to maintain its social-democratic welfare state in three main ways. First and foremost, joining the EU would mean a more stable economic environment and greater possibilities for increased growth and reduced unemployment, which would in turn reduce the economic and political pressure on the welfare state. Second, outside of the EU the international environment had become so harsh that individual nation-states had no ability to control their economies or protect their welfare states. Within and through the EU, these international forces could be blunted and redirected, creating the space for the maintenance of the welfare state.[57] Third, only by joining the EU and using one's voice within it that could Norway pressure the EU to build up its social dimension and employment policies.[58] By staying out, Norway would leave itself in a weaker economic position, in a harsher international environment, and without a voice in that environment.

For the anti-EU traditionalists, the consequences of joining the EU entailed a very negative effect on the Norwegian welfare state. They stressed the neo-liberal aspects of the EU, especially the strength of the EMU and weakness of the social dimension, and argued that the EU would damage employment and would therefore weaken Norway's ability to defend its welfare state.[59] Moreover, they argued that the free market nature of the EU stressed internal EU competition and privatisation that pressured the boundaries of the welfare state.[60] Norway would also lose its tax base, especially its massive taxes on alcohol and tobacco, if sales taxes were harmonised. Finally, if Norway did become a member it would be subject to much more neo-liberal rules than it had to face outside of the EU and because of its small size, would have virtually no influence in the EU government. In short, by joining, Norway would give up its remaining national controls and lock itself into a neo-liberal organisation with virtually no ability to influence or alter the direction of that organisation.[61]

Clearly, in the Norwegian case, the social-democratic structure and popularity of the welfare state and its linkage to the development of the DNA made it central to the current EU debate. Modernists argued that joining the EU was the only way to save it. Traditionalists argued the opposite. One can therefore conclude that the more social democratic nature of the Norwegian welfare state combined with the continued strength of the DNA and traditionalism within the party, were the key elements in explaining the importance which the Norwegian debate placed on the welfare state.

CONCLUSIONS

The influence of this divergence between distinct historical developments and a more social-democratic Norwegian context and a less social-democratic British context was clearly reflected in the development of the labour parties' debates over their EU policies and the role of the welfare state in those policies. Despite the growing international pressure on Norway, the neo-liberal EU had very little to offer the deeply entrenched social-democratic Norwegian society and was much more of a threat to the Norwegian social-democratic welfare state. The Norwegian social-democratic movement was doing relatively well, basic elements of national corporatism remained intact, the financial system was changing but not drastically, the Norwegian industrial relations system and electoral system continued to benefit the social democrats, traditionalists maintained a strong voice in the party, and the social-democratic welfare state remained very popular. Even Norway's substantial oil revenues gave it an added degree of policy autonomy and freedom to pursue options outside of the EC/EU.[62] What could the EU, or by implication globalisation, offer when its neo-liberal orientation seemed to threaten most if not all of this success?

On the other hand, the EU offered opportunity and hope to the beleaguered and demoralised British Labour Party in the late 1980s and early 1990s. Through the Social Dimension and Social Charter, it gave the party a chance to shift its focus on industrial relations, provide a basis for social-policy floor in the face of a seemingly unstoppable Conservative legislative onslaught, and even open up a 'second front' against Thatcherism in defence of the welfare state. Further, in theory, as EMU developed and the EU took over the monetary controls of Britain, Labour would no longer have to be electorally responsible for the use of those controls. It would become a non-issue for Labour. Finally, as the Conservative Party became increasingly divided over Britain's relationship to the EU (leading to the dismissal of Margaret Thatcher in 1990), the electoral advantages of a pro-EC/EU policy became obvious. Rather than being a threat, the EU and globalisation were a general boon to the Labour Party and its successful modernisation wing.

THEORETICAL IMPLICATIONS

The most obvious implication from this work is that the relationship between globalisation and the welfare state is extremely complex and dependent on historical and institutional factors at the international, European, and national levels. Nevertheless, as I have argued throughout this work, growing structural constraints at the international level remain relatively secondary in determining the particular policies of national parties. Not only did these factors fail to force the relatively small and seemingly helpless DNA into adopting a more unified pro-EU position and liberal welfare state, but they did not provide a sufficient explanation of why the British Labour Party became so pro-European.

This is not to argue that the international and European levels have no impact, but rather that the impact is filtered through the national level. A currently popular strategy for conceiving the relationship between national, European, and international forces and actors is the multi-level game approach.[63] In this strategy the basic assumption is that the various levels are of equal weight and that forces at one level are relatively similar in impact to forces at another level. With respect to EU policy formation and the role of the welfare states for the British and Norwegian labour parties, this is a faulty assumption. The international and European levels constrained and offered opportunities to the domestic actors, but did not determine their choices. A better way of conceiving of the relationship between national party policy and the international/European level is to view the formation of party policy as a domestic game played out in a multi-level context. National parties may be constrained by or take advantage of developments at the European and international levels, however the primary focus is still national.

In short, in the British and Norwegian cases the strength of the historical developments and national social-democratic contexts were more important in determining the particular party policy outcomes than international or European developments. Certainly, international and European factors cannot be ignored. In fact, often times national analyses and comparative works go too far in ignoring European and international forces. However, with regard to the relationship between globalisation and the welfare state, pressure from globalisation does exist, but it is not a hegemonic force. Where it gains its power is when it coincides with political forces at the national level. As has been shown, the forces of globalisation interacted in a symbiotic relationship with the less social-democratic British context and Labour Party modernisers, while they were a disruptive force for the Norwegian context and DNA. Moreover, national contexts may increasingly 'lock in' strategies of acceptance of, or resistance to, the forces of globalisation. As the British Labour Party increasingly abandons any attempt to create a more traditional social democratic welfare state (mirroring the Clinton welfare-reform strategies in the USA) the neo-liberal agenda of the EU and globalisation is increasingly imprinted on the British institutional framework and political ideology. Meanwhile, as the DNA continues to maintain its social-democratic welfare-state orientation, a political and institutional tradition of resistance to globalisation is increasingly enmeshed in Norwegian society. Therefore, instead of welfare-state convergence, one should expect to see continued divergence as these international forces interact with different national contexts and encourage them along different paths of development.

NOTES

1. The term 'de-commodifying' comes from the work of Gøsta Esping-Andersen. He uses the term to explain the effect of a social democratic welfare state on the releasing of individuals from the constraints of the commodifying effects of markets and market institutions. See G. Esping-Andersen, *Politics Against Markets* (Princeton UP 1985) p.31.
2. I borrow this tripartite typology of national welfare states from Gøsta Esping-Andersen, *The Three Worlds of Welfare Capitalism* (Princeton UP 1990).
3. Examples of this position include: David Andrews, 'Capital Mobility and State Autonomy: Toward a Structural Theory of International Monetary Relations', *International Studies Quarterly* 38 (1994); John Goodman and L. Pauly, 'The Obsolescence of Capital Controls? Economic Management in an Age of Global Markets', *World Politics* 46 (Oct. 1993). OECD, *The OECD Jobs Study* (Paris: OECD 1994); Kenichi Ohmae, *The Borderless World* (NY: Fontana 1990); Michael Stewart, *The Age of Interdependence: Economic Policy in a Shrinking World* (Cambridge: MIT Press 1984). For an excellent review of works in this area see: Benjamin Cohen, 'Phoenix Risen: The Resurrection of Global Finance', *World Politics* 48 (Jan. 1996).
4. See Geoffrey Garret and Peter Lange, 'Political Responses to Interdependence: What's 'Left' for the Left?', *International Organisation* 45/4 (Autumn 1991). Robert Geyer *et al.* (eds.) *Globalisation, Europeanisation, and the End of Scandinavian Social Democracy?* (London: Macmillan 1998); David Gordon, 'The Global Economy: New Edifice or Crumbling Foundations?', *New Left Review* 168 (March/April 1988); John Lambert, 'Europe: The Nation-State Dies Hard', *Capital and Class* 43 (Spring 1991); Duane Swank, 'Politics and the Structural Dependence of the State in Democratic Capitalist Nations', *American Political Science Review* 86 (March 1992); Wessel Visser and Rien Wijnhoven, 'Politics Do Matter, but Does Unemployment?', *European Journal of Political Research* 18 (1990).
5. The EEC/EC/EU has gone through a series of name changes during its history. For simplicity, I will use the abbreviation EC to denote the European Community throughout the 1970s and 1980s. I will use the term EU to denote the European Union from 1993 onwards.
6. Despite its distinctive beginnings, in the post-World War II period the British Labour Party has taken on an increasingly social-democratic profile. With its organisational combination of a political party and trade union movement and emphasis on traditional social-democratic strategies, it easily falls into the general parameters of social democracy. The Norwegian Labour Party has clear historical links to the German social democracy and is in many ways a proto-typical social-democratic party.
7. It is important to note that the Labour Party was not the hegemonic political actor behind the formation of the British welfare state. The British welfare state began forming before the Labour Party ever obtained governmental power and Labour was only in power for 18 of the 50+ years since the end of World War II. On the history of the British welfare state see: Samuel Beer, *Modern British Politics* (London: Faber 1965); Paul Pierson, *Dismantling the Welfare State? Reagan, Thatcher and the Politics of Retrenchment* (Cambridge: CUP 1994); Richard Titmuss, *Social Policy: An Introduction* (London: Allen & Unwin 1974).
8. See Robert Erikson *et al.* (eds.) *The Scandinavian Model: Welfare States and Welfare Research* (London: Sharpe 1987); Gøsta Esping-Andersen, *Politics Against Markets* (Princeton UP 1985); Stephen Graubard (ed.) *Norden – The Passion for Equality* (Oslo:

Norwegian UP 1986); Bent Greve (ed.) *Comparative Welfare Systems: The Scandinavian Model in a Period of Change* (NY: St Martin's Press 1996).

9. Historical institutionalism (or 'new institutionalism') is a theoretical approach with a long history within political science and economics. It argues that historical trajectories and social institutions play an essential role in the development of a nation-state's political and economic evolution. Historical institutionalism is not inherently limited to national level analyses. However, given the historical predominance of the nation-state and the rich institutional legacy that exists there, historical institutionalism is strongly drawn to national level analyses. Works in the historical institutional tradition include: John Campbell, J. Hollingsworth, and L. Lindberg (eds.) *Governance of the American Economy* (NY: CUP 1991); G. Hodgson, *Economics and Institutions: A Manifesto for a Modern Institutional Economics* (U. of Philadelphia Press 1987); M. Panic, *National Management of the International Economy* (NY: St Martin's Press 1988); Andrew Shonfield, *Modern Capitalism: The Changing Balance of Public and Private Power* (London: OUP 1969).

10. There are at least five works which explore the post-World War II relationship between the British Labour Party and European integration: Kevin Featherstone, *Socialist Parties and European Integration: A Comparative History* (Manchester UP 1988); Robert Geyer, *The Uncertain Union: British and Norwegian Social Democrats in an Integrating Europe* (Aldershot: Avebury 1997); John Grahl and Paul Teague, 'The British Labour Party and the European Community', *The Political Quarterly* 59/1 (Jan./March 1988); Michael Newman, *Socialism and European Unity: The Dilemma of the Left in Britain and France* (London: Junction Books 1983); L.J. Robins, *The Reluctant Party: Labour and the EEC 1961–75* (Ormskirk: Hesketh 1979).

11. See David Reynolds, *Britannia Overruled: British Policy and World Power in the 20th Century* (London: Longman 1991) Chs.7, 8; Stephan George, *Britain and European Integration since 1945* (Cambridge: Blackwell 1991) Ch.2.

12. See The Labour Party, *European Unity* (London 1950).

13. R. Bilski, 'The Common Market and the Growing Strength of Labour's Left Wing', *Government and Opposition* 12/3 (1977) and M. Newman, *Socialism and European Unity* (London: Junction Books 1983) argue that whenever Labour went into opposition, the Left was strengthened due to the implicit need for change in order to be reelected. Hence, when in government Labour moderates had more power and could push the party to support EC membership. When the party was out of power, the Left was strengthened and anti-EC opinion dominated. Eric Shaw, *Discipline and Discord in the Labour Party* (Manchester UP 1992) argues that there was also a general trend towards the Left during the 1970s and towards less deference to party leadership and central control during that period.

14. See Anthony King, *Britain Says Yes: The 1975 Referendum on the Common Market* (Washington DC: American Enterprise Inst. 1977) Ch.1.

15. The Alternative Economic Strategy was the Labour Left's nationalist strategy for bringing Britain out of the economic difficulties of the 1970s. Key works that formed the basis of the AES include: F. Cripps *et al.*, *Manifesto: A Radical Strategy for Britain's Future* (London: Pan Books 1981); Stuart Holland, *The Socialist Challenge* (London: Quartet 1975).

16. For more information on the 'policy review' and the 'modernisation' of the Labour Party see Richard Heffernan and Mike Marqusee, *Defeat from the Jaws of Victory* (London: Verso 1992); Colin Hughes and Patrick Wintour, *Labour Rebuilt: The New Model Party* (London: Fourth Estate 1990); Eric Shaw, *The Labour Party Since 1979* (London: Routledge 1994); Martin Smith and J. Spear (eds.) *The Changing Labour Party* (ibid. 1992).

17. The basic elements of the EC's social dimension are summed up in: Commission of the European Communities, 'The Social Dimension of the Internal Market: Interim Report of the Intergovernmental Working Party, Special Edition of *Social Europe* (Luxembourg 1988).

18. See The Labour Party, *Meet the Challenge, Make the Change* (London: Labour Party 1989) p.7.

19. See Anthony King *et al.*, *Britain at the Polls, 1992* (Chatham, NJ: Chatham House 1993).

20. See Andrew Geddes and J. Tonge (eds.) *Labour's Landslide* (Manchester UP 1997).

21. A brief selection of works on this period include Hilary Allen, *Norway and European in the 1970s* (Oslo: Universitetsforlaget 1979); Nils P. Gleditsch and O. Hellevik, *Kampen om EF*

(Oslo: NAVF 1977); Jostein Nyhamar, *Nye utfordringer 1965–1990* (Oslo: Tiden Norsk Forlag 1990); Nils Orvik (ed.) *Fears and Expectations: Norwegian Attitudes toward European Integration* (Oslo: Universitetsforlaget 1972); Helge Pharo, 'The Norwegian Labour Party', in R. Griffiths (ed.) *Socialist Parties and the Question of Europe in the 1950s* (NY: E.J. Brill 1993).

22. Skaug is quoted in ibid. p.204.

23. See Atle Hellevik, *Det Ansvarlige Opprør: AIK og EF-motstanden i Arbeiderpartiet* (Oslo: Universitetsforlaget 1979).

24. For an excellent overview of the pro- and anti-EC positions see: Olav Vefald, 'The 1971 EEC Debate', in Orvik (note 21) Ch.6.

25. Since the 1970s, the Norwegian party system has had seven main parties. From left to right, they are: the Left Socialist Party (SV, Sosialistisk Venstreparti), the Norwegian Labour Party (DNA, Det Norske Arbeiderparti), the Centre Party (SP, Senterpartiet), the Liberal Party (V, Venstre), the Christian People's Party (KrF, Kristelig Folkeparti), the Conservative Party (H. Høyre), and the Progress Party (FrP, Fremskrittspartiet).

26. As Hilary Allen noted in *Norway and Europe in the 1970s* (Oslo: Universitetsforlaget 1979) p.208, regarding EC policy in the 1970s: 'The subject of relations with the EEC had become surrounded by taboos which scarcely anyone in active political life seemed to dare to defy ... With a few notable exceptions, most Norwegians appeared to have stopped thinking seriously about what was happening in the EEC or the long-term implications of alternative developments there for themselves. Much of the responsibility for this lay with the Labour Party and the Labour government of these years.'

27. See St. meld. nr.61, (1986–1987) *Norge, EF og europeisk samarbeid*: released from the Norwegian Foreign Affairs Department, 22 May 1987.

28. Torill Egge Grung (ed.) *Norsk Utenrikspolitisk Årbok 1989* (Oslo: Norsk Utenrikspolitisk Institutt 1990) p.161.

29. The former anti-EC umbrella organisation 'Nei til EF' reformed itself under the name 'Nei til EU' and the anti-EU segments of the DNA organized themselves into a group under the name 'Sosialdemokrater Mot EU' (SME).

30. The party attempted a similar strategy in the prelude to the 1972 referendum as well.

31. It was amazing the degree to which every issue was debated for its EU implications. For example, in 1991 a Swiss-owned brand of Swedish ice cream began to break into the protected Norwegian ice-cream market. Norwegian producers ran a national campaign arguing that Norwegian jobs were being undermined by the international competition and that if Norway joined the EU, Norwegian ice cream would be completely wiped out.

32. My personal favourite and theoretically the most encompassing of the anti-EU groups was 'Blondes against the EU'.

33. See Robert Geyer, 'Traditional Norwegian Social Democracy and the Rejection of the EU: A Troublesome Victory', *Scandinavian Studies* 69/3 (summer 1997); Robert Geyer and Duane Swank, 'Rejecting the EU: Norwegian Social Democratic Opposition to the EU in the 1990s', *Party Politics* 3/4 (1997).

34. This result would seem to demonstrate the success of Norwegian modernisers and the adoption of a pro-EU position by the party. However, it is important to note that polls shortly before the referendum and shortly after it saw the split within the party as much closer to 50–50. This momentary change in support for the EU is supported by a Norwegian poll (*Dagbladet*, 29 Nov. 1994) that noted that 86 per cent of EU opponents had held their position for more than one year. Meanwhile, only 66 per cent of EU supporters had held their position for more than three weeks.

35. For more on current DNA élite attitudes to the EU and divisions within the DNA over the EU see: Robert Geyer, 'Just Say No! Norwegian Social Democrats in the European Union', in idem *et al.* (eds.) *Globalisation, Europeanisation, and the End of Scandinavian Social Democracy?* (London: Macmillan 1998).

36. See Philip Armstrong *et al.*, *Capitalism Since World War II: The Making and Breakup of the Great Boom* (London: Fontana 1984); Thomas Biersteker, 'Evolving Perspectives on International Political Economy: 20th Century Contexts and Discontinuities', *International Political Science Review* 14/1 (1993); Wolfgang Hager, 'Protectionism and Autonomy: How

to Preserve Free Trade in Europe', *International Affairs* 59/3 (1982); John Goodman and Louis Pauly, 'The Obsolescence of Capital Controls: Economic Management in an Age of Global Markets', *World Politics* 46/1 (1993); Robert Reich, *The Work of Nations* (NY: Vintage 1991); Herman Schwartz, *State Versus Markets* (NY: St Martin's Press 1994).

37. See Richard Cooper, *The Economics of Interdependence: Economic Policy in the Atlantic Community* (NY: McGraw-Hill 1968) p.148.

38. See Paul Kennedy, *The Rise and Gall of the Great Powers* (NY: Vintage 1989); Nicholas Colchester and David Buchan, *Europower* (London: Economist Books 1990).

39. Generally, leftists within the social-democratic and socialist traditions have been sceptical of this neo-liberal orientation since early in the 1992 Project period. Examples include: Tony Cutler *et al.*, *1992 – The Struggle for Europe: A Critical Evaluation of the European Community* (NY: Berg 1989); Francois Colpin and Gerard Streiff (eds.) *Europe 1992: Marche de Dupes* (Paris: Messidor 1989); George Ross, 'Confronting the New Europe', *New Left Review* 191 (Jan./Feb. 1992).

40. See Wolfgang Streeck and Philip Schmitter, 'From National Corporatism to Transnational Pluralism: Organized Interests in the Single European Market', *Politics and Society* 19/2 (June 1991).

41. See Robert Geyer, 'EU Social Policy in the 1990s: Does Maastricht Matter?', *Journal of European Integration* 20/1 (Spring 1997).

42. By the term 'social-democratic movement', I mean the combination of the labour party and its trade union affiliates.

43. See David Cameron, 'Social Democracy, Corporatism, Labour Quiescence, and the Representation of Economic Interest in Advanced Capitalist Society', in J. Goldthorpe (ed.) *Order and Conflict in Contemporary Capitalism* (Oxford: OUP 1984); Sarah Vickerstaff and J. Sheldrake, *The Limits of Corporatism* (Aldershot: Avebury,1989); H. Wilensky and L. Turner, *Democratic Corporatism and Policy Linkages* (Berkeley: Institute for International Studies 1987).

44. See Andrew Cox (ed.) *State, Finance and Industry* (Brighton: Wheatsheaf 1986); Jan Fagerberg *et al.*, 'Structural Change and Economic Policy: The Norwegian Model under Pressure' (Oslo: NUPI Notat 456, Feb. 1992); John Zysman, *Governments, Markets and Growth* (Ithaca, NY: Cornell UP 1983).

45. See Ken Coates and T. Topham, *Trade Unions in Britain* (London: Fontana Press 1988); Jan Dølvik and A. Steen (eds.) *Making Solidarity Work? The Norwegian Labour Market Model in Transition* (Oslo: Scandinavian UP 1997); David Marsh, *The New Politics of British Trade Unionism* (London: Macmillan 1992); Lars Mjøset, 'Nordic Economic Policies in the 1970s and 1980s', *International Organisation* 41/3 (Summer 1987).

46. Despite the name, the modernisers have a long history in the Labour Party. In many ways their position and situation parallels that of the Gaitskellite 'pragmatists' against the Bevanite 'fundamentalists' during the 1950s.

47. This would seem to confirm Andrew Moravcsik's theory in 'Preferences and Power in the European Community: A Liberal Intergovernmentalist Approach', *Journal of Common Market Studies* 31/4 (1993) – that the EU can augment the power of national governments rather than undermine them. I agree with this position. However, I would add that since the EU has taken on an increasingly neo-liberal orientation, then those policies and areas of national power which the EU is most likely to augment will tend to be neo-liberal policies and powers, while undermining social-democratic ones. For more on this see: Robert Geyer, *The Uncertain Union: British and Norwegian Social Democrats in an Integrating Europe* (Aldershot: Avebury 1997).

48. For more information on the growth of the modernising faction in the DNA see Erik Eriksen, 'Ap's styringsfilosofi i 1970- og 80-arene', *Nytt Norsk Tidsskrift* 3 (1992); Knut Heidar, 'The Norwegian Labour Party: 'En Attendant l'Europe'', in Richard Gillespie and W. Patterson (eds.) *Rethinking Social Democracy in Western Europe* (London: Frank Cass 1993); William Lafferty, 'Den sosialdemokratiske stat', *Nytt Norsk Tidsskrift* 1 (1986); William Lafferty, 'DNA's Nye Retning', ibid. 4 (1987).

49. One may wonder why Brundtland and the modernisers chose to pursue the pro-EU policy when it seemed so obvious that it would be opposed by substantial segments of their party. I

see three main reasons for this. First, when they first took this position in the late 1980s and early 1990s, Norwegian opinion was becoming more pro-EU, so they assumed that this trend would continue. Second, they were greatly entranced by the activity and the possibilities that were presenting themselves at the EU, not only personally in terms of job opportunities, but also in terms of the development of some form of European social democracy. Third, like other European élites, the DNA leadership had a more pro-EU opinion than the majority of its voters and assumed that Norway would lose out if it did not join.

50. See D. Ashford, *The Emergence of the Welfare State* (Oxford: Basil Blackwell 1986); Norman Birnbaum, *Comparing Welfare States* (London: Sage 1992); Alan Cochran and J. Clarke (eds.) *Comparing Welfare State: Britain in International Context* (London: Sage 1993); Robert Erikson *et al.* (eds.) *The Scandinavian Model: Welfare States and Welfare Research* (London: Sharpe 1987); Esping-Andersen, *Three Worlds of Welfare Capitalism* (note 2); Peter Flora and A. Heidenheimer (eds.) *The Development of Welfare State in Europe and America* (London: Transaction Books 1981).

51. Esping-Andersen (note 2) p.27.

52. See Ivor Crewe, 'Has the Electorate Become Thatcherite', in R. Skidelsky (ed.) *Thatcherism* (London: Basil Blackwell 1988).

53. See: Trades Union Congress, *Europe 1992: Maximising the Benefits, Minimising the Costs* (London: TUC 1988) and Trades Union Congress, *Unions After Maastricht: The Challenge of Social Europe* (London: TUC 1992).

54. See Esping-Andersen (note 2) p.28.

55. At present, a major example of this social-democratic welfare-state predicament can be found in Sweden where growing unemployment has led to the sky-rocketing of public debt.

56. As Grete Knudsen, the former DNA Minister of Trade, has argued: 'The main rule in the EU is that security systems and health systems are seen as a *national question* that lies outside of the community's competence. *We can therefore conclude that if we have our economic foundation in order, there is nothing in the EU that will hinder us from making the welfare state that we want*' (her emphasis, my translation). This quotation was found in: Odd Nordhaug and O. Søilen (eds.) *Et Sosialdemokratisk Ja til EU* (Oslo: Tano 1994) p.63.

57. As Jan Grund has argued in ibid.: 'The strong internationalization of the economy places the national welfare state in a completely new situation. It is much more difficult – maybe impossible – to secure the economic basis for the welfare state with nation-state arrangements ... We can best defend our national welfare policy by being active in the international economic and welfare-state organisations and arrangements pprimarily the EU] that will set the context for our nation' (my translation).

58. As Per Kleppe, former DNA finance minister, has argued in ibid. p.53: 'Together with the current EU countries that have a similar priority (high employment and strong welfare state), this group of countries could press for the increased importance of employment policy as a main goal of EU policy' (my translation).

59. As stated in a major publication of Social Democrats against the EU (SME), *Sosialdemokratisk Alternativ* (Oslo 1993) p.8–9: 'The EMU, with its central bank, common currency, goal of low inflation, no development of a finance policy centre in the EU and reduced ability for finance policy in the EU member states, could result in unemployment reaching much higher levels' (my translation).

60. See *Solidaritet for alle*, A-info, 23/94, p.11, Programforslag, published by the DNA. This was the position of the anti-EU minority in the DNA following the DNA's June 1994 national meeting.

61. As argued in ibid. p.24: 'If we become a member of the EU the EU's influence on the Norwegian society will be much bigger than our influence on the EU. With membership, Norway will be changed in important areas, but there is little to indicate that our membership will significantly influence EU policy. It is more important that Norway maintains its freedom to pursue a different, more social-democratic policy' (my translation).

62. I would emphasise that the oil revenues were only a relatively minor factor contributing to EU opposition. See: Robert Geyer and Duane Swank, 'Rejecting the EU: Norwegian Social Democratic Opposition to the EU in the 1990s', *Party Politics* 3/4 (1997).

63. Key examples of this multi-level approach include: Wayne Sandholtz, 'Membership Matters:

Limits of the Functional Approach to European Institutions', *Journal of Common Market Studies* 34/3 (Sept. 1996); R. Putnam, 'Diplomacy and Domestic Politics: The Logic of Two-Level Games', *International Organisation* 42 (1988); Dale Smith and J. Ray, 'The 1992 Project', in D. Smith and J. Ray (eds.) *The 1992 Project and the Future of Integration in Europe* (NY: M.E. Sharpe 1993).

The Politics of Currency Crises in Sweden: Policy Choice in a Globalised Economy

JONAS HINNFORS and JON PIERRE

In the two-pronged debate on 'globalising markets' the 'society-centered' perspective claims nation-states are losing economic control whereas the 'state-centred' perspective holds that 'business as usual' is possible. Both views are oversimplified. Looking at Sweden's 1992 currency crisis, we suggest that studies over time provide insights about the significance of political craftsmanship. We argue that market influence on domestic policy making should be regarded as a variable contingent on a fortuitous (from the point of view of market actors) confluence of political and economic circumstances. Our analysis suggests that this confluence, to some extent, can be controlled or manipulated by the state.

UNDERSTANDING THE STATE IN A GLOBALISED ECONOMY[1]

A significant consequence of the deregulation of financial and currency markets in the Western European political economy has been aggressive speculation against different currencies. Governments and central banks in Italy, Spain, Sweden and the United Kingdom, and more recently several Asian countries have experienced extraordinarily complicated problems in defending their currencies, often with negative results. These processes highlight the limits of nation-state macro-economic policies and the shifting balance between the state and 'the market' in an era of globalisation and footloose capital.

The globalisation of the financial market and other markets during the late 1980s and 1990s has presented almost as challenging problems for social scientists as it has for the nation-state. There is profound disagreement regarding what analytical model best conceptualises the current international political economy of the advanced states, what will be the nature of the future international political economy, and, indeed, whether globalisation is an essentially 'good thing' or, conversely, a necessary evil. Much nuance and context has been lost in the debate, partly because of the ambiguity of the issue itself and partly because of the

West European Politics, Vol.21, No.3 (July 1998), pp.103–119
PUBLISHED BY FRANK CASS, LONDON

normative dimensions which characterise these issues.

There are two main strands of thought in this debate. One set of arguments could be called the globalisation approach. This economy-centred perspective portrays the state as embedded in a volatile economic system albeit with some latitude to implement welfare-provision policies. In the American debate, this view on the contemporary political economy is referred to as 'embedded liberalism',[2] whereas the European conceptu-alisation is that of 'society-centred' models of political economy.[3] According to this perspective, nation-states face the choice between adapting to the changing nature of international competition or experience economic decline. Furthermore, the pressures of the internationalised finance and capital sectors force domestic policy makers to factor in and anticipate considerations about how different policy options will be evaluated by international market actors.[4]

The evolving international political economy, according to 'globalists', pits nations against one another in fierce competition for foreign investment. In order to be able to compete for such investment, nation-states seek to provide favourable conditions for private capital, including low taxes on private businesses, low wages and minimal social overheads. While another strategic option would be to attract foreign investment by offering superior infrastructure, high-skilled labour and welfare programmes that may help encourage experts and skilled personnel to live in a country – what Betchermann[5] refers to as the 'high-road' strategy in international economic competition – most nation-states seem to go for the 'low-road' strategy and compete by keeping production factor costs low.

Another important ramification of the current international political economy on domestic politics manifests itself either through speculation in the foreign-currency market against weak currencies, or in the form of speculation based on nation-states' international financial borrowing.[6] In a world in which most advanced nation-states – Norway being the notable exception – accumulate foreign debts by generating annual budget deficits, the international market for loans and credits is fertile ground for speculation against nation-state debt and interest-rate fluctuations.

This perspective on the current international political economy triggered a host of state-centric analyses taking issue with the extent and significance of the globalisation.[7] According to this second view on the international political economy, while acknowledging the political clout of international capital, nation-states still enjoy substantive leeway to manoeuvre and genuine domestic policy choice.[8] Some of this literature offers not only an empirical but also a normative defence of the state *vis-à-vis* the economy; an example of these sentiments is the argument that 'the domination of financial markets can and must be reversed'.[9]

The state-centred perspective has been accused of being a nostalgic reflection of the heyday of welfare-state expansion and redistribution through the state.[10] The decline of the nation-state – if true – would mean that redistribution and social welfare would no longer be possible political projects. Furthermore, although the globalisation view has been overly dismissive of political institutions in the economy, it is regions more than states which offer the main current expressions of collective interests. This argument ties the growing importance of economic regions to political and institutional change granting more political and economic autonomy to subnational governments. Capitalising on industrial and entrepreneurial synergy and an assertive strategy of positioning the region in the international arena, regions bring together political entrepreneurship and economic growth.[11]

Finally, the nation-state and its role in the economy is believed to be challenged by an ethnically driven regionalism. Typically, this attack on the nation-state paradigm draws on research on regions such as northern Italy, Catalonia, Quebec and Scotland. However, the argument could also include the rapidly increasing international initiatives at the local level.[12]

There are, however, three basic conceptual and theoretical problems in this slightly confused debate. First, we need a clear analysis from both sides of the argument of the theoretical consequences of their perspective on the changing international political economy. Advocates of the state-centred perspective clearly overlook (or downplay) what most observers would recognise as fairly obvious consequences of international, deregulated markets. By the same token, 'internationalists' or 'globalists' take indications of nation-state response to transnational economic forces as unambiguous validations of their perspective.

Second, and more importantly, the discussion on globalisation treats nation-states and national political economies in a similar and undifferentiated way. However, national economies and domestic institutional arrangements differ extensively with regard to how globalisation affects them and offer different preconditions for nation-state responses to global economic pressures. Differences in trade dependence, institutional arrangements, inclusion of organised interests in the policy process and domestic economic regimes – just to give a few examples – are factors which make a tremendous difference with regard to the degree to which global economic change impacts on the domestic economy.[13]

Finally, both the society-centric and the state-centric discourses need to address much more thoroughly than hitherto the issue of the development of the state. The society-centred perspective argues with little nuance that the nation-state is bound to lose control over its economy; its institutions will become increasingly incapable of resolving its problems; and the state will eventually fade into oblivion. In the state-centred perspective, on the other hand, 'business as usual' is assumed to be a likely path of development for most nation-states. We believe that both these scenarios are misleading and incomplete at best, and essentially false at worst. As Anthony Payne recently pointed out, 'the state is not disappearing; it is simply that its role is changing'.[14] This process of change is propelled by both international and domestic forces and the interplay between these drivers of change will vary from one national context to the other.

The controversy between state-centred and society-centred perspectives is intriguingly similar to the perennial argument about actors' freedom in various structural and institutional settings. As Peter Hall argues, 'national economic policy is influenced most significantly, first, by what a government is pressed to do, and secondly, by what it can do in the economic sphere. To a large extent, the former defines what is desirable in a democracy and the latter defines what is possible.'[15] Thus policy formulation can be seen as the combined outcome of, on the one hand, long-term international economic trends such as trade (goods, services, capital) conditions and, on the other hand, domestic capabilities to sustain a given institutional order.

Looking at the domestic–global exchange in this perspective, contextual factors such as political entrepreneurship and skill and the configuration of corporatist features come to play. While individual nation-states are unable to govern the international economy, they have a wide range of alternatives on how they should respond to international economic change. These choices have profound ramifications on the domestic economy. Furthermore, these choices are essentially ideological or political choices, hence different government reactions will yield different short-term and long-term outcomes.

Another source of frustration is that on both sides of the debate the relationship between standpoint and evidence is unclear. Thus, there is a strong tendency in both camps to perceive the most extreme events in the international political economy as the most typical, namely, to use extraordinary events as proof of either irreversible globalisation of economies or, conversely, of nation-state resilience to these forces as evidence supporting a more general perspective. We need to know to what extent the cases and events we are observing are integrated parts of consistent, long-term processes of change or to what extent they are anomalies caused by a contextual state of affairs which is not very likely to repeat itself. Thus, we need to recognise the difference between short-term, acute crises and their political management, on the one hand, and the more gradual, but continuous, reshaping of the international political economy on the other.

CLEARING THE CONCEPTUAL JUNGLE

We have probably only witnessed the first exchange of blows in what appears to become a rather lengthy battle between the society-centric and state-centric models of the international political economy. Meanwhile, we need to outline a robust analytical framework for an understanding of state–global exchange and interdependence. Here, the literature identifies four different themes. One group of studies highlights the degree to which nation-states can exercise control over the currency exchange rate.[16] Another perspective focuses on welfare states in a globalised economy and nation-states' capacity to sustain such programmes[17] or, more broadly defined, policies which do not serve to enhance national competitiveness.[18] A third approach is focused on 'policy styles' and models of interest representation in economic policy.[19] The fourth group of studies, finally, looks at the limits of politics *vis-à-vis* markets.[20] We will assess these four themes in greater detail below.

This article takes a 'dual' view on the issue of the impacts of globalisation, on the one hand, and nation-state capabilities to accommodate the effects of this globalisation on the other. Domestic political and economic factors are essential to an understanding of three crucial problems in this context. First, we suggest that trade dependence – particularly export dependence – is a crucial factor in understanding the variations among countries with regard to the impact of the globalised economy. Nation-states whose economies to a large extent depend on the international competitiveness of their core products are more susceptible to changes in these markets compared to other economies. Interestingly, most of the advanced corporatist political milieux (e.g. Austria, the Scandinavian countries, and Switzerland) belong to the category of extremely trade-dependent economies.[21] Thus, nation-states are unequally susceptible to market speculation against currencies and interest rates due to different institutional arrangements of the economy,[22] size of the public sector and the nature of organised interest involvement in policy making.

Second, fluctuations in international markets are (albeit to a varying degree and in different forms) mitigated by nation-state institutions.[23] However, we suggest that much more analytical work can be done on the nature of this mitigating process. These countries constitute a distinct type of political economy, displaying continuous involvement of organised interests throughout the policy-making process coupled with industries which control only minor shares of world markets and are, therefore, 'price-takers' much more than 'price makers'.[24]

Such corporatist arrangements have two different types of effects on nation-states' ability to control speculation against the currency. On the one hand, corporatist models of policy making normally involve various forms of 'domestic compensation' among constituencies directly or indirectly exposed to foreign competition.[25] In such compensatory policy making, keeping budget deficit or inflation under close control is not a top priority and the model may therefore well contribute to weaken currencies which, in turn, exacerbates problems of financial markets' influence on domestic policies. On the other hand, corporatist arrangements may also help implement and generate support and legitimacy for policies necessary to alleviate problems of financial market influence.[26]

Finally, we suggest that a contextual and actor-based factor as sheer political skill and ingenuity can make quite a difference with regard to how nation-states alleviate acute situations of dependence on volatile markets. Speculation in currency exchange rates or interest rates is by definition a matter of weighing risk against anticipated profits and hence relies to a large extent on making correct assessments of statements and actions by the political élite. Thus speculators and investors are more dependent on political decisions and actions – even postures – by the political leadership than is often recognised. Since in the case of Sweden at least an interactive relationship emerged between currency-market speculators and political decision makers such perceptions among both actors have a strong influence on their future actions.

One of the perennial problems in international political economy is the different levels of analysis it embraces, which presents a major challenge in bringing observations together in a coherent multi-level analytical framework.[27] The politics of defending the currency's exchange rate certainly illustrates this problematic. The perspective adopted here is focused on the exchange between government and market. Analysing what economic conditions triggered speculation against the Swedish krona and the government's response to the number of related crises which this speculation entailed will shed new light on this exchange. Thus, in the present context we are less interested in market dynamics and market behaviour *strictu sensu*.

We will return to these issues in the closing section of the article. First, however, we will look at the Swedish experience of currency speculation and the political handling of a major economic crisis.

THE CASE OF THE 1992 CURRENCY CRISIS IN SWEDEN

In the autumn of 1992, the Swedish government faced one of its deepest and most complicated economic crises in modern history. In the wake of the Danish anti-Maastricht referendum the full thrust of the international currency crisis hit the Swedish economy. During a few turbulent – perhaps even tumultuous – months interest rates – rocketed, and a huge budget deficit in the state's finances was accumulated. The government spent a fair amount of its time prowling the international money-lending markets, taking up loans at an annual rate of 200 billion kronor (approx. £20 billion) in order to balance its national budget. In addition, tens of thousands of jobs were lost; major construction companies collapsed each leaving billions of kronor in losses, and major banks were on the brink of bankruptcy. For a short time, the Swedish economy was essentially free falling.

Already during the summer of 1992, the public-sector budget deficit rose alarmingly, placing upward pressure on interest rates. When the Finnish central bank decided to float the mark in September, tremendous pressure was immediately put on the Swedish krona. As a result, interest rates reached all-time high levels, while the stock market went into the doldrums.

In spite of unprecedented inter-bank marginal-rate levels, the currency flow out of the country continued to grow dramatically. Earlier government efforts to act firmly during the spring – severely criticised by the Social Democrats in opposition – such as a 30 billion kronor (approx. £3 billion) budget cut and a 20 billion kronor (approx. £2 billion) aid package to save the publicly-owned merchant bank, Nordbanken, from collapse proved insufficient: the entire banking system was on the verge of collapse.

Various measures were implemented to prevent complete disaster. The central bank raised the inter-bank marginal rate while the government met informally with labour-market representatives in order to keep wage increases at a moderate level. After two weeks of continued market pressure which forced the central bank to an unprecedented inter-bank marginal rate of 500 per cent, the 'bourgeois' coalition government entered negotiations with the Social Democratic Party on how to end the crisis.[28]

Three days later, at an historical joint party conference, the parties presented an agreement on an extensive austerity programme. All in all, some 45 billion kronor (approx. £4.5 billion) were to be cut from the public budget. Some of the cuts were to be effective immediately with others implemented later. After some favourable market reactions – which at the time was the key evaluative instrument of the efficiency of the measures to reduce the pressure on the currency – the central bank reduced the inter-bank marginal rate to 50 per cent. While that remains an extraordinarily high level by all standards, the crisis seemed to have been at least temporarily resolved. Ten days later, however, renewed speculation against the krona triggered a second all-party agreement comprising once again extensive welfare-state cuts, a rise in VAT and the cancellation of two days of paid national holidays. After yet another disastrous week of car-factory lay-offs affecting 6,500 workers, extensive building-society bankruptcies and renewed speculation against the krona which triggered a renewed 500 per cent inter-bank marginal rate, the central bank had to give up its fight for a fixed exchange rate for the krona.

The unprecedented all-party agreements aimed explicitly at sending a signal to 'the market' that the politicians remained in charge of the economic situation and that the situation was under control. However, in spite of the strong political will and extremely costly attempts to keep the krona currency rate pegged to other currencies, these efforts failed.[29] Unique public-sector austerity measures such as record-high interest rates and unparalleled co-operation between the cabinet and the opposition over budget cuts had seemingly proven insufficient to fend off speculation against the krona. Finally, after a series of further speculative shocks in November, the government had no choice but to float the krona which ensued in an immediate 20 per cent effective depreciation. Prime Minister Carl Bildt described the events as a 'complete failure'.[30] All in all, speculation drained the national budget of some 95 billion kronor (approx. £9.5 billion).[31]

The process of crisis development and management highlighted a novel and very interesting pattern; the market had become *interactive* with the political élite. Each government measure to calm the situation generated immediate responses in the currency market. Similarly, any development in the market was instantly commented upon and reacted to by the political élite.

The government's reference to 'the market' as the root and cause of austerity measures to which the politicians 'considered' themselves 'bound' left little doubt about the source of authority over public policy in Easton's perspective.[32] Ironically, the traditional image of the Swedish 'mixed economy'[33] had taken on a new meaning; while the traditional notion of the 'mixed economy' could be described as a coexistence between two insulated spheres of society (the political and the economic) rather than integration, the deregulated international economy and the speculation against the krona had created a truly mixed, interactive political economy.

The nature of the interaction and the allocation of power and authority between the political élite and market actors is to an important extent in the eye of the beholder; as soon as politicians perceive the market as authoritative, it *de facto* enters the sphere of politics. The market's status as an authoritatively binding actor was driven home by the *Financial Times* which commented that 'the financial markets are likely to approve the choice of Mr Persson [for PM] who has won their confidence'.[34] Thus, in terms of democratic legitimacy, the system faced the risk of completely losing its electoral foundation. Market actors appeared to have become not only the main constituents of public policy,[35] but also the architects of those policies.

Currency instability, which provides the very basis of market speculation, was acute. The leeway left to politicians appeared to be extremely limited. With no clear grasp of either who exactly constituted 'the market' or what its objectives were, politicians were left to act typically short-term and, indeed, inconsistently. In so far as the typical 'style' of Swedish policy making saw all major interests present at the bargaining table, this situation in which one of the most important actors (the market) was absent from the table offered a whole new type of challenge. The notions that a balanced economy will fend off speculators and that even the faintest rumours of devaluation will trigger massive currency trade had been confirmed.[36] In these respects, globalisation as a relentless force undercutting political authority and control is indeed corroborated by the data.

However, the opposite picture – the nation-state perspective – may also find empirical support in the Swedish case. Looking at the relationship between the government and 'the market' over a longer time period, it becomes obvious how quickly the Swedish economy has regained strength. Figures 1–5 show different indicators on the remarkable post-1992 economic recovery.

FIGURE 1
SWEDISH GNP/YEAR, 1981–96
(ONE-YEAR INTERVALS, PER CENT)

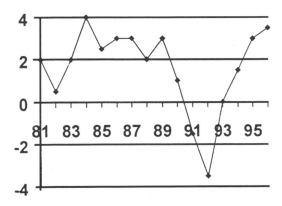

Source: Statistics Sweden.

FIGURE 2
SWEDISH ANNUAL INFLATION RATE, 1981–96
(PER CENT)

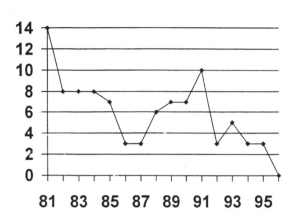

Source: Statistics Sweden.

FIGURE 3
SWEDISH ONE-YEAR GOVERNMENT SECURITIES, 1993–96
(HALF-YEAR INTERVALS, PER CENT)

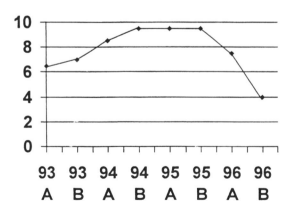

Source: Statistics Sweden.

FIGURE 4
SWEDISH FIVE-YEAR GOVERNMENT BONDS, 1993–96
(HALF-YEAR INTERVALS, PER CENT)

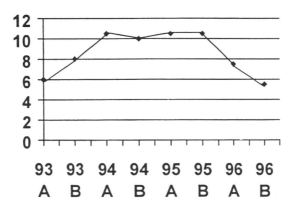

Source: Statistics Sweden.

FIGURE 5
SWEDISH FIVE-YEAR HOUSING INTEREST, 1993–96
(HALF-YEAR INTERVALS, PER CENT)

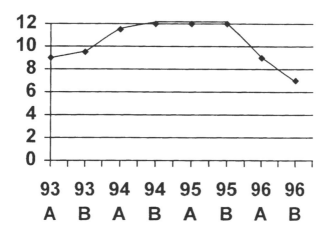

Source: Statistics Sweden.

Four years after the 1992 turmoil the Swedish GNP was growing at an annual rate of around three per cent. True, unemployment remains a major problem, with neither any immediate improvements achieved since 1992 nor any bright prospects for the future. On the other hand, inflation has been largely eliminated, interest rates have dropped substantially and the krona has regained at least half of the strength it lost in 1992. Furthermore, the 1998 national budget is largely balanced. Indeed, the Swedish economy, by early 1998, was meeting most of the convergence criteria for EMU (European Monetary Union).

Some of the economic recovery is clearly attributable to the austerity programmes outlined during the 1992 crisis. The crisis probably provided a 'policy window' for the government to implement austerity measures which would not have been politically possible under normal political and economic circumstances.[37] Since some cuts affected core sectors of the welfare state, this applies not least to the Social Democrats. For them, the crisis was a 'win–win' type of situation; by supporting the Conservative-led government in a time of crisis they showed statesmanship and responsibility, while at the same time they could not be held accountable for cuts which they at some level probably deemed necessary in the longer term.[38]

The economic recovery has contributed to a re-emerging sense of political control and latitude. These sentiments have manifested themselves not least in several (fiercely contested) issues such as the 1996 Social-Democratic government's decision to restore benefit levels in a couple of major income-related social-insurance programmes, and the 1997 commitment to target SEK 10 billion (approx. £800 million) to sustain the health-care sector. This becomes all the more noticeable as most of the 1992 cutbacks were aimed at reducing the extensive welfare state. A short time perspective would no doubt have generated the conclusion that globalisation entails overwhelmingly powerful challenges to the social-democratic welfare state. In the longer term, however, such a conclusion has to be modified, given the clear political will to defend core sectors of the welfare state.[39]

The 1992 crisis displayed, at a glance, the capacity of global markets to narrow domestic political discretion and control. Both actions and words by the political leadership substantiated that they were authoritatively bound by the market. Unique all-party agreements ensued. However, in spite of the extensive parliamentary co-operation in economic matters between the now Social Democratic government and the Centre Party for the past couple of years, the overall consensus on economic policy has clearly come to an end.[40]

Without overinterpreting the data, it appears as though the political élite interpreted the economic recovery as so stable and sustained that renewed party conflict would not jeopardise the economy. Put slightly differently, the political parties seem to be confident that there is now some latitude for the nation-state, in other words, that more than one economic policy is conceivable and that the consensus which was integral to the crisis management choked political debate. Thus the nation-state perspective holds true at least as much as the globalisation perspective does.

ANALYSIS

We now need to review the theoretical arguments from the introductory section of the article to see what new insights the case study on Swedish crisis management have yielded. First of all, what the case of Sweden brings out very clearly is that the domestic–global exchange is a highly dynamic relationship. The 1992 crisis triggered, in a fashion unique to Swedish political history, a series of extensive and profound cutback measures which effectively reduced speculation against the krona. Even so, however, there was leeway for the political élite to choose a currency-stabilising strategy rather than a path of continuous instability.

However, we argue that market influence on domestic political decision making is more contextual and contingent on a fortuitous (from the point of view of market actors) state of circumstances, some of which appear to be reasonably easily manipulated by domestic political institutions. Therefore, global market influence should not be regarded as fixed but rather as contingent on political and economic circumstances. It is the confluence of such factors which creates potential for speculation. Nation- states, to some degree, can control that confluence, for instance by exercising a strict fiscal and budgetary policy, by creating institutional preconditions for stable political leadership with sufficient parliamentary central bank discretion from elected officials (as was implemented in 1997 in Britain), and by showing unambiguous political determinism in following through economic policy.

Second, the case study shows the importance of looking at the exchange between nation-state governments and market actors *over time*. A short-term perspective would have produced a strong plea for the society-centred school of thought with international speculation against the nation's currency effectively leaving the government with very limited discretion and few options except playing the game defined by the market. In the longer term perspective, however, the government's macro-economic policies have effectively reduced the scope for speculation.

Third, the handling of the 1992 crisis highlights the importance of the political marketing of counter-measures to speculation against the currency and hence the significance of political craftsmanship and skill. Most of the measures announced by the government during the crisis were actions which would not be fully (or even partially) implemented until several years after the crisis. Moreover, by presenting the 'crisis packages' with senior representatives of all major political parties at the table, images of continuity and firmness were clearly conveyed. While the effect of such image building is impossible to assess, it would be misleading not to acknowledge the ingenuity of the strategy.

The Swedish case describing the interactive relationship between policy makers and market actors, and market changes as the key evaluation of political measures, might easily lead the observer to conclude that market actors have a distinct political agenda. However, market actors involved in currency speculation are not in the game for the sake of mustering political clout, but for the sake of making money. The awkwardness for the government of designing its policies for a group of actors which does not have any identifiable (and indeed, which can normally not even be identified in the first place) political goals is amazing.

By the same token, in so far as market actors were influential over the decisions made by the government, they can never be held accountable in any way for the consequences of the decisions over which they exerted influence. This marks yet another profound difference compared with the traditional, corporatist model of policy making. In that 'policy style', all key players are involved in policy making as well as policy implementation, and they share a fairly clear idea about what objectives are on the other actors' agenda. The corporatist model also implies some degree of shared accountability – effective if not formal/legal – of all involved actors. During the 1992 crisis, however, one of the most powerful actors did not seem to have any clear political objectives, nor was it politically accountable. Thus, both the type of challenge and the process through which it was addressed and resolved were new to the Swedish political élite.

Finally, the 1992 crisis made it clear that a national economy as dependent as Sweden's trade and creditors is extremely vulnerable to market-based evaluations of its macro-economic policies. No matter how clever or skilled the politicians happen to be, they must always consider these conditions.

CONCLUDING REMARKS

Much of the current economic literature offers little more than a very general and aggregated framework for more detailed analyses of how governments respond to challenges by international markets. A deeper understanding of the relationship between markets and political actors must be based on an analysis at several different levels. As mentioned above, this remains a salient problem in all research areas of international political economy. In the type of problem investigated here, however, the levels of analysis we have in mind range from that of how individual policy decisions are made and the broader context of such decision making to an analysis of markets and market actors. We need to look at the micro-politics as well as the macro-politics of crisis management. On a more general note, there is a need for more empirical case studies of similar processes in different types of national economies. Much of the debate so far has been conducted in a theoretical and reductionist language.

Second, neither the society-centred nor the state-centred approach tells the whole story. It is not the case – for the advanced Western democracies at least – that the globalised economy dictates domestic policy choice but, by the same token, such policy choice cannot be understood unless global economic forces are factored into the analysis. Instead, the most rewarding – but also most tedious – approach seems to be to focus on the exchange between the domestic and global over time.

Finally, it remains an historical irony that the current discussion about the linkages between domestic policy choice and the international economy ignores the political economy discourse of the late 1970s and early 1980s. As Nicos Poulantzas – one of the leading figures in that debate – pointed out – 'since Max Weber, all political theory has constituted either a dialogue with Marxism or an attack upon it'.[41] Indeed, the currency crises experienced by many Western European and Asian countries during the 1990s could be seen as incentives to revisit the debate on the economy as 'the last instance', eschewing the dead weight of functionalism,[42] but profiting on some of its conclusions concerning the capacity of the state to act within the confines of the economy. Welfare states, in that debate, were believed to be particularly dependent on a capitalist economy.[43] Then, it was the capitalist 'mode of production' which generated that dependence; today it is the footloose nature of private capital which pits countries in competition against each other, as society-centred accounts argue. Are those differences sufficiently important to maintain that the debate in the late 1970s does not have anything to inform current analyses?

NOTES

1. This article is a revised version of a paper presented at the Joint Sessions of the European Consortium for Political Research, Bern, 27 Feb.–4 March 1997.
2. J.G. Ruggie, 'International Regimes, Transactions and Change: Embedded Liberalism in the Postwar Economic Order', *International Organization* 36 (1982) pp. 37–415.
3. R. Stubbs and G. Underhill (eds.) *Political Economy and the Changing Global Order* (London: Macmillan 1994).
4. K. Ohmae, *The End of the Nation State: The Rise of Regional Economics* (London: Harper Collins 1995); W. Streeck, 'Public Power Beyond the Nation-State', in R. Boyer and D. Drache (eds.) *States Against Markets: The Limits of Globalisation* (London and NY:

Routledge 1996) pp.299–315; R.B. Reich *The Work of Nations* (NY: Vintage 1991).

5. G. Betcherman, 'Globalisation, Labour Markets and Public Policy', in Boyer and Drache (note 4) p.261.

6. S. Strange, *States and Markets* (London and NY: Pinter Publishers 1988).

7. Boyer and Drache (note 4); E. Helleiner, *States and the Reemergence of Global Finance* (Ithaca, NY and London: Cornell UP 1994); P. Hirst and G. Thompson, *Globalisation in Question* (Cambridge: Polity Press 1996); E. Kofman and G. Youngs (eds.) *Globalisation: Theory and Practice* (London: Pinter 1996).

8. P. Evans, 'The Eclipse of the State?: Reflections on Stateness in an Era of Globalisation', *World Politics* 50 (1997) pp.62–87.

9. Boyer and Drache, 'Introduction', in idem (note 4) p.15.

10. G. Esping-Andersen (ed.) *Welfare States in Transition: National Adaptations in Global Economies* (London: Sage 1996); M. Keating, 'Regional Autonomy in a Changing State Order', *Regional Politics & Policy* 2 (1992) pp.45–61.

11. M. Keating and J. Loughlin (eds.) *The Political Economy of Regionalism* (London: Frank Cass 1997).

12. E. Fry, L. H. Raudebaugh and P. Sodatos (eds.) *The New International Cities Era* (Provo: David M. Kennedy Center for Int. Studies, Brigham Young U. 1989); M. Keating, *Nations Against the State* (London: Macmillan 1996); S. Sassen *Cities in a World Economy* (Thousand Oaks, CA and London: Pine Forge Press 1994).

13. P. Evans, *Embedded Autonomy: States and Industrial Transformation* (Princeton UP 1995).

14. A. Payne, 'Globalisation and Modes of Regionalist Governance' (paper delivered to the First Sheffield/Pittsburgh Colloqoium, University of Sheffield, 16–17 May 1996) p.6; cf. Evans (note 8) pp.62–87; C. Navari, 'On the Withering Away of the State', in idem (ed.) *The Condition of States* (Milton Keynes and Philadelphia, PA: Open UP 1991) pp.143–66.

15. P. Hall, *Governing the Economy* (NY and Oxford: OUP 1986) p.232.

16. E. Helleiner, *States and the Reemergence of Global Finance* (Ithaca, NY and London: Cornell UP 1994); E.B. Kapstein, *Governing the Global Economy: International Finance and the State* (Cambridge, MA: Harvard UP 1994); P. Krugman, *Currencies and Crises* (Cambridge, MA: MIT Press 1994).

17. Esping-Andersen (note 10).

18. Boyer and Drache (note 4); Kofman and Youngs (note 7).

19. T.J. Anton, *Administered Politics: Elite Political Culture in Sweden* (Boston, MA: Martinus Nijhoff Publishing 1980); E. Damgaard, P. Gerlich and J.J. Richardson, *The Politics of Economic Crisis: Lessons from Western Europe* (Aldershot: Avebury 1989); G.P. Freeman, 'National Styles and Policy Sectors: Explaining Structured Variation', *Journal of Public Policy* 5 (1985) pp.467–96; P.J. Katzenstein, *Small States in World Markets* (Ithaca, NY and London: Cornell UP 1985).

20. C. Lindblom, *Politics and Markets. The World's Political-Economic Systems* (NY: Basic Books 1977); D. Easton, *A Framework for Political Analysis* (U. of Chicago Press 1979); Hall (note 15).

21. P.J. Katzenstein, *Corporatism and Change* (Ithaca, NY and London: Cornell UP 1984); Katzenstein (note 19).

22. Hall (note 15).

23. P.L. Knox and P.J. Taylor (eds.) *World Cities in a World System* (Cambridge and NY: CUP 1995).

24. Katzenstein (note 21).

25. P. Gourevitch, *Politics in Hard Times* (Ithaca, NY and London: Cornell UP 1986).

26. Katzenstein argues that one of the main virtues of corporatism is its ability to generate support for policies among all major constituencies by virtue of organised interest representation and participation in the making of policy. Thus, the key point here is that in the 'Katzenstein democracies', traditional corporatist arrangements are part of the problem as well as part of the solution. The combination of trade dependency and 'political style' which tends to make the currency susceptible to global speculation but which also is geared to ameliorating the problems they create for themselves is an interesting type of political economy in the context of nation-states' autonomy in globalised economy. Cf. Katzenstein (note 21).

27. G. Underhill, 'Introduction: Conceptualizing the Changing World Order', in Stubbs and Underhill (note 3).
28. G. Persson, *Den som är satt i skuld är inte fri* [He who is in debt is not free] (Stockholm: Atlas 1997); A. Wibble, *Två cigg och en kopp kaffe* [Two cigarettes and a cup of coffee] (Stockholm: Ekerlids Förlag 1994).
29. B. Sundelius and E. Stern, 'Sweden's Twin Monetary Crises of 1992: Rigidity and Learning in Crisis Decision Making' (paper presented at the Nordic Political Science Conference, Helsinki 15–17 Aug.1996).
30. The Swedish prime minister was not alone in acknowledging this type of defeat by the market. Following the 'Black Wednesday' (16 Sept. 1992) in Britain – a crisis which shares several similarities with the Swedish experience – the British government decided to take the sterling out of the ERM. John Major believed this to be such a serious political failure that he seriously considered resigning from office, *The Times*, 7 Oct. 1997.
31. Sundelius and Stern (note 29) p.16.
32. Charles Lindblom's (note 20, p.8) observation that 'much of politics is economics, and most of economics is also politics' had become the order of the day in Swedish politics. Given Easton's definition of 'politics', the market had clearly entered the sphere of politics: 'What distinguishes political interactions from all other kinds of social interactions is that they are predominantly oriented towards the authoritative allocation of values for a society ... An allocation is authoritative when the persons oriented to it consider that they are bound by it'. [Easton (note 20) p. 50].
33. H. Heclo and T. Madsen, *Policy and Politics in Sweden: Principled Pragmatism* (Philadelphia, PA: Temple UP 1987).
34. *Financial Times*, 6 Dec. 1995.
35. J. Moses, 'Abdication from National Policy Autonomy: What's Left to Leave?', *Politics and Society* 2 (1994) p.139; Streeck (note 4) p.310.
36. Krugman (note 16) Ch.4.
37. J. Kingdon, *Agendas, Alternatives, and Public Policies* (Boston: Little, Brown 1984).
38. Damgaard, Gerlich and Richardson (note 19).
39. G. Garrett, 'The Politics of Structural Change: Swedish Social Democracy and Thatcherism in Comparative Perspective', *Comparative Political Studies* 25 (1993) pp.521–47.
40. The Centre Party decided to discontinue its co-operation with the Social Democrats in late 1997 on the ground that the overarching objective of the co-operation – restoring the balance in the economy – had been attained.
41. N. Poulantzas, *State, Power, Socialism* (London: Verso 1980) p.11.
42. R. Mishra, 'The Welfare of Nations', in Boyer and Drache (note 4) p.317.
43. I. Gough, *The Political Economy of the Welfare State* (London: Macmillan 1979); C. Offe, *Contradictions of the Welfare State* (Cambridge, MA: MIT Press 1984).

Cities and States in Europe

PATRICK LE GALES and ALAN HARDING

The article assesses the rise in importance of cities in Europe, which are relying on their demographic and economic dynamism, on the one hand, and their political strategies on the other. In most European countries, urban élites are trying to implement medium-term development strategies and to fight against fragmentation. Globalisation represents both a constraint and an opportunity for cities; it does not determine their strategies or policies. Though often in the background, the state remains an important factor in the evolution of cities in Europe, but not a dominant one. This emergence of the city as a player goes hand in hand with processes of identity redefinition and collective strategies.

Claims about the ungovernable quality of societies in the West are often linked to the increasingly marked differentiation and autonomisation of sub-systems in society, to the fragmentation of the state and the proliferation of networks, each being able to resist the state's injunctions. This has led to growing interest not only in government, in its powers and instruments, but also in alternative negotiating mechanisms between various groups, networks and sub-systems that can variously facilitate or resist the actions of government. 'Territories' – cities and regions in particular – have emerged as potential levels at which the regulation of interests, groups and institutions can take place, even if these entities do not possess the characteristics of the nation-state.

Historically speaking, European cities, and in particular the most independent among them, have owed their power to the local concentration of wealth, that is, to the accumulation and mobilisation of capital. In the Middle Ages, low prosperity and financial difficulties considerably weakened cities, which gave sovereigns a chance to incorporate them in their kingdoms or principalities. In the last 30 years, wealth and population have been concentrated once more in European cities, notwithstanding a short-lived lull in the 1970s.[1] From the time when the efficacy of European nation-states was first called into question, that is roughly from the 1970s onwards, it was logical that interest in cities and, more generally, in the local, territorial, and regional levels that had somewhat disappeared from

West European Politics, Vol.21, No.3 (July 1998), pp.120–145
PUBLISHED BY FRANK CASS, LONDON

social science, should be rekindled. Indeed, as market regulation grew in importance *vis-à-vis* state regulation, thus marking a weakening of the nation-state, cities – especially the most prosperous among them – could not fail to make their political voice heard more clearly.

Raising the question of the pressure exerted by cities in the context of the partial decline of states in Europe requires the highlighting of certain ambiguities:

(1) In Europe, for the moment, cities are constitutionally and legally inferior to states, even if European norms overlap. However, the relationships between the various levels of government are everywhere marked by ever stronger horizontal and vertical interdependence; hence the studies on multi-level governance. It would therefore be wrong to refer to, or indeed wish for a return to, city-states without considering their environment. Neither should we look at the question in terms of 'cities against the state'. In most cases, cities need states in order to confront their problems and realise their ambitions. On the other hand, states need cities because it is in cities that the majority of inhabitants live and where both the production of wealth and social problems are concentrated. The numerous examples of 'urban' public policies bear witness to these interactions.

(2) The 'city' category is not simple or straightforward. It is not possible to portray European cities in general as triumphing over declining national states. Whether one is dealing with institutional or economic dynamics, it is also clear that transformations are occurring relatively slowly in the nation-states of Europe. The changes described here do not represent fundamental breaks of the kind described by those who, adopting one version of regulation theory, refer to dichotomies between a fordist and a 'post-fordist' period.

(3) The theory of the end of territories or deterritorialisation – which is enjoying a certain resurgence – also appears simplistic once it is applied to public policy and politics rather than international relations. Granted, there are norms and flows running through territories, calling into question an idealised vision of the local level. However, to accept this is not to argue against the possible social and political construction of territories, especially cities, as political and social players. Of course, if the question of 'the political' and 'territory' is defined to that of 'the instrument of domination within society'[2] – and of the legal apparatus that goes with it – territory then means idealised national territory, and any other entity at the regional, city, or local level will only be defined negatively and defensively, in relation to this absolute whose passing is

mourned. It appears to us that the primacy given to the normative system is not a must, that the state has partially lost its centrality in certain European countries and that the overlapping of various levels and logics renders this vision of politics and territory somewhat suspect. As Gianfranco Poggi points out, 'one of the distinctive features of the modern political environment – that politics is the matrix of policy – has become less and less credible in the last phase of the state's story'.[3]

Following this brief reminder of the way in which the domination of the state over cities has been analysed, this article describes the changes which give cities renewed importance and, under certain circumstances, the opportunity to assert themselves as political and social players. It suggests that broader transformations – and globalisation in particular – are important influences in this process, but by no means are they necessarily decisive. The restructuring of national states which cities are taking part in calls for a fresh look at the links between market, state and society.

STATE VERSUS CITY

In Western Europe, the modern state developed in opposition to cities; effectively, the voracious states got the better of the obstructing cities.[4] In his book *Contraintes et capital dans la formation de l'Europe 990–1990* (Constraints and capital in the formation of the State 990–1990), Charles Tilly takes a critical look at the classical theories that seek to explain the formation of the state in Europe. He argues that state formation in Europe arose out of the constraints caused by war. The success of the nation-state model can be explained by its superior ability to mobilise the human, technical and financial resources needed to wage war on other states (and not necessarily just national ones). There was not, however, a uniform process across Europe. Several types of state organisation, for example, coexisted in France before the fifteenth century. Empires, kingdoms, principalities and city-states were all in conflict with one another. According to Tilly, the existence of cities – places, first and foremost, where wealth is accumulated – represents the second type of constraint for the formation of nation-states. He thus elaborates an analytic framework that endeavours to identify several types of state-formation processes according to the weight of the constraint and of the capital.

In developing the role played by cities, Tilly and Blockman[5] took up these questions and advanced a somewhat Manichean vision of the history of the formation of the state which tends to present medieval European cities solely as conservative powers hindering the formation of 'good' nation-states. For those who defend the state, the city is always presented negatively, for example as being run by small-fry local dignitaries. Though they are seen as economically dynamic, cities are always suspected of being captive of local trading societies and, therefore, far removed from the noble ideal of a political community (which, of course, exists only nationally).

By the twelfth century in Europe, cities had become a political and economic force. Between the thirteenth and fourteenth centuries, the feudal system remained dominant wherever urbanisation was weak, for example in Spain, France, the Celtic parts of Great Britain, eastern Europe and Scandinavia. But in what was already the urban centre of Europe, in southern England, the United Provinces, western Germany and northern Italy, cities dominated or resisted the land-owning gentry either by associating themselves with the sovereign (England), by creating leagues (Germany), or becoming powerful city-states (Genoa, Venice) occasionally vaguely attached to an empire. That national governments recognised the power of cities can be seen in the way they associated themselves, in some cases, with the city's middle classes, giving them charters or exempting them from taxation in order to fund foreign and domestic wars. (The Republic of United Provinces, for example, hardly existed outside of the assembly of cities and provinces.) In Poland, the rural nobility that elected kings managed to prevent cities from playing too significant a role. States used various means to control cities: legitimacy disputes, the creation of national ideologies, force, heavy taxation, the bestowing of peerages and privileges upon urban élites, and political integration.

Tilly and Brockman demonstrate the failure of cities and their collective strategies to maintain their privileges (and their wealth). Too often guided by short term economic and political interests, they were unable, in most cases, to resist the processes of nation-state formation except when the feudal system was particularly weak (The Netherlands, Switzerland), or when it was a question of city-state or dense city networks (Italy, parts of Germany). Even in the latter case, cities proved incapable of containing the rise in military power of France, Spain and England. The rise to ascendancy of nation-states did not erase the pre-existing urban system. The urban structure that existed before nation-states continued, and still continues, to have an effect despite the strategies undertaken by the national states.

The dominance of the state over cities grew. Beyond the legal and constitutional constraints binding cities, the industrial revolution, the great wars and the development of the welfare state contributed across the board to accentuating the dominance of central government over local authorities including cities. The formation of a professionalised state civil service on the Weberian model, which was more or less widespread by the late nineteenth century, and the absorption of an increasing proportion of national GDP by the state – state spending accounted for less than 10 per cent of GDP at the start of the century but is between 40 to 45 per cent in the large European countries today – are key factors that reinforced the dependence of the city on the state. Thus, in Germany, for example, the experiments in municipal socialism of the late nineteenth and early twentieth centuries, original political experiments in urban management and relative political autonomy regarding public action were gradually abandoned or eroded. In Great Britain, where such experiments were numerous, political conflicts and legal control, as well as the national success of the Labour Party, overcame these local experiments, sometimes causing conflict as in the famous Borough of Poplar. In France, municipal socialism in the northern part of the country and in the Paris suburbs on the one hand, and a wish for social or economic interventionism on the part of other large municipalities such as Lyons on the other hand, were systematically reduced by the republican state and its armed support, the prefect and the Conseil d'Etat. The European national state became all-powerful in the twentieth century and reduced cities' margins of autonomy, even in those cases where the state is federalised or relatively weak.

Trends in social science approaches to cities reflected the declining autonomy of cities. The classical definitions of the state emphasise the autonomisation of a political sphere on the controlling of borders, the monopoly over legitimate violence and the institutionalisation of power. Political science has too often followed the letter of the law, having no interest in local autonomy under the pretext that the legal domination of the state little or no autonomy to cities (this is particularly true for the old centralised countries such as Great Britain and France). One strand of the Marxist literature in the 1960s and 1970s, which tended to produce accounts of the state as a monolithic and undifferentiated agent of capital, also paid little attention to intermediate levels of government. State-centred accounts, similarly, emphasise the national rather than the local level. In *The State and the City*,[6] Gurr and King propose a theoretical model to counter the American Marxists and pluralists who highlighted the coalitions of interest determining urban policies. Inspired by classical research into the state, this particular state-centred approach argued that: (i) the state is the main factor which determines the long-run decline or prosperity of cities; (ii) it is in the state's interest to intervene in cities to ensure the maintenance of public order, to ensure an adequate flow of state revenues, and in the interest of state civil servants to develop policies which support these aims; and (iii) civil servants have a large degree of autonomy in deciding and implementing public policies.

In other words, it is in the interests of the political and bureaucratic élites to ensure the continuity of the state and to guarantee its authority. Gurr and King's argument is state centred in the sense that the economy is seen as a constraint on state action, but not as a deciding factor.[7] Similarly cities impinge upon the actions of the state but are seen to have little in the way of an independent role. Given that European countries are overwhelmingly urbanised, nation-states cannot ignore the fates of cities; the places where wealth is produced and where the major civil services operate. Since the middle or late nineteenth century in Europe, the state (or the federal states) has taken charge of the large institutions and the production of collective goods which contribute to the well-being of city dwellers.[8]

Both historical and contemporary accounts of the role of the state, then, tend to argue that cities had lost all legal and constitutional autonomy in the process of becoming politically and financially dependent on the state. The question of urban or local autonomy, as a result, became marginalised in social science. Certain changes have arisen, however, which call this way of seeing things into question.

CITIES VERSUS THE STATE?

For 20 years now, a great many articles and books have been written which challenge the idea that the state should be the only, or even the main, level of study of social and political phenomena. In most European countries, the growing importance of cities on a political level has been highlighted. If it is not merely a coincidence this evolution deserves some clarification. The wealth but also the diversity of arguments mobilised in favour of this type of theory have often clouded the debate. Often, the question of cities and states is seen in the perspective of 'globalisation' processes[9] in economic, political, social and cultural terms. This process is invariably taken to be associated with neo-liberal ideology and opposition to state intervention. The vast majority of comparative research about the changing relationships between cities and states highlight the fact that recent change is intimately related to global economic reorganisation. The presentation of the argument is twofold: on one hand economic globalisation processes reduce the state's capacity to manage the economy as well as its legitimacy, which opens up new perspectives for cities; on the other, this evolution leads to 'entrepreneurial' forms of urban governance.

Globalisation and Mobilisation of Cities

How persuasive are the two parts of the globalisation scenario for cities? It is certainly clear that economic pressure has led to a restructuring of the relationships between states and cities as the state's role in national economic management has become progressively less effective. In the process, local efforts in the field of economic development have grown substantially, become more legitimate, and been associated with distinctive new forms of governance. Before swallowing the globalisation scenario whole, however, let us subject it to greater scrutiny.

First, it has now become axiomatic that economic globalisation has considerably reduced the national state's room for manoeuvre. Liberalisation, deregulation or privatisation are now features of national governance in most other European countries. The multiplication of economic and financial flows and the interweaving of transnational companies makes it difficult to speak any longer of 'national economies'. The national states have gradually given up their support of traditional industrial sectors in difficulty, with massive social and economic effect on some industrial cities. This dropping of support has occurred both in southern Europe, for example with a liberal government in Portugal, a socialist one in Spain, and in Italy where the Northern Leagues pushed for the ending of voluntarist policies in favour of the South. The same pattern has occurred in northern Europe. The British case is probably the best known but France, Sweden and Austria, too, have called the policy of the 'stretcher-bearing' state into question, albeit whilst accepting responsibility for transition costs.

The state has, therefore, lost much of its ability to direct the economy, to make some of the decisive choices in terms of industrial investments as well as sectoral and territorial choices. The market, Europe, and the financial institutions have largely taken its place. That does not mean it has disappeared: it has reorganised itself by promoting supply-side improvements, particularly for small and medium-sized companies, and styling itself as a 'strategist' – according to the terms of the *Commissariat au Plan* in France – which regulates in order to defend the country's interests and guarantee its competitiveness.

Second, in spite of the anti-urban ideology of the 1970s, and the prospect of the 'end of urban concentrations' which some argue is made possible by new technologies, the idea that cities are regaining an important role as an economic development factor, or accumulation centre, is being supported. At least five facets of this argument have been identified.[10]

(1) A trend in analysis describes the global cities or world cities as benefiting from the tendency for world economic-command centres to concentrate, especially the head offices of banks and transnational companies.[11] Saskia Sassen takes this argument furthest and demonstrates that the production of certain services (advertising, financial and legal services, leisure) is monopolised by these cities,[12] in Europe that is Paris, London and, to a lesser extent, Berlin and Frankfurt.)

(2) Cities, above all, offer 'flexibility guarantees'[13] as their environment and diversity allow companies to lessen their risks and to have access to vast expertise, financial, infrastructure and labour-market resources.[14] This reduces their uncertainty margins in the face of the ups and downs of world economic competition which would otherwise multiply the risks that companies face.

(3) The production of innovation and its rapid diffusion are invariably done in cities where one finds both a dense network of research centres and networks of small and medium-sized companies likely to create 'innovative environments'.

(4) If the globalisation of the economy occurs through the development of exchanges, networks and flows, then the infrastructures that link the points of the network are vital. The economic logic of networks (for transport or information) is to maximise their use between the 'key nodes' in order to minimise the risk of making very costly infrastructural investments, involving ever more technology. Cities are becoming crucial accumulation centres for the industries connected to infrastructure (in the environmental field for example). This logic, which operates beyond the national sphere, leads to more concentration around the large urban centres.

(5) Finally, as far as the job market is concerned, the double activity of couples and the hierarchy of labour markets depending on the city leads to a concentration of the middle and upper classes (especially within the private sector) in cities.

We might expect, then, that the globalisation of the economy would lead to more and more urban concentration. This trend has largely been confirmed, that is a concentration of economic activities and population in cities, especially the large European cities, and this, since the 1950s, despite a lull in the 1970s. Only a few large depressed industrial cities on the rim (such as Liverpool, Glasgow or Naples) have suffered an increased decline. The body of the arguments outlined here *a priori* concern the largest cities. Geographers have highlighted both the concentration processes identified above in the largest cities and the spatial dispersion processes around these cities, which gives rise to vast urban regions with a dense fabric of medium-sized towns around the capital, such as the south-eastern region of Great Britain, Lombardy around Milan and the Paris region. This can vary from country to country. In Italy or France, for example, urban centres with a population of 50,000 to 150,000 are considered true cities, which is not the case in Germany, Great Britain or The Netherlands. However in several countries and especially in France the same evolution has been observed at regional level, that is the growth of regional capitals in regions characterised by decline or stagnation (e.g. Toulouse, Montpellier, Nantes, Rennes).

Consequently, cities are finding a new legitimacy, a role in terms of economic development, and the globalisation of flows and exchanges means that their economies are no longer so intrinsically bound up with what happens in the 'national' economy. In other words, certain cities at least can be argued to be privileged places for the accumulation of capital and the production of wealth.

But change has not just been economic. Nor has all policy change been led from the national level. Urban local authorities have mobilised themselves in favour of economic development since the 1960s. When local development policies appeared in the mid-1970s, they were primarily responses to the consequences of the recession, a challenge to state's role, and a reflection of the aspirations of key social classes in the 'post-1968' generation. Defending jobs in the face of industrial reorganisations was the most often quoted reason for supporting local authority, city and occasionally regional intervention. In most cases states provided tools for intervention in the most serious cases, while the traditional tools of regional policy or territorial development were either abandoned or at least seriously called into question.

In this way, local officials came into contact with company directors and banks, to negotiate with the private sector players the conditions for the state's intervention. They experimented with new ways of acting; they started carrying out studies into the dynamics of local economies and formed networks with economic partners. Finally, they gradually undertook economic intervention which took the shape of indirect aid to companies and the buying back of buildings and land. This mobilisation took place particularly in German, British, French, Dutch and Belgian cities, where the trend had been adopted as early as the early 1980s and later in Italy, Ireland, Portugal or the Scandinavian countries for reasons to do with limited autonomy in terms of skills, political legitimacy or funds.

The cities' economic development policies took three main directions:[15] the defence of jobs and active training policies; participation in the development of companies (creation, modernisation, networking, financial support); improvement of the environment to attract companies; and competition to attract investments and privileged social groups (such as executives). The latter point became increasingly important. David Harvey has particularly highlighted the logic of inter-urban competition in a global economy.[16] Economic globalisation means an increase in the mobility of capital and the ability for capitalists, to a certain extent, to overcome spatial constraints. Paradoxically, this overcoming goes hand in hand with an increased sensitivity to territory, especially cities as possible sites for investment and living. This marks a new phase in the development of capitalism, in which the latter takes the advantage over national states, and allows the process of creative destruction through the de-industrialisation of cities and regions to take place. Within this framework, competition between urban regions reflects the decline in state regulation. Cities – or, more accurately, the governing coalitions which form within them and on their behalf – are attempting to position themselves: in the context of the international division of labour (especially in terms of social relations and organisation of town planning), as consumption centres (which means developing prestige, status, culture to attract visitors and tourists) and as competitors for transnational-company command centres, prestigious public bureaux or other forms of public and private investment, such as in the social field

For Harvey, cities' bids to be distinctive result, paradoxically, in the same sorts of project being seen everywhere. Harvey insists on the capitalist logic of the 'discipline' exerted by inter-urban competition, since this leads to a transfer of public money towards the support of companies and executives, to the setting up of 'a business-friendly environment' that excludes excessive taxation, too many unions, strikes and social problems. In a viewpoint closer in inspiration to Weberian and public-choice approaches, Peterson[17] heads in the same direction. For him, American urban governments depend on private companies for their resources, the value of land, jobs, and economic development in the broad sense of the term. The higher interest of cities demands that they improve their position on the prestige scale, the wealth scale and the political-weight scale in inter-urban competition. These two visions, the one Marxist, the other public choice share the argument that city politics hardly matter. For one, the transition to urban entrepreneurialism reflects the logic of the broader economic system. For the other, growth-orientated government is the result of the freedom of movement of capital and labour, on one hand, and the particular structures of American governance on the other. In both cases, cities are assumed to have little space to manoeuvre.

Are these arguments consistent with the idea that it is the national, rather than local, level of the state which is enduring the most marked crisis? Beyond economic pressures, flows of all sorts (pollution, information, immigration, culture) and the processes of globalisation contribute to limiting the state's autonomy[18] or signal the end of the state's territory.[19] All these flows, which cities are also a party to, constitute pressure on the state. The spreading of local authorities' programmes and policies (especially urban ones) to favour economic development is occasionally derided. Apart from the fact that a literary trend has highlighted, under certain circumstances, that these interventions were not necessarily completely absurd from a strictly economic point of view (in the case of development of localised industrial systems, or that of attraction of public and private investment), this is not the crux of the matter. This mobilisation reveals not only the weight of the constraints identified earlier, but also the strategies carried out and the political choices made by the urban élites in many cities. In other words, there is a role for local politics. And not all of the changes in local politics can be 'read off' from changes in the global economy or the form and functions of nation-states.

Entrepreneurial Urban Government in Europe?

The evaluations identified above would not have determined but rather allowed a transformation of the government of European cities to take place. Using regulation theory, and particularly the notion of the transition to 'post-fordism'[20] in a stimulating and interesting way, Margit Mayer has attempted to identify the features of a 'post-fordist' entrepreneurial urban government which could apply to European cities.[21] Bob Jessop has theorised this postfordist transformation of the state as being from the Keynesian welfare state to the Schumpeterian workfare state.[22] This new state form is said to concentrate upon two main functions: through supply-side policies, to promote innovation in terms of products, processes, organisation, and markets in the globalised economies in order to reinforce the countries' competitiveness, and the subordination of social policies to the flexibility requirements of the labour market. This obviously means a calling into question of welfare states as they are currently known and, for cities, a restructuring of the local forms of welfare state to reinforce economic competitiveness. Following Harvey, Jessop sees in the 'hollowing out of the state' a victory for market logic over politics. These works on post-fordism are nevertheless strongly marked by what has been observed in the United States and Great Britain. The European situation is much more diversified. According to Mayer, this post-fordist urban governance would be characterised as follows: (i) a mobilisation in favour of economic development; (ii) a restructuring of social policy, of the local welfare state, and privatisation of urban services; and (iii) the development of new forms of local politics and urban governance in terms of arrangements and exchanges between public and private players (the famous public–private partnerships in areas of growth), association members, which can make the mobilisation of new social actors and groups possible.

  This model does at least fit into the theoretical framework, and it does indicate empirically verifiable transformation;[23] we shall examine the propositions one by one.

(a) Mobilisation of Cities in Favour of Economic Development. We have partially dealt with this aspect above. It seems possible to indicate a single direction of change in this sense in most European countries, even if this requires nuancing. Mobilisation in favour of economic growth in cities varies as much *within* states as *between* them. Thus, in most European countries, capital cities have been only slightly mobilised in favour of economic development as in Paris, Rome, Madrid, Copenhagen or Dublin. In the last two examples, it is the state itself that launched the bulk of economic development policies and programmes, sometimes against the wishes of at least some of the urban political élite (as in Copenhagen). It appears that this mobilisation was more pronounced in the regional capitals, large provincial towns which grasped the opportunity to distance themselves from the central state. This mobilisation is all the more important since the city political élites have financial resources at their disposal, power, political legitimacy, influence on national policies, in other words, room to manoeuvre. Thus this mobilisation of cities in favour of economic development has been particularly significant in German, French and Dutch cities (where low financial autonomy is compensated by close co-operation between central government and cities), but also in British and Spanish ones. On the other hand, in Ireland and Portugal, two centralised peripheral countries, mobilisation has remained weak.

It was necessary to wait for the DG XVI's large European programmes to see this type of mobilisation develop, encouraged as it then was by the state which was anxious to respect the criteria laid down by Europe for obtaining funding. In Italy, this mobilisation in favour of economic development was impeded by the extreme financial dependence of cities and fragmentation. The remarkable examples of economic development in medium-sized Italian cities like Bergamo in Lombardy, the cities of Emilia-Romania or the Venice region generally owe little to city politics. In northern Europe, the weight of urban local authorities in running the welfare state, and the stability of the traditional social democrat élites has obstructed this mobilisation (as in the case of Swedish cities or in Copenhagen). On the contrary, in France, Great Britain and Germany, the different types of 'new urban left', that are younger, more educated and less working class, have heightened this evolution, for example in Manchester, Sheffield, Edinburgh, Lisbon, Hamburg, Barcelona, Montpellier, Rennes or Grenoble.

This mobilisation in favour of economic development does indeed come within the framework of competition between cities to attract companies, investment, executive populations, in short, factors of wealth, production and consumption. Even if this logic of competition has apparently become inevitable in the majority of European cities, however, it could hardly be said to be the single, overriding priority of those cities. There is a strong contrast, here, with the American situation, with the European system being characterised by a stronger role for the state and lesser reliance by city governments upon the market – through business taxes or local incomes – for their expenditures. Mobilisation takes different shapes in different cities – promotion, support for companies, strategic planning, etc. – and it does not exclude, replace, or dominate other types of policy. However, the stricter the financial constraints are, as in Great Britain or Denmark during the 1980s, the more brutal are the choices between economic development and social politics forced upon cities from the centre. On the contrary in France, which stands as an exception, the golden financial age of local authorities since 1980 has allowed cities not to have to make such difficult choices.

(b) Restructuring the Welfare State to Promote Economic Competitiveness between Cities. This tendency does not appear to us to be verified in most European countries. Of course, decentralisation reforms were carried out in several countries, particularly with a view to decentralising the regulation of social spending, very much on the increase, for example in France. British cities have also been obliged to make substantial budgetary cuts regarding education, policy relating to the elderly, youth, support for communities and areas in difficulty, social policies of all types. However, these readjustments were only made under the forceful constraint imposed by central government. This reduction in social spending has, moreover, brought about much conflict between local authorities and central government in the early 1980s, a conflict which ended with the victory of the Thatcher government, especially after its third electoral win. These adjustments also caused serious conflicts within the municipalities, especially Labour municipalities which control the majority of cities in Great Britain. In most cases – Britain included – urban governments have done all in their power to retain or increase social spending and protect themselves from budget cuts that affect the welfare state. In Amsterdam, Rotterdam, Copenhagen, Lisbon, Dublin, and French cities, the leading élites in cities sought to demand and obtain extra resources from their central governments: low-cost/council housing, schools, day-care centres, hospitals, hostels, social workers, and even certain services for people in difficulty concentrated in cities.

Contrary to the previous statement, it appears to us that the majority of European city leaders are anxious to protect their populations (and therefore their electors) from the hardships of economic reorganisations and the effects of the transformations to the labour market. It is only when forced by the central government that local authorities implement restrictive policies in the social fields. Although such adjustments are underway in Germany, that can largely be explained by the massive transfers of funds from the *Länder* of the West to those of the East. These massive transfers have often penalised the big cities, their social politics and their infrastructures.

One can understand the reticence on the part of urban élites to restructure the welfare state at local level. City-dwellers are electors and they are the first to be affected by a reduction in social services, the absence of housing and the closing down of schools or hospitals. In a good many European cities, for example the traditionally social-democratic left-wing cities in northern Europe, there are governing coalitions that rely on well structured networks of welfare-state professionals, low-income clienteles who are dependent on local services, and the unions which help provide them. Even in cities that are not governed by the Left, for example in France or in Italy, city élites are often efficient defenders of the local welfare state. Radical political changes in welfare, therefore, tend to be forced, rather than voluntarist, and to be led – if at all – from the national level.

A nuance may be necessary to complete this observation. European integration will probably contribute to a widening of the gap separating the richer and poorer regions and cities. One could therefore imagine that certain cities would try to play the social-dumping card, as some American states or cities have done, thereby contributing to maintaining low wages and above all low taxation to attract companies. The effect of such a strategy is hardly compatible with the development of social services, but this type of strategy is thinkable and may well play a part in the future in Europe's peripheral cities and regions.

(c) From Urban Government to Urban Governance. The argument put forward by Mayer here is twofold. On one hand, we can see a multiplication of the coalitions between public and private players and of non-public forms of management of public services. She takes up the arguments developed to suggest a new urban governance. On the other hand, she suggests that new forms of urban governance, in which the local authority is but one among many players, is going to make way for a renewal in local politics and the formation of coalitions with various groups, associations, social movements and a renewal of local élites. These two arguments are examined separately.

As far as urban governance is concerned, we have sought to demonstrate above that this evolution in urban government towards urban governance may have some relevance for France[24] and for Great Britain.[25] The argument seems equally valid for some large German and Dutch cities. However, the stability of the traditional forms of bureaucratic, hierarchical local authorities still seems to be dominant in Portugal, Ireland, Sweden, Norway and Belgium. If one takes the development of public-private partnerships for example,[26] their spreading assumes very different shapes and their degree of importance in particular differs considerably. Even in the case of

Great Britain, where these partnerships structure policies and often
dominate the development politics of urban areas, their importance is a
subject of debate. There was a considerable number of significant such
partnerships in the cities of the 1980s during the period of growth and real-
estate speculation.[27] On the other hand, they disappeared from a good many
cities with the recession. These partnerships are likely to become more
important as the economic environment supports and favours large-scale
prestige urban projects with a real estate thrust. Cities in decline sometimes
have great difficulty in setting up partnerships in spite of their
determination, through lack of interest from private investors. On the
contrary, Barcelona in the 1980s had ample freedom to set up such
partnerships. The local authorities in Danish and British cities committed
themselves in this direction under the influence of neo-liberal voluntarism
on the part of central government unlike the local Scandinavian authorities,
for example.

These public-private partnerships are encouraged by the ideology of the
state at least, by competition between cities, financial constraints, the
politics of the central state and technological development. As far as urban
services are concerned for example, Lorrain distinguishes those countries
where there is a strong political plan for local public management as in
Germany, Great Britain with its strong political plan for private
management and privatisation and France with no strong political plan
where the dynamics of the system and the strategies of large public-service
bodies have brought about a 'silent revolution' and the delegated private
management of a good many services. Public management is also dominant
in northern Europe and Italy, and in Spain despite strong pressure for
change.[28] In most European cities, public or quasi-public structures can be
seen to be emerging, which causes considerable confusion as to the
boundaries, objectives and ways of acting publicly and privately. The new
forms of horizontal and vertical arrangements of the various interests in
cities have been highlighted with the renewal of strategic spatial planning
and the modes of co-operation that have been adopted. In Barcelona, Lyons,
Rotterdam or Birmingham, these plans reveal the cities' strategies and
forms of governance where public and private players are closely
interlinked as regards long-term strategic decisions concerning the city.
Finally, in most large European cities a significant fragmentation can be
seen: multiplication of public and private agencies, contractual links
binding one another, opposition with various forms of political legitimacy,
rivalry at different levels, forms of co-operation and competition with the
state. This issue of urban governance is consequently valid for European
cities. It must be stressed that many of the partnerships which are
developing in countries such as France, Sweden, Denmark, Belgium or even

Germany are partnerships between various public players.

The second dimension of new urban politics, that is the appearance on the local political scene of groups that are not traditionally a party to local power, warrants more scepticism. In Germany, there is no doubt that the rise of the Greens as political players and the changes in the left-wing in cities like Hamburg have made it possible for debates and élites to exist, as well as all different sorts of groups to arrive on the urban political scene. Through a completely different route, the political earthquake in Italy has also favoured the arrival on the political scene of progressive coalitions in Rome, Turin, Venice and Palermo with new élites and new groups. In the first half of the 1980s, certain local authorities in Britain (caricatured as 'the loony left' by their political opponents) carried on similar experiences, but their strategies, if not also their membership, soon changed. Elsewhere, as in Spain, Belgium, France, Scandinavia (without exception), Portugal and Ireland the above renewal does not seem to be marked. If the transformations identified by Mayer as characteristic of post-fordist urban politics are occurring, they remain merely a possibility which has only rarely materialised. On the contrary, we can see, in some urban regions, urban technocracies forming which would tend to be moving away from any renewal of democratic life. In France for example, the arrangements between mayors and certain private enterprises, encouraged by the systematic use of consultants, for large-scale urban development operations have rather impeded any renewal of local politics. Non-democratic practices and secretive decision making by closed élites have also assumed a high profile in the UK. Considering the importance of the stakes for large-scale urban development operations, the élites in big cities often do better to play at secrecy than transparency, or to move between the two depending upon the audience.

It appears to us that these two changes are both heading in the direction of fragmentation of urban governance even if, paradoxically, this also leads to increased visibility for urban political leaders, given the considerable political work they have to achieve to try to go beyond this fragmentation, to preserve a little territorial coherence and to organise the conditions of collective action that may make effective public action possible.

The model of entrepreneurial urban governance therefore rests on propositions which are not altogether confirmed. Three other elements could nonetheless be mobilised in this direction:

(1) The development of cities' international relations, the renewal of twinning operations and economic co-operation agreements, the multiplication of city networks (such as Eurocities) and the attempted development of interests common to European cities via these networks.

Following the example of regions, but to a lesser extent, European integration has made it possible to give cities a new political legitimacy. The DG XVI has subsidised several big and medium-sized city networks or thematic networks (such as *quartiers en crise* – areas in crisis) which allowed mayors to reassert their political legitimacy in Europe and to develop forms of co-operation independently from the state. The European programme URBAN, implemented by the DG XVI is a direct result of pressure exerted by these city networks despite the reserves of management that has always privileged the regional echelon. The elected officials of big cities are seizing this opportunity to revive a prestigious past, to rewrite their history free from the state. Ancient trading routes or financial networks are being reactivated at least symbolically to assert that Europe will be a Europe of cities and exchanges. The energy devoted by the élites in Turin and Lyons to creating a TGV link is based on this European way of seeing that predates the reinforcement of national states. All the border zones are under pressure to ensure co-operation between Barcelona and Montpellier, between cities and regions which often co-operate (Saarlorlux).

(2) The growing dependence of big city finances upon international financial markets (in Great Britain and France for example), though this is far from being the case everywhere (not in Italy, the Netherlands, Ireland, Portugal). In these cases, cities are subject to 'marks' from international agencies and can end up being dependent upon financial institutions.

(3) The fact that in several countries, the mayors of big cities are tending to see their political weight increasing at national level within the political parties. This phenomenon seems more palpable in southern Europe, Spain, Italy, Portugal and France. In Germany we observe the elected officials of big cities forming coalitions with private enterprises and other interests in order to give large urban regions more political weight, as in the 'Greater Stuttgart' project which is not dissimilar to the wish to create a 'Greater Bordeaux, Lille, Lyon'.[29]

These developments, and especially the greater political weight of cities, leads to a relationship between cities and states which is more and more negotiated and moving further away from the hierarchical centre-periphery model which once dominated approaches to understanding state–city relationships. Consequently, cities in Europe are developing strategies that are increasingly independent from national states, and closely linked to companies, local institutions and associations. The question of the state remains to be examined. It seems to us that this question is too frequently tackled from an Anglo-Saxon point of view, especially American, which tends not to take sufficient account of different state traditions in other European countries.

CITIES WITH THE STATE

The Weakened but Unavoidable State in Europe

Cities can, to a certain extent, oppose the state and play out their own strategies. This is not necessarily in their best interest as they need the state. Indeed, the weight of the state in most European countries, remains higher than that which can be observed in the USA. Consequently, legitimacy problems aside, the national European states play a more significant role in public services, infrastructures and, above all, the welfare state. One must also consider the fact that the interplay between cities, the market and the state is not the same in Europe as in the United States. Even if the competition between cities and, as an oblique result of this, the entrepreneurial strategies of cities are greater than before, European cities are not American cities. Private enterprise generally plays a less important political role. At least three arguments point in this direction:

(1) The much weaker role of private companies in political life, for example in supporting or choosing key candidates for political office;

(2) The centralisation in the organisation of private interests in countries like France or Great Britain and of capital in general. Until the 1980s, there were relatively few cases of urban organisation of private interests or companies that could play a decisive role in urban politics (except in Germany and Italy);

(3) The dependence of local authorities regarding private enterprises is also weaker as a much more significant part of local authorities' income in Europe comes from state transfers.

It should be added that the autonomy of cities varies considerably from one country to another, either in terms of financial room to manoeuvre, skills or political legitimacy. Both unitary and federal states have resources which make them key players in urban politics, even if their spheres of influence have been curtailed in other fields. This process has particularly been translated into a whole range of reforms which have modified the distribution of powers and resources, invariably in favour of local authorities, not necessarily cities.[30]

The weight of the state is particularly visible when one looks at the political organisation of national capitals. In several cases, the state has intervened directly or indirectly to prevent a powerful metropolitan government from existing or developing.[31] This was the case, for example, in Sweden, the UK, France and Denmark. In other cases, the state intervenes directly in the strategic choices made by the capital city, as in for instance Madrid, or Dublin. On the contrary, the national state can intervene in a bid to reinforce the governing of big cities and encourage them to join in with European competition as in France with the objective charters, the City Pride programme in Great Britain or Law 142 in Italy. Finally, it can happen that the most unfavourable situation for a city's autonomy is the existence of a federal tier of government: German, Belgian and Spanish cities have their autonomy limited by the power of regional authorities or *Länder*, although co-operation can be seen in some circumstances, albeit conflictual (the Generality of Catalonia and Barcelona). On the other hand, in Scandinavia, Italy, France or Great Britain, the relative weakness of the regional echelon is a factor which works in the cities' favour. For that matter, one must stress that the national states have not given up the old rule 'divide to govern'. In most European countries, the national states maintain broad capacities of arbitration by playing inter-city rivalries off against one another, or by alternately seeking support from regions and cities to prevent coherent territorial political blocs from forming that may oppose them. The British government, for example, long played on the rivalry between Edinburgh and Glasgow in order to splinter and contain the demands of the Scots. The Spanish state, similarly, seeks to accentuate the division between Catalonia and Barcelona. The French state is skilled in playing off regional capitals against one another, and the conflicts that invariably oppose regional councils and cities, and the German *Länder* use medium-sized cities to counter big cities.

Although the state remains powerful, particularly in terms of the politics of welfare, this represents a major resource. Indeed, in most European countries, the majority of cities are experiencing more or less pronounced forms of urban crisis and decline of certain areas and groups within cities. This is why the big city élites often call upon the state (or the European Union) to help them cope with growing social problems and new forms of poverty which considerably increased across Europe in the 1980s and 1990s. Our argument is, therefore, that one must not merely examine urban governance from an economic point of view. Social exclusion is also a major constraint for city governments and these frequently turn to the state in an attempt to tackle the problem. Urban policies are one of the answers provided by national states.

Cities Weakened by Economic and Social Problems Need the State

The state, through its leading role in running the welfare state, holds crucial resources for cities, which they would be hard pushed to do without. The example of urban politics illustrates this interaction, which is more and more negotiated, between the state and cities in terms of public action.

Over the past 20 years, the effects of economic restructuring, of the reorganisation of the labour market, the end of the growth in the welfare state have caused old and new forms of poverty to appear. These are especially concentrated in cities, and particularly in certain city districts. Urban politics then deals with social and spatial segregation, the 'urban crisis', the fight against exclusion, poverty and the urban as a new social issue. In another sense, urban politics refers to infrastructures, policies of economic development, strategic planning and policies aimed at attracting people and businesses. Finally, in most European countries, a restructuring of the role of the state is underway, which manifests itself through a reduction in the provisions of the welfare state, or at least, through a revision of the social policies (in the name of improving management or local experimentation) and through a more or less pronounced withdrawal of public power in favour of the market or non-profit-making organisations.

Most European cities must confront exclusion processes affecting certain populations and the deterioration of certain districts. The European cities where this poverty is most widespread are the old industrial cities of the nineteenth century, which have suffered the most from the economic restructuring: cities in the North and Midlands of Great Britain, Wallonia, north-eastern France, industrial ports such as Liverpool, Marseilles, Genoa and Bilbao. But there are significant pockets of concentrated disadvantage and exclusion in even the wealthiest urban regions, for example in London, Brussels, Copenhagen, Barcelona, Paris, Frankfurt, Rotterdam, Rome, Lyons and Hamburg. Some southern-European cities experienced both traditional forms of poverty, especially linked to growth and rural exodus, and suffered the effects of economic restructuring such as Athens, Naples, Bari, Seville, Lisbon and Oporto.

Until recently, urban policies related to policies carried out by the national states in cities. Behind the imprecise term of urban politics, only Great Britain and France (and to a lesser extent the Netherlands) had urban policies that were relatively well defined. Elsewhere, the state had often played a key role in developing social housing. City politics *à la française* comes under the scope of politic that aims to mend the social fabric and prevent groups and areas from entering the spiral of decline. 'The global approach' in city politics and the mobilisation of various players may have taken the edge, at least in terms of political flag-waving, but the Ministère de l'Equipement and the Corps des Ponts et Chaussées have not disappeared, nor has their role, their weight in infrastructure, transport, housing and territorial development. For them, it is a question of large-scale urban policy (particularly for the development of amenities and town planning) of which city politics is merely a minor sub-division.

An opposite way of thinking prevails in Great Britain where the support given to big cities in terms of straight social redistribution has given way to urban regeneration in which a centrally managed system of intra-urban competition is linked to money for economic and physical initiatives through which, it is hoped, social problems will be solved. In the 1970s, a classical urban social redistribution policy had the particular effect of causing a redistribution of social services of various types in favour of the big city populations, and taking into account the effect of economic restructuring. Since 1979, the logic of urban policy has radically changed. The private sector and market mechanisms are seen as the long-term solution to urban problems and the role of the public sector has been redefined as being to provide short-term programmes to correct market failure. The creation of wealth, the development of a culture of entrepreneurs, and adaptation, however hard it may be, to the rules of the market must replace the development of the welfare state. Redistribution of wealth towards zones hit by crisis is only justified if it is short term and produces longer term 'self-sustainability'.

A brief panoramic look at Europe reveals the diversity of the urban policies carried out by national states. In the Netherlands, urban policy essentially means social housing policies as this sector is one of the broadest in Europe (40 per cent of housing). The vigorous rehabilitation campaigns carried out over the last 15 years or so go hand in hand with active policies for integrating immigrants, transport and culture. In the Nordic countries, the appearance of 'new poverty' came later given the importance of the welfare state and a relatively stable employment situation until the mid-1980s (except in Finland). Since then, specific programmes have been implemented such as the social development programme, SUM, set up in 1988 by the Danish government in co-operation with the local authorities and cities in particular. This local initiative support programme places the emphasis on support of local networks fighting poverty, group projects in some areas, social life and the maintenance of links between generations to avoid isolation and reorganisation of the social and administrative services. As in France, emphasis is placed on projects, innovative approaches, transversality. In Italy, finally, there is no urban policy (except for infrastructure) as the social policies for redistribution are hallmarked by aid given to people and not by a priority given to a city or area. In several centralised peripheral countries such as Ireland and Portugal, urban policy does not exist as a clearly defined field of public action. Invariably, the leading élites in cities request more resources, especially in terms of social policies, as regards social problems or economic restructuring. Urban policy then means redistribution of economic resources first of all in favour of big cities.

Now, local officials are directly confronted with these difficulties. Following the example of national states, they have positioned themselves within the logic of economic competition, while mobilising themselves to limit the effects of poverty and exclusion. This mobilisation is less significant in the southern European cities where traditional forms of poverty persist, where the welfare state is less developed and where traditional family networks play an important part in supporting poor populations. This mobilisation has also been rather late in coming in the most centralised countries like Ireland or France where the fight against exclusion was considered to be the responsibility of the state. On the other hand, in the northern European countries, either because the urban crisis is older and more pronounced (as in Great Britain), or because the welfare state was more important and city resources more important (Germany, the Netherlands), the organisation of the fight against exclusion through the urban policies of the cities themselves was more premature. However, the urban policies carried out by cities encounter the same problems of capacity to act, mobilisation of networks and fragmentation of the state. In the most significant cases, certain cities have established genuine anti-poverty strategies in order to mobilise their services as well as all the players, including employers or unions and state services if there are any. The northern European cities are particularly sharp on this subject. In other countries, like France, it has been considered that urban policy for fighting poverty should either be discrete or in the hands of the state.

The challenge is clear for European cities: what can be done so that in 10 or 20 years certain groups are not excluded on a quasi-permanent basis and gathered in more and more isolated and branded areas? Already in some European cities among the largest or most affected by economic restructuring, this situation is not far off being prevalent. The support of the state and its social programmes are indispensable if the worst is to be avoided. Beyond the urban policies, any restructuring of redistributing social policies risks having a major effect on cities. European cities are therefore fragile and their élites do not wish, for the most part, to obtain too great an autonomy which would expose them without support to the rigours of economic restructuring.

On the other hand, states need cities that run smoothly in terms of social integration, economic development and keeping the peace. The economic competitiveness of national states is realised largely through cities. The

state and the cities are, therefore, to a certain extent profoundly dependent
on one another, which no doubt explains the multiplication of forms of non-
hierarchical arrangements between cities and state in public policy. If the
approaches in terms of entanglement are familiar to the observers of
German or Dutch political systems, they are also becoming equally
important in the centralised states such as Great Britain and France. In both
these countries one can see a multiplication of the contracts between the
state and cities in various sectors, as well as a reinforcement of the regional
state in an attempt to maintain territorial coherence.[32]

CONCLUSION

Even if this point has not been thoroughly demonstrated, it appears to us
that we are witnessing a rise in the importance of cities in Europe, which are
relying on their demographic and economic dynamism, on the one hand,
and their political strategies on the other. In most European countries, urban
élites are trying to implement medium-term development strategies and to
fight against fragmentation. However, we do not support the views
concerning the appearance of a post-fordist entrepreneurial urban
government as outlined above. It seems to us that this model relies on a
pattern which is too deterministic and too global. Globalisation represents
both a constraint and an opportunity for cities, it does not determine their
strategies or policies. The most global theories about change in cities seem
too general to us and unsuited to European cities where it is necessary to
bear in mind local situations and the different state traditions.[33]

Though often in the background, the state remains an important factor in
the evolution of cities. However, we do not share the analysis of Gurr and
King as it appears to be a static vision which does not take the evolutions,
the changes we have identified into account. Even if urban hierarchies are
evolving slowly, even if the state plays an important role, it is not certain
that it is the major factor in the evolution of cities. The term 'glocalisation'
used by Swyngedouw[34] renders nicely both globalisation and the role of the
local level, especially in cities.

If there is no direct link between globalisation and cities, we suggest that
the withdrawal, albeit relative, of the state, opens up new opportunities for
cities, yet it does not determine a universal new localism movement which
has been rightly criticised by Lovering.[35] Nevertheless, if the networks are
causing territories to lose all significance and, for example, the scattering of
economic activities concentrated in large urban regions makes the whole
idea of the city as a political and social player null and void, in some cities
there are social and political regulations which enable them to emerge as
political players within the European Union. Whether one adopts the

language of urban political regimes, growth coalitions, institutional thickness or the more sociological language of localities, the fact remains that some cities are characterised by a stability in the arrangements between social groups and institutions, a model of development, and a capacity to integrate various local and external interests in a collective strategy, as well as a capacity to represent them externally.

This emergence of the city as a player goes hand in hand with processes of identity redefinition and collective strategies. In the analysis we have presented, we have sought to demonstrate that if the state plays a role, it is not the dominant one. In other words, the differences within a country are likely to be just as significant as between countries. Thus in the Netherlands, for example, the process of coalition-building and the arrival at élite consensus has generally been easier to achieve in Rotterdam than it has been in Amsterdam for reasons which are less to do with the priorities of national governments than with local culture and politics. One of the interesting phenomena linked to European integration is the emergence of a kind of 'European city' standard which may include a certain number of cultural, economic, demographic and social criteria, a goldmine for international consultants. The 'city as player' does not necessarily mean acting in competition with other cities. Urban élites can conceive original compromises between social cohesion, environmental protection and economic and cultural development. But, as ever, they cannot do so in situations of their own choosing.

NOTES

A first version of this article was published in French in V. Wright and S. Cassese (eds.) *La recomposition de l'Etat en Europe* (Paris: La Découverte 1996).

1. M. Parkinson *et al.*, *Urbanisation and the functions of cities in the European Community* (Brussels: European Commission (DG XVI) 1992).
2. B. Badie, *La fin des territoires* (Paris: Fayard 1995) p.12.
3. G. Poggi, 'La nature changeante de l'Etat', in Wright and Cassese (eds.) *La recomposition de l'Etat en Europe* (Paris: La Découverte 1996).
4. W. Blockman, 'Voracious states and obstructing cities: an aspect of state formation in preindustrial Europe' in W. Blockman and C. Tilly (eds.) *Cities and the Rise of States in Europe* (Boulder, CO: Westview Press 1994).
5. Ibid.
6. T. Gurr and D. King, *The State and the City* (London: Macmillan 1987).
7. Ibid. p.9.
8. H. Wolman, M. Goldsmith, *Urban Policy and Politics, a Comparative Approach* (Oxford: Blackwell 1992).
9. We have developed this point in A. Harding and P. Le Galès, 'Globalisation and Urban Politics,' in A.Scott (ed.) *The Limits to Globlization* (London: Routledge 1997).
10. Ibid.
11. P. Knox and P. Taylor (eds.) *World Cities in a World System* (Cambridge: CUP 1995).

12. For a discussion of Sassen's hypotheses, see *Le Débat* 80 (1994); S.Sassen, *The Global City* (Princeton UP 1991).
13. M. Savy and P. Veltz (eds.) *Economie Globale et Réinvention du Local* (Paris: DATAR/Editions de l'Aube 1995).
14. A.J. Scott, 'L'économie métropolitaine: organisation industrielle et croissance urbaine', in G. Benko and A. Lipietz (eds.) *Les territoires qui gagnent* (Paris: PUF 1992).
15. Fox Przeworski, J. Goodard, M. De Jong (eds.) *Urban Regeneration in a Changing Economy* (Oxford: Clarendon Press 1991); H. Heinelt and Margit Mayer (eds.) *Politik in europäischen Städten* (Berlin: Birkhäuser 1992); A. Harding, 'The Rise of Growth Coalitions, UK Style?', *Environment and Planning C Government and Policy* 9 (1991); P. Le Galès, *Politique urbaine et développement local. Une comparaison franco-britannique* (Paris: L'Harmattan 1993).
16. D. Harvey, *The Urbanisation of Capital* (Oxford: Blackwell 1985) Ch.6; idem *The Conditions of Post-Modernity* (ibid. 1989).
17. P. Peterson, *City Limits* (U. of Chicago Press 1981).
18. D. Held and A. Macgrew, 'Globalisation and the Liberal Democratic State', *Government and Opposition* 28/2 (1993).
19. Badie (note 2).
20. A. Amin (ed.) *Post-Fordism* (Oxford: Blackwell 1994).
21. M. Mayer, 'The Shifting Local Political System in European Cities', in M. Dunford and G. Kakfkalas (eds.) *Cities and Regions in the New Europe* (London: Belhaven Press 1992).
22. B. Jessop, 'Post-Fordism and the State', in Amin (note 20).
23. Our basis of comparison is the 28 case studies produced for the report 'Urbanisation and the Functions of Cities in the European Community', EEC, DG XVI, which we both took part in. Some have been published in A. Harding *et al.* (eds.) *European Cities towards 2000*, (Manchester UP 1994). We have also used our own case studies produced in Great Britain, France, Italy, Denmark, the Netherlands and Germany as a basis, as well as existing comparative studies, such as M. Harloe, C. Pickvance and J. Urry (eds.) *Do Localities Matter?* (London: Unwyn Hyman 1988); J. Logan, and T. Swanstrom, *Beyond the City Limits. Urban Policy and Urban Restructuring in Comparative Perspective* (Philadephia, PA: Temple UP 1990); E. Préteceille and Chris Pickvance (eds.) *State Restructuring and Local Power* (London: Pinter 1991); D. King and J. Pierre (eds.) *Challenges to Local Government* (London: Sage 1990); Heinelt and Mayer (note 15); M. Parkinson and D. Judd (eds.) *Leadership and Urban Regeneration* (London: Sage 1990); M. Keating, *Comparative Urban Politics. Power and the City in the United States, Canada, Britain, and France*, (Aldershot: Elgar 1991).
24. P. Le Galès, 'Du gouvernement des villes à la gouvernance urbaine', *Revue Française de Science Politique* 1 (1995).
25. A. Harding, 'Is There a New Community Power and Why Should We Need One?', *International Journal of Urban and Regional Research* 20/4 (1996); Gerry Stoker has made the argument in many publications related to the ESRC 'Local Governance programme'. See also A. Cole and P. ohn, 'Urban Regime and Local Governance in Britain and France', *Urban Affairs Review* 33/3 (Jan. 1998).
26. W. Heinz (ed.) *Partenariats public-privés dans l'aménagement urbain*, (Paris: L'Harmattan 1994).
27. Harding (note 15).
28. D. Lorrain and G. Stoker (eds.) *Urban Privatisations in Europe* (London: Pinter 1997) esp. chapter by Lorrain.
29. V. Hoffman-Martinot, 'La relance du gouvernement métropolitain en Europe, le prototype de Stuttgart', *Revue Française d'Administration Publique* (1996).
30. This aspect is not dealt with here.
31. J. Sharpe (ed.) *Metropolitan Government* (Chichester: Wiley 1994).
32. P. Le Galès and J. Mawson, 'Contracts versus competitive bidding, rationalizing urban policy programmes in Britain and France', *Journal of European Public Policy* 2/2 (1995).
33. A. Bagnasco and P. Le Galès (eds.) *Villes en Europe* (Paris: La Découverte 1997); A. Harding, 'Urban Regime in a Europe of the Cities?', *European Journal of Urban and*

Regional Studies 4/4 (1997).
34. E. Swyngedouw, 'The Mammon Quest. "Glocalisation", Interspatial Competition and the Monetary Order: The Construction of New Scales', in Dunford and Kafkalas (note 21).
35. J. Lovering, 'Creating Discourse Rather than Jobs: The Crisis in Cities and theTransition Fantasies of Intellectuals and Policy Makers,' in P. Healey *et al.* (eds.) *Managing Cities, the New Urban Context* (Chicester: Wiley 1995).

Government or Governance?
The Case of the French Local Political System

HERVE MICHEL

The structure of the local political system has completely changed since decentralisation. However, the presentation of peripheral power made by Pierre Grémion before decentralisation has not really been updated. Most academic research concentrates on either rural or urban issues. From the analysis of the current attempt of the French state to enhance co-operation between communes, it is possible to make a general presentation of the current decentralised political system. Local authorities are increasingly part of a multi-actor system combining many public and private institutions. However, they also are developing a specific political mode of organisation and relationship with one another. Local governments are the political cores of the multi-actor system, in charge of local management.

The concept of local power in France is controversial; there is no agreement over a concrete definition. To help us in our analysis, it is, however, possible to define it as the capacity for action of the legal local authorities: commune (local council), *département* (departmental council), *région* (regional council). Recent analysis of this capacity for action has focused mainly on its external determinants. Influenced by state and local social groups, local authorities must now work with the European Union (EU) and with private companies. Their power is shaped by legal unilateral norms, contractual policies, and old and modern forms of social representation.

Local authorities' capacity for action is subject to the local social background. In the rural areas, it is dependent on the activities of dynamic social networks established through historical events, such as the French Revolution, the Resistance and through political traditions. A study by Marc Abélés has shown the impact that local societies have on local management.[1] However, most studies concentrate on the effect of the modern principle of action rather than on historical and social influences.

Local authorities are increasingly inserted into a multi-actor system, combining local elected authorities (the aforementioned *régions*,

West European Politics, Vol.21, No.3 (July 1998), pp.146–169
PUBLISHED BY FRANK CASS, LONDON

départements, communes) but also, among others, the state, the EU, private enterprise and associations. Since the 1980s, the local political system has accorded growing importance to private enterprise and to market principles.[2] First, the conception, building and implementation of public services are being increasingly delegated to companies in the private sector. Second, the principles of private management increasingly influence local administration. Therefore, the local political system is being transformed by a gradual privatisation process.

At the urban[3] and regional[4] levels, the concept of governance expresses the political consequences of this process. According to Patrick Le Galès, it refers to the various capacities of local actors to co-ordinate their strategies in order to solve their conflicts and to increase their influence in their relationship with the state, the EU and the other local authorities. As a result, the power of local elected representatives seems to be diluted in the new local action framework (multi-actor system) and also in the new framework for the analysis of local power (governance). However, the capacity for action of the local authorities is not completely subject to such external forces; local authorities, and especially local leaders, still manage to retain their independence.

An analysis of the implementation of the law concerning the territorial administration of the Republic (ATR law dated 5/02/1992) reveals the existence and the development of political centres of gravity inside the multi-actor system.[5]

The division of the local system into rural and urban sub-systems, observed by P. Grémion before decentralisation,[6] still applies. The local system can now be divided into three spatial dimensions: metropolitan, medium-sized cities and rural areas. In metropolitan areas, new intercommunal organisations, which are led by the mayor of the largest city, are emerging as a real local government. In medium-sized cities and their surroundings, intercommunal government can also be created if the local leaders (the mayor of the city and the departmental councillors) agree. In rural areas, the departmental council (*conseil général*) controls the communes' management. However, its territorial leadership is increasingly being challenged by the regional council (*conseil régional*) and the major cities.

Local governments consist of hierarchical and autonomous groups of political actors who implement, in a more or less competitive and interactive way, various intercommunal policies for protecting (departmental council), enforcing (regional council) or enlarging (major cities and medium-sized cities) their institutional territory. The strategies of local governments are based less on cultural legacies, objective economic necessities and financial constraints than on political ventures generated by the local system.

The concept of local government defines local political power: it refers to the political capacity of local authorities, sheds light on the specific political mode of organisation and on the relationship between these local authorities. Finally, the concept of local government expresses the political structure and the logic existing in the multi-actor systems rooted in local societies.

A HIERARCHICAL AND CLOSED POLITICAL STRUCTURE

The architecture of local governments becomes apparent from studying the implementation of the law concerning the territorial administration of the Republic (ATR law). This law invites local councillors to renew their intercommunal structures and practices. It creates two new devices: the *communauté de communes* and the *communautés de villes*. These intercommunal organisations have two distinguishing characteristics. First, they are not dependent on the communes; they have autonomous financial power. To finance their operations, they must levy local taxes. Second, they have some compulsory political functions – that is, they are responsible for local economic development.

The plan of the state is to push local councillors into transforming their traditional intercommunal organisations. The single purpose *syndicats* (*syndicat à vocation unique,* SIVU), the multi-purpose *syndicats* (*syndicat à vocation multiple*) and the *districts*, funded by communal subsidies to provide public services (the cleaning and supply of water, refuse collection and disposal, public transport, etc.) are being encouraged to give way to integrated intercommunal structures. These are mainly the new *communautés de communes* and *communautés de villes*, or at least the previous more or less integrated formula, the *communauté urbaine* and *district,* able to levy local taxes in order to manage public services and especially to implement local development policies. To promote the creation of the new structures, the law provides some financial incentives and imposes the creation of a departmental board of intercommunal co-operation (*Commission départementale de coopération intercommunale*, CDCI).

Finally, an analysis of the conditions of the creation and management of the new intercommunal organisations reveals the changing structure of local governments. The implementation of the ATR law is being monopolised by local councillors. However, all local elected representatives do not have the same influence and role; there is a division of political tasks.

A Division of Political Tasks

The decision-making process for the creation of new intercommunal organisations is elitist. On the other hand, intercommunal management is rather pluralistic; it involves the participation of every commune and many other actors.

Elitist Decision Making. In institutional and systemic positions of decision making, the local political élite controls the renewal of the intercommunal organisations. In rural areas, the *départements* or departmental councils are accustomed to overseeing the communal management. Created in 1789, departmental councils and the communes have developed an intimate relationship by the intermediary of the départemental councillors elected (by a majority system) in the cantons. The departmental councils more or less control the management of the rural communes.

Legally established as local authorities in 1982–83 by the laws of decentralisation, and politically strengthened in 1986 by election (through proportional representation in the departmental constituency) of their representatives, the regions are trying to develop an intercommunal relationship with the rural 'communes'. They are working towards the emergence of intercommunal projects or structures on the scale of socio-economic areas, consisting of several cantons. After a period of 'breaking in', most of these new institutions wish to draw up a real territorial strategy, and these regional policies challenge the territorial departmental leadership.

However, departmental councils have, on the whole, controlled the implementation of the ATR law.[7] Helped by a few elected and administrative colleagues, the chairman of the departmental council defines the territorial orientation which enables or prevents the creation of new intercommunal organisations.

When the departmental council is in favour of the intercommunal renewal, it encourages it financially, technically and politically. To this end, it establishes various devices that offer immediate financial advantages and creates the possibility of local development. The implementation of such policies is carried out within the cantons by departmental councillors, aided by the departmental staff. They work together in order to unite local councillors (the mayors and other municipal elected representatives) and, finally, create new intercommunal organisations.

If the departmental councillors implement departmental guidelines, they act simultaneously in their own interest. Intercommunality is a crucial political resource for the departmental councillors. Based on the constituency of the canton, intercommunality transforms their constituency into an institutionalised area of management. Situated in their domain (canton), intercommunality is an opportunity for strengthening or imposing their political leadership. Therefore, by discipline and interest, departemental councillors are, with the help of departmental staff, the major actors of intercommunal renewal.

When the chairman of a departmental council is hostile to this renewal, the departmental institution can usually prevent the implementation of the ATR law. The political influence of the chairman, the non-existence of facilitating devices for political intercommunality, and the departmental subsidies of technical intercommunality are sufficient to dissuade the usually individualistic local councillors from developing their relationship with their neighbours.

Integrated into the departmental system of government, the management of the rural communes cannot change at present without the authorisation and the support of the departmental council (the agreement of the chairman and the local departmental councillors and the benefit of departmental expertise and subsidies). More precisely, the departmental council can forbid, promote or prescribe the intercommunal renewal. The level of intercommunal renewal demonstrates this. A determined departmental strategy in favour or against the implementation of the ATR law leads either to a fast and complete[8] or a slow and nearly non-existent renewal.[9] Between these extreme stances, an intermediate position, authorising the creation of the new structures but without any strong (political and material) incentives, leads to a progressive but incomplete renewal.[10]

There are two fundamental methods of governing rural territory: either through constraint (in the case of the imposition of and the banning of intercommunal development) or in a more liberal manner (such as a strategy based on incentives without coercion).

The borderline between rural and urban areas is not easy to establish. However, an analysis of intercommunality reveals the territory that is controlled by the departmental council and also the urban areas where its influence decreases. The notions of rural communes, medium-sized cities and conurbations assume some demographic differences. Nevertheless, they are useful mainly to qualify and demarcate the areas where various methods of government are exerted. If the departmental council itself oversees the development of rural intercommunality, it is forced, in those areas close to cities, to collaborate with the more or less autonomous urban political élite.

In the areas of the medium-sized cities, the departmental council is still influential through the mediation of its local representatives. Rivalries between departmental councillors from the rural canton and the mayor of the city may block the intercommunal project. On the other hand, agreement between local leaders compels the mayors to come to a compromise for the creation of a *communauté de communes* or a similar intercommunal organisation. For this purpose, they deploy a political and technical strategy of mobilisation of the local councillors. They activate their political networks and try to justify their project with expertise. Organised around a city which is already autonomous from a technical, financial and political point of view, this new organisation seems to be able to manage its territory. Stemming from the federation of local leaders, this new intercommunal structure has its own fiscal power in order to define and implement a local development policy on a rather autonomous socio-economic and political territory. Its aim is to reshape communal power on the intercommunal scale. A new system of action and power is emerging from this.

In the conurbations of a territory unified by urban growth, the departmental council is no longer influential since urban departmental councillors do not really share its rural preoccupations. The urban élite is formed by the political leaders who are generally the mayors of the largest cities. Urban communes are more autonomous than the rural, because they are usually richer and not included in the territorial priorities of the departmental council. However, they have to deal with the effect of the concentration of economic activities and the population on their territory. Urban growth creates the need for public infrastructure and services; urban communes are more or less dependent on one another to manage their responsibility towards local development. This problem has always existed. Through the strategies of the major cities, this has now become an acute issue.

Metropolitan territory forms a real system of action and power which is being reorganised by intercommunal renewal, triggered by the creation of the syndicats (SIVOM) or districts. This intercommunal process is dependent upon the strategies of the major cities. Indeed, the largest cities use intercommunal integration to extend their territorial perspective of development and share with the peripheral communes the financial cost of their project.[11] Intercommunal integration is also used to develop financial solidarity between the communes. However, this objective is secondary compared with the project of territorial and financial extension aimed at by the major cities. Intercommunal solidarity is designed to lessen the territorial conflicts between the centre and the periphery, the rich and poor communes in order to facilitate the implementation of the project of the largest cities. Mayors of the major cities are leading the intercommunal process. The success of their strategy depends on their ability to rally the peripheral communes. Without unveiling their real motivations, the metropolitan élite is trying to demonstrate the convergence of communal and intercommunal interests, and is drawing up political and technical strategies with a view to uniting the local representatives.

In the conurbations, political opposition and discipline are strong. Mayors of the largest cities, as chairmen of intercommunal organisations, use their political influence and networks to diffuse their guidelines. They use also the technical expertise of the intercommunal services, especially of the *agences d'urbanisme*. Intercommunal expertise establishes and legitimises metropolitan projects for intercommunal renewal. First, experts insist on the socio-economic interdependence of the communes. Second, they try to demonstrate the financial, economic and even political compatibility of communal and intercommunal interests. Third, they assert the possibilities of intercommunal development. Finally, focusing the debate on the immediate material benefit for the communes and the intercommunal perspectives of development, intercommunal experts rationalise a political question: is it necessary to concentrate communal power at a collective level?

Through this, the mayors of the major cities are succeeding, little by little, in creating intercommunal government. Of course, intercommunal renewal differs according to the conurbations and the political configurations. Nevertheless, the tendency is towards the emergence of metropolitan governments, based on hierarchical and autonomous groups of political actors, entitled to levy local taxes in order to define and implement intercommunal development policies. Mayors of the largest cities are the leaders of the progressive reorganisation of communal power at intercommunal level.

An analysis of the processes of intercommunal renewal reveals the existence and the strategies of local political élites. It highlights three areas of government: within conurbations under the direction of the mayors of the main cities; in the areas of medium-sized cities according to the agreement of the local leaders (the mayor of the city and the departmental councillors); in the rest of the territory under the direction of the departmental councils (which control the management of the rural communes) through the intermediary of their local representatives and field staff.

Pluralistic Management. A hierarchy exists within the structure of local political power. It is necessary to distinguish between actors who have positive power and those who possess negative power. The local political élites (mayors of the main cities or medium-sized cities, chairmen of departmental and regional councils) have the power to orientate local management. They use intercommunality to consolidate or establish their fiefdoms, their local governments. Within local governments, the rank and file of elected representatives are not only in charge of implementation, but also have a specific power: they have less of a capacity for action than a capacity of reaction, of resistance to the changes required by the local élite. Mayors and departmental councillors can behave like counter-powers.

Mayors are being subtly led to renew their intercommunal structures. However, after the creation of the new organisations, at the stage of management, these mayors usually defend their territorial interests. Thus, intercommunal policies are deformed by communal strategies: first, mayors more or less protect their own communes from communitarian devices, by using them in a communal perspective or by slowing down their implementation. Second, they often use intercommunal policies to promote their own territory. They agree to co-operate when the collective game is not a constraint or when it becomes a source of communal advantage (financial support for the construction of welfare buildings, the creation or transfer of trading estates, and, more generally, technical co-operation). Third, they negotiate overall for their participation in the implementation of intercommunal policies by asking for support in return.

Mayors are torn by communal (electoral and territorial) reflexes and communitarian (political and rational) impulses. In spite of this communal schizophrenia, the tendency is towards the rationalisation of local management, especially in the urban areas; it is towards the improvement of intercommunal integration – that is, towards the effective transfer of power from the communal to the intercommunal level. Therefore, an integrated, intercommunal form of management, based on the definition of norms and plans of development, is in the process of replacing the traditional, communal form which is more informal and more in touch with the population. Mayors are following the guidelines of the élite by creating *communautés de communes*, or renewing *districts*. However, at the stage of intercommunal management, they more or less avoid constraining intercommunal policies and exploit those which offer advantages. Within their local governments, rural and peripheral mayors intervene less to define projects than to protect their territory. They act as counter-powers, but, at the same time, are able to implement the projects of the élites. Rank-and-file mayors are less the decision makers of intercommunal changes and policies than the adjustors of intercommunal integration on their territory.

In rural areas, departmental councillors implement departmental guidelines. At the same time, they exploit them to protect, create or strengthen their electoral fiefdoms. That is why most new intercommunal organisations are based on the cantons. However, on the whole, it is not possible to state whether departmental councillors possess the power of initiation within departmental government. When departmental policies endanger their territorial domain, they can collectively censor them, by creating obstructions to departmental policies which destabilise their position in their constituency.[12] Departmental councillors are against all attempts to include their constituency in a wide area. They do not usually co-operate with one another, unless a local leader is able to unite them, and they normally manage to preserve their domain from departmental interference.[13]

Led by some of the élites which define general guidelines, local governments also comprise rank-and-file elected representatives, who usually implement elitist policies, but who may also sometimes neutralise them. Normally managers, departmental councillors and mayors sometimes behave as counter-powers when their territorial and electoral interest are endangered. 'Shared' in a hierarchical manner, local political power is also monopolised by local elected representatives.

Political Hegemony

Other public and private actors are not really associated with the implementation of the ATR law. The state is adapting itself to the political decision of either intercommunal renewal or stagnation, while private actors are usually only spectators.

The Adaptation of the State. Within the state apparatus, the prefects (representatives of the state at regional and departmental level) are the only actors really involved in the implementation of the ATR law. In principle, they have to promote the creation of new intercommunal structures. In reality, even when they are paying more attention to metropolitan and urban issues, they are compelled to monitor and adjust themselves to the territorial strategies of local governments. Like chameleons, they are adapting themselves to their environment.

The strategies of local leaders structure their intervention. Decentralisation has 'dethroned' them, and has now forced them to follow the orientations of the local governments. When departmental councils resist intercommunal renewal, they can merely register and observe intercommunal stagnation. Departmental inertia prevents the attempt of the prefects to activate the departmental commission of intercommunal co-operation (CDCI). On the other hand, when a departmental council agrees with the ATR law, they can more easily enhance the creation of new intercommunal organisations; they can amplify the strategies of the local governments.

In the conurbations, the prefects intervene personally to facilitate intercommunal renewal. They authorise some legal adaptations, for the creation or transformation of the intercommunal organisations and they invite local leaders to sign intercommunal contracts with the state (*convention ville-habitat, contrat de ville, charte d'objectifs*).

Through the intermediation of the prefects, the state accompanies the intercommunal process controlled by local governments. The power of the prefects is dependent on the capacity for action that local political élites allow them: they can be completely neutralised or more or less explicitly authorised to enforce departmental and urban strategies.

However, the state does not suffer any loss of sovereignty. Indeed, its strategy of modernisation of territorial administration is increasingly efficient. The laws of decentralisation are based on a conception of change which is premised on the participation of local élites. These laws tend to be very efficient: the territorial strategies of local governments are increasingly leading to the transformation of the intercommunal structures. As a result, the state no longer has to prescribe and impose, but it has rather to invite and underpin an inescapable development generated by the logic of the decentralised political system.

During the short period of the emergence and implementation of the ATR law (1989–97), the power of the local governments has proved to be real. Their various intercommunal strategies are at the root of the extreme geographical differences of intercommunal renewal. Under these conditions, the prefects themselves are forced to adapt; they must follow local political orientations. However, in the long run, a process of intercommunal integration, organised by the state since the 1950s, is likely to remain in force.[14] Technical local functions are already collectively managed; the intercommunal management of political affairs (mainly planning and economic development) is improving. If this intercommunal process continues, it will achieve the strategy of the state. Under these conditions, it would be better to talk about a functional local autonomy rather than actual local governments and territorial administration of the state rather than prefectoral subordination to local leaders.

Seen in the short term, local power exists: it neutralises or underpins, more or less actively, the project of the state. From this perspective, one can say that 'except when acting as a referee and a producer of legal frameworks, the state cannot do anything other than allow local actors to develop their strategies in order to come to local arrangements'.[15]

Seen in the long run, local power appears to be diluted in the process of intercommunal integration organised by the state. Local governments are more or less the disciplined executants of the state guidelines. From this perspective, one can argue that:

> The laws of decentralisation of 1982 have not been such a revolutionary reform. They comply with the conception of delegation on which the operation of the French state is based ... power has not been decentralised in France, responsibilities of management have only been transferred ... In France, we are still thinking through a unitary framework. As a result, decentralisation is thought of only as a delegation of management. We are still in a system based on a centre and a periphery.[16]

The Absence of Private Actors. Private actors are not involved with the intercommunal decision-making process. The population is rather indifferent to this problem. Local business people are more or less worried by the fiscal consequences of this process. However, private sector companies working for the urban local authorities seem to be more aware, and are concerned by the effect of intercommunal strategies. On the whole, they are only spectators to this process. Local elected representatives are not particularly prone to associate themselves with private actors. Of course, there are occasionally attempts to inform the population through the medium of local newspapers and meetings. However, these are the exceptions to the rule. The French local political system is characterised by a weak version and conception of participatory democracy.[17] If some local representatives regret the passivity of the population, they are generally far from involving it in the intercommunal decisions which they monopolise. Their proclaimed aspirations for the development of a local direct or participatory democracy, contrast with their attachment to a representative political system.

This political monopolisation does not facilitate the involvement of the private actors. Local residents and business people are nevertheless interested by an intercommunal renewal which usually entails a fiscal increase, but the intercommunal issue is treated in such a way that most private actors cannot put forward their own point of view – is it necessary to manage a wide range of technical and political functions in an intercommunal organisation endorsed with an autonomous financial power? Which fiscal formula has to be selected? Are the creation of the *communautés de communes* and the renewal of the *districts* necessary for local development? In reality, most private actors are unable to understand these technical issues.

The situation of private companies working for the urban local authorities is different. Their influence on the intercommunal process is indirect, and difficult to establish. First, the question is whether they have financial interests in the concentration of local power. The answer depends on the level of participation of the companies with local management. The next question is whether they can concretely influence the decision-making process of the creation of the new intercommunal organisations. In reality, they may propose projects to local elected representatives, which require a financial power that intercommunal integration can attain. Through this, they may nurture and amplify the entrepreneurial strategies of metropolitan leaders. However, their capacity to make proposals about the renewal of intercommunal organisations is difficult to establish. Local actors do not admit to this.

On the other hand, by promoting the normalisation of public management, they foster the depolitisation, of the relationship between the communes.[18] Therefore, they contribute to the creation of a state of mind which fosters intercommunal integration. However, their power is only one of suggestion – one cannot say that it influences directly decisions about intercommunal renewal. Within their technical field, the power of these companies is definitely increasing. Nevertheless, it does not seem determinant in the implementation of the ATR law. It has only a subterranean and indirect effect on the political decision process of intercommunal restructuring. Whatever the reasons for their absence, private actors are not really involved with the decisions relating to the creation of *communautés de communes* or *districts*.

This analysis of the implementation of the ATR law enables us to assess the concept of governance. This concept has been introduced in France by Patrick Le Galès.[19] According to Le Galès, urban governance has two dimensions: internal and external.

> The internal dimension refers in the city to the capacity of integration of the organisations, the actors, the social groups, the different interests. In certain cities, there is a capacity to integrate most of the public and private actors in order, for example, to launch a collective strategy or to elaborate a number of policies. Certain social groups can either be included or left out from governance. There is no necessity for integration ... This only reveals the existence of local rules that help the actors to solve their conflicts. The external dimension of governance deals with the capacity of local actors to define a collective and unified strategy in their relationship with the state, the European Community and the other local authorities. For example, it can implicate strategic planning and a collective perception of the city. The governance refers to the capacity of the local actors to form a collective, political and social actor.[20]

Under these conditions, the concept of governance is not relevant to explain the various processes of implementation of the ATR law. Intercommunal integration reveals the field of 'communal foreign affairs'. If mayors share their responsibilities more and more with their deputies, they still monopolise issues concerning relationships with other communes.[21] In contrast with governance, the analysis of the implementation of the ATR law demonstrates the specific political strategies within the local management. It reveals the core of local political power. A political centre of gravity exists inside the 'multi-actor system where, amongst others, the local authorities, the state and certain associations try to co-operate in order to develop overall action in their territory'.[22] The renewal of intercommunal organisations does not depend on a process of governance – neither in metropolitan and urban areas, nor in rural areas;[23] it depends on the territorial strategies of local governments, which devise communal decisions.

A POLITICAL LOGIC

The first part of this article has tried to show the structure of local governments. This second part will attempt to determine the logic of their strategies. In reality, the logic of the operation of the decentralised political system constitutes the basis of the strategies of the local governments. It especially structures the behaviour of the political élite.

Local authorities have a functional vocation: they have to provide public services and infrastructures in order to facilitate economic and social activities.[24] However, the local political system has its own rules of operation. Its purpose is to create the political and administrative conditions for local development. Nevertheless, political actors do not fundamentally act under economic pressure or cultural influences. In fact, local governments produce some useful policies, but their strategies are based more on political motivations than according to economic, financial and cultural factors.

The local political system (such as is revealed by the analysis of the implementation of the ATR law) is not structured by market principles or by local historical influences. The decisions that create intercommunal organisations which are able to levy local taxes for local development are not based on objective, economic, financial and technical necessities. The autonomous financial power of these new organisations (*communauté de communes* or new *districts*) facilitate only local management. Technical public services (water supply and sewage, refuse collection and disposal, public transport, etc.) were already supplied by some multi-purpose syndicates or districts, funded by communal subsidies. With respect to political functions (planning and economic development), intercommunal integration creates only some uncertain possibilities for local development and for the rationalisation of communal strategies.

From a cultural point of view, the case of the western areas of France suggests the absence of significant influence of professional agricultural traditions and political legacies on the strategies of local governments. These cultural variables represent contextual elements rather than explanatory factors of political behaviour.

Finally, the decisions of intercommunal restructuring are less the result of economic necessities and cultural pressures than political ventures. Local governments are more guided by utilitarian objectives imposed by the decentralised political system than by economic constraints and cultural specificities. The local political system has always enjoyed autonomy over its own operations. Decentralisation and the myth – or the reality – of European urban competition have generalised and exacerbated an entrepreneurial and territorial dynamic, forcing local elected representatives to tackle socio-economic problems.

An Entrepreneurial Dynamic

As long as the territorial strategies of the state and those of local leaders differed, all attempt to modernise territorial organisation failed.[25] Indeed, the projects for regionalisation (1964, 1969, 1972), the law concerning the merger of the communes (1971) and all attempts at intercommunal integration (1959, 1966, 1976), were neutralised before decentralisation by local leaders.[26] The departmental and communal structures of the local system blocked the territorial strategy of the state, paralysing in particular its plan for intercommunal integration. Already bypassed by certain urban practices before decentralisation, this local system is being completely transformed by decentralisation and by European integration.

Urban demographic and economic growth has changed the strategies and the condition of the management of cities.[27] This growth has legitimised the mayors of the major cities in their relationship with the state. It has allowed them to request new financial support, and it also allowed them to negotiate directly with ministries wishing to experiment with new procedures and policies. Before decentralisation, a silent change was already happening. According to Dominique Lorrain, it arose from the renewal of local councillors and from the incentives produced by the state in favour of the development of new strategies.[28] Before decentralisation, the urban strategies bypassed, and therefore broke down the departmental and communal organisation of the local political system.

In 1982–83, the laws of decentralisation completely undermined the traditional local system. They invested local elected representatives with the responsibility for local development, which they still hold. At the same time, they lessened the control of the prefects on local authorities. By modifying the structure of the local system, decentralisation made obsolete the previous overlapping mode of relationship between the elected and administrative fields.[29] It invited local elected representatives to give up their habits of being secret mediators and to act as dynamic entrepreneurs, as most of them now tend to be. Decentralisation promotes a certain logic of adaptation to socio-economic changes.

The changes to the structure of the local political system involve various new political behaviours. The function of the elected representative is now less to negotiate secretly with the state for the adaptation of the rules and policies defined by the state; rather, it is to manage local development with other local authorities and actors. The discreet but influential mediators between the local and national levels are being replaced by dynamic managers of their own territorial interests. The legitimacy of the local elected representatives is based increasingly on action. Established through election, a certain form of sociability and close relationship with the population, the republican legitimacy has not disappeared.[30] However, it has been weakened and challenged by a rhetoric of local economic development. Most local speeches and policies (culture, environment, communication, etc.) now refer to this norm of development.[31]

Legally responsible for local development, elected representatives can no longer shift the blame for local problems on to the state. The logic of the decentralised political system is forcing them to transform their strategies. They must now actively tackle local development. If they do not behave or present themselves as good managers of their territory, they offer an opportunity to their political opponents to criticise them, and also lessen their chance of electoral success. Based on secret and defensive strategies of the local notables (elected leaders and prefects) against the central state, the peripheral power[32] has been transformed in local governments, which deploy public and offensive strategies in order to preserve and consolidate their own territorial interests.

The logic of the decentralised political system has highlighted the behaviour and strategies of local elected representatives. Of course, one should not overestimate the impact of decentralisation and underrate the effect of social changes. However, the entrepreneurial dynamic of the decentralised political system needs to be emphasised.

Before decentralisation, the local political system generated a behaviour of mediation. It favoured also the individualistic strategies of the communes. According to Pierre Grémion, in order to solve their problems, local elected representatives developed personal relationships with the field services of the state. As they were not always successful, the departmental council intervened to compensate the inequalities of subsidies between the communes.[33] Therefore, the logic of this political system favoured the individualistic strategies of the communes.

The new local system does not directly promote intercommunality. However, by breaking completely the previous organisation, decentralisation has overcome the structural obstacle preventing intercommunal renewal. It has placed local elected representatives at the centre of the local system by investing them with responsibility for local development and by reducing the power of the prefects. It has generated new forms of political behaviour and strategies.

> If we had to summarise the decentralisation of the 1980s, we could qualify it as an example of an incremental radical process of reform in opposition to a synoptic or overall process which would have completely elaborated an overall solution. Concerning decentralisation, a number of local changes have preceded the intervention of the central decision maker. The central decision maker elaborated a law

which has changed one aspect of local organisation, only one, but a significant one. The implementation of this reform is quick. However, local actors are free; they can push the reform further, and experiment with various strategies. The central decision maker is still observing the local situation and assessing the changes in order to encourage those it was looking for.[34]

The incremental process of reform has continued with the ATR law which offers new resources to local elected representatives in order to help them in their strategies.

Finally, the differences of socialisation of local élites may contribute to an explanation of the different territorial strategies of local governments. Rather influential in rural areas, the heirs of the republican model of administration (the local system before decentralisation) tend to behave as protectors of the status quo: helped by their syndicates, the communes can perfectly manage local (technical) affairs. On the other hand, the advocates of decentralisation are modernisers: communes must create integrated intercommunal organisations to manage local development. The renewal of local elected representatives contributes to the diffusion of the entrepreneurial logic of the decentralised political system. Dependent on the mode of socialisation of the local élite, intercommunal strategies of the local governments are, however, mainly shaped by territorial configurations.

A Territorial Dynamic

Urban Competition. After a period of communal individualism, the mayors of the major cities 'understood' at the end of the 1980s that the development of their cities had to be organised at the intercommunal level. Almost completely occupied by residential areas and trading estates, their territory could no longer be further developed. The mayors of the major cities lack available space to fulfil their development strategies. Restricted in their territory, they have use of intercommunal integration to enlarge their territorial perspective of development.

At the same time, in a climate of European urban competition, the cities are increasing the numbers of infrastructures of international dimension. The projects of business areas, 'technopolitan' sites, TGV railway stations, modern urban public transport, big cultural and sporting facilities are realised in most of the larger French cities[35] and, on a proportional scale, in the medium-sized cities. Aiming at economic development, these urban policies are, however, *not* regulated by market principles. They arise less from an economic necessity than from political objectives that obviously have to be funded. To finance these expensive, offensive and competitive strategies, intercommunal renewal is the only realistic solution.

Metropolitan élites are also using intercommunal integration to share their investments with other communes.

Caught in an entrepreneurial and territorial dynamic, the major cities are exploiting intercommunal integration to extend their financial power in order to fund and continue their uncertain development strategies.

The Rivalry between the Departmental Councils and the Major Cities. The territorial interests of the departmental council and the major cities tend to be different. Departmental councils try to organise and develop rural areas while the big cities attempt to give a European dimension to their territory. In fact, departmental councils and the cities compete more or less explicitly to control local territory. These territorial competitions have some effect on intercomunal renewal. Of course, the city is in a dominant position. Although its legal area of intervention is bound by communal and intercommunal borders, its socio-economic influence forces and legitimises it progressively to plan and manage its own development on a wider scale. Challenged in its territorial leadership, the departmental council can develop a strategy of resistance to metropolitan growth. Before decentralisation, Pierre Grémion had already noted the departmental distrust of urban expansion. He observed that this situation might lead to the alliance of rural elected representatives and local civil servants against the major cities.[36]

Today, intercommunal renewal may be analysed as a response to the intensity of the territorial tension between the departmental council and the major city. An open conflict generates intercommunal development. A latent opposition produces intercommunal stagnation.

Destabilised by socio-economic and institutional expansion, certain departmental councils are deploying a territorial strategy designed to contain urban growth. They use intercommunality as a fence to control sprawling metropolitan development. Intercommunality is simultaneously supposed to stimulate rural development and to create institutional ramparts around the growing cities. These departmental councils exploit it to govern their territory: they are tending to reactivate and reinforce their relationship with rural communes. There usually results from this type of departmental strategy, a rapid and complete intercommunal renewal.[37] On the other hand, when departmental councils are not disrupted by metropolitan growth, they do not develop any territorial strategy of resistance. In this situation, intercommunality does not represent an important political resource for the departmental élite, and departmental councils do not deploy any offensive intercommunal strategy; they provide support for the local projects without any strong incentives. In the absence of open territorial competition between the departmental council and the major city, there arises a slow and incomplete rural intercommunal renewal.[38]

There is potential territorial competition between major cities and departmental councils. On one hand, socio-economic urban development legitimises the metropolitan strategy of governing a wide territory and also poses the question of intercommunal co-operation. On the other hand, urban growth calls into question the vocation of the departmental councils to manage their territory. Some departmental councils exploit inter-communality to maintain their territorial influence.

The Opposition between Departmental Councils and Regional Councils (State and EU). Through the conservative or modernist guidelines of its chairman and the territorial anchor of its departmental councillors, the departmental council still controls the management of rural communes.

In spite of its institutional handicaps, the regional council has an increasing influence in the rural areas, but it suffers from a deficit of political legitimacy. The regional problem is territorial and electoral; regional councillors are elected through proportional representation in the departmental constituency. The regions are also organised as a conglomeration of *départements*. The regional voting system prevents at the top and the bottom the development of a real regional institution. The combination of the departmental constituency and the system of proportional representation deprive regional councillors of the territorial anchor and proximity which benefits departmental councillors elected in the cantons on a majority system. Thus, the regional voting system weakens the democratic and territorial legitimacy of the regional councillors. It disconnects them from their electoral and territorial base. Too large to anchor the regional councillors in the local societies, the departmental constituency is also too small and dependent on the departmental structure to promote the regional dimension and interests. Therefore, the regional council is blocked at the top by its departmental constituency.

To exist, the regional council has to construct and conquer its own independence. For this purpose, regional institutions can use intercommunality. On the whole, they have no influence over the implementation of the ATR law. However, certain regional élites have, from the beginning (1986), attempted to differ their strategies from the departmental framework, by developing a number of specific intercommunal policies. In these regions, intercommunal renewal has occurred as a consequence of the competitive territorial strategies of regional and departmental councils. The struggle between these institutions for control of territory can also structure intercommunal renewal.[39]

Regional councils now increasingly reshape their territorial policies on the basis of a wide socio-economic intercommunal area. They try to overcome communal, cantonal and sectorial approaches to local management. They provide support, under condition of the definition of intercommunal projects or structures, at the level of several cantons. For this purpose, they can lean on the support of the state and EU. The 'leader-programmes' (EU) and the policy of the state promoting the *pays* (law dated 5 February 1995) have encouraged the creation of wide socio-economic intercommunal territories compatible with regional interests. Under these conditions, the territorial strategies of regional councils, the state and the EU are often opposed to the departmental mode of local management. On the one hand, the departmental council is still controlling the management of rural comunes. It organises it on a cantonal intercommunal basis through the intermediary of the departmental councillors. On the other hand, the EU, the state and regional councils are in favour of the extension of the territory of rural management to socio-economic areas. However, these institutions, and especially regional councils, do not have the territorial anchor and legitimacy of the departmental councils to implement their strategies.

In fact, the definition of the relevant territory for rural management calls into question the role of departmental councils, and its prevailing partnership with the rural communes. Apparently neutral, because of its economic implications, the issue is deeply political; it poses a question regarding rural territorial leadership: which institution (*département* or region) is going to be the main partner of rural communes? How is the local political system going to evolve? Will the departmental councils keep their position as local governments, or are they going to be dethroned by regional councils which may take advantage of the convergence of their territorial strategy with those of the state and the EU? Is the tendency towards the emergence of a sort of rural 'condominium system' of government, associating departmental and regional councils over wide intercommunal areas, protecting the traditional departmental borders? It is too soon to answer these questions, but it is possible to underline the increasing influence of regional councils on the local political system. Supported by the EU and the state, regional councils deploy various intercommunal strategies which challenge the management habits of most of the departmental councils. Justified by local development objectives, their strategies force rural communes to extend their departmental and cantonal framework of co-operation into a wider socio-economic area.

Potential territorial conflicts exist between the local authorities (regional council, departmental council and the major city) whose territories overlap. Departmental councils are obviously the most unstable institutions; they can be endangered by regional ambitions and also suffer from the sprawling socio-economic and institutional development of the conurbations. Encouraged by the policies of the state (*pays*) and the EU (leader), regional councils are trying to emancipate themselves from departmental and cantonal structures in order to reinforce their territory and functions. Under the influence of the myth or the reality of the European urban competition, major cities are undertaking many attempts to extend their financial and territorial dimensions in order to achieve their developmental objectives. To preserve or defend (departmental council), extend (cities) or appropriate (regional council) their institutional territory, local authorities may use intercommunality. Combining material incentives with political authority, their strategies encourage communes to co-operate according to their institutional interests. They also try to consolidate (departmental councils and cities) or to develop (regional councils) their relationship with communes within their area of influence. They try respectively to maintain or to insert the rural communes into departmental or regional government, and to integrate peripheral communes into metropolitan and urban governments. Intercommunality is a political resource used by this existing, or emerging, local government in order to control, enlarge, or reinforce their territory.

The political system is definitely subjected to institutional struggles. One may also suggest, using the words of Gaxie, that:

> Local authorities constitute an 'Hobbesian' universe, where everyone tries to extend their own function and field of intervention, at least in fields considered relevant, to control and maximise their share of local taxes and subsidies ... This institutional universe can be qualified as 'Hobbesian' because it is characterised firstly by a general struggle, and secondly by the existence of a superior instance of arbitration and regulation that is, in fact, rejected.[40]

This analysis of the implementation of the ATR law enables us to present Gaxie's view with more precision. On the one hand, the 'Hobbesian world' deals less with a struggle between all local authorities than with a competition between local governments. On the other hand, this struggle is only potential; more precisely, it has different levels of intensity ranging from open warfare to vigilant collaboration. It depends on the territorial configuration – namely, the rapport between the departmental council and the city, and between the departmental and regional councils – as well as the mode of socialisation of local élites – heirs of the previous local system or advocates of decentralisation. Territorial competition is not general and systematic, but is shaped by the logic of the decentralised political system.

CONCLUSION

Overall, the intercommunal integration process is improving. As a result, the communal and rather informal mode of local management is being progressively replaced by an intercommunal one, one which is more integrated, technical and planned.

This development stems from the territorial offensive strategies of local governments, replacing the secret and defensive strategies of negotiation deployed by the local 'notables', in order to adapt the rules and policies defined by the central state.

The regulation of the local political system is now less overlapping than decentralised and territorial. Local authorities collaborate within their own local government, and local governments have a more or less competitive relationship. Negotiations occur now less with the state than between local authorities that form local governments. Potential rivalries are now rather between local governments than between individual local governments and the state.

This study of intercommunality sheds light on the changing structure of local political power: peripheral power has been transformed into local governments. Local governments refer to the hierarchical and autonomous groups of interdependent political actors, who define and implement offensive intercommunal policies of local development, in order to strengthen (departmental councils), extend (cities), or appropriate (regional council) their institutional territory.

The local political system is formed by local governments potentially competing for the control of local territory. Under these conditions, intercommunality is a major political resource. It allows departmental councils, regional councils, the large and the medium-sized cities to develop some relationship, either with the rural or peripheral communes, in order to anchor themselves within the territory, to constitute a local government.

Local governments form the political centre of gravity of the local system. This concept does not explain all the dimensions of local power, but it expresses the political core of the multi-actor system, bringing together the other local authorities, the state, the European Union, private enterprise and associations.

Finally, this study calls into question the concept of governance. The development of the relationship of collaboration between the public and the private actors is improving.[41] However, the power of local political élites is not dissolved by governance. Local political leaders are perfectly able to take their distance from the multi-actor system to manage their political affairs and, on the contrary, may take advantage of it when they need it.

This article also questions the idea of the growing importance of the market principle on local management.[42] Intercommunal integration is based less on objective financial and economic necessities than on the search for financial advantages to manage the political strategies of development.

Last, this article calls into question the role of the mayors who are less able to create projects than to manage and sometimes create obstacles for regional, departmental, metropolitan and urban territorial strategies. The capacity for action of entrepreneural rank-and-file local elected representatives[43] is structured particularly in rural areas by political orientations and the financial, administrative and political incentives of local governments.

NOTES

1. M. Abélés, *Jours Tranquilles en 1989: Ethnologie Politique d'un Département Français* (Paris: O. Jacob 1989).
2. D. Lorrain, 'France, le Changement Silencieux', in D. Lorrain and G. Stocker (eds.) *La Privitisation des Services Urbains en Europe* (Documentation Française 1995).
3. P. Le Galès, 'Du Gouvernement des Villes à la Gouvernance Urbaine', *Revue Française de Science Politique* 1 (April 1995).
4. R. Balme, 'La Région Française Comme Espace d'Action Publique'. Paper given at the international conference, *Les régions en Europe*, Rennes, 4–6 Oct. 1995.
5. H. Michel, *Intercommunalités et Gouvernements Locaux,* (Paris: l'Harmattan 1998). This article develops the theoretical elements of this empirical research.
6. P. Grémion, *Le pouvoir p018ripherique* (Paris: Seuil 1976).
7. The example of the French western *départements* demonstrate this. On the other hand, the experience of the Picardie and Rhône-Alpes areas show that some dynamic regional councils can be more influential at the early stage of the intercommunal renewal.
8. The example of the *département* of Ille-et-Vilaine can illustrate this kind of strategy. Integrated into its rural plan of development, the intercommunal policy of the departmental council of Ille-et-Vilaine is based on devices promoting the creation of intercommunal trading estates near the motorways, offering financial incentives to sustain the creation and operation of the intercommunal structures for local development, and the creation of a new service (SIDEL) in order to implement this policy. The departmental council is also trying to change the communal individualistic mentality of the local representatives. To this end, between 1989 and 1992, it instituted a departmental plan of development which insists on the necessity of improving rural co-operation by touristic and residential intercommunal policies. This departmental strategy has led first to the multiplication of the *syndicats* with an economic purpose between 1988 and 1991, and, second, their transformation into *communautés de communes* from 1992. Following the departmental guidelines, these new intercommunal organisations have opted for residential and touristic functions.
9. For example, the departmental council of Morbihan is chaired by a senator hostile to intercommunal renewal, and because of this, it promoted technical intercommunality. It did not materially sustain co-operation for local development. In addition, it discouraged it by political pressure. Some rural elected representatives have disclosed their attachment to the guidelines of the chairman. During 1992–96, only eight new intercommunal organisations were created. Most rural communes continue to co-operate within their traditional intercommunal structures, the *syndicats*.
10. The majority of departmental councils deploy this intercommunal strategy.
11. The case of the urban district of Rennes illustrates this strategy perfectly. With the agreement of a small group of local representatives from the centre and the periphery, the mayor of Rennes became the chairman of the district in 1989, in order to modernise the intercommunal structure. Created in 1970 to plan and study the development of the metropolitan area, the district was transformed between 1989–93 into a real intercommunal structure of development. The intercommunal strategic planning was re-triggered. The functions were extended (public transport, refuse collection and disposal, economic development). The territory was enlarged (from 27 communes to 33). However, the first preoccupation of the

urban élite has been since then to free the district from the financial dependence on the communes. From 1991, the district has had an autonomous financial power. To fund its policies, it has to levy local taxes. In 1992, its fiscal system was again modified. Based on the *taxe professionnelle communautaire*, the district is now the main partner of the local companies. It is very much involved in the local development, because the level of its funds depends on the level of the local economic activities.

12. For example, in the *département* of Mayenne, the chairman wanted in 1996 to organise the merger of the *communautés de communes*, based on the *cantons*, into some new intercommunal organisations established on wider socio-economic areas. At the same time, he wanted to reshape the departmental policies according to these new intercommunal organisations. He also wished to transform the method of departmental support to the communes and *cantons* into an intercommunal and multi-cantonal model. The collective opposition of most of the departmental councillors forced the chairman to give up the project.

13. However, their position can change if they are at the same time regional councillors or chairmen of an intercommunal organisation established on a   multi-cantonal basis.

14. Since the 1950s, the state has multiplied devices in order to develop intercommunal co-operation. Between 1955 and 1995, the formula of the multi-purpose *syndicat* (*syndicat à vocation multiple*, 1959), the *district* (1959), the *communauté urbaine* (1966), the *syndicat d'agglomeration nouvelle* (1970), the *syndicat à la carte* (1988), the *communautés de communes et de villes* (1992), the *pays*'(1995) were created. On the whole, these devices increasingly invite local councillors to create integrated intercommunal structures – i.e, able to levy local taxes, for the management of technical and political functions, on the basis of wide socio-economic territories.

15. P. Durant and J.C Thoenig, 'L'Etat et la Gestion Publique Territoriale', *Revue Française de Science Politique* 4 (Aug. 1996) p.621.

16. E. Friedberg, 'Il faut Accompagner le Polycentrisme Naissant de la Société Française', *Pouvoirs locaux* 29 (June 1996) pp.97–100.

17. J.C Thoenig, *'Les Contre-Pouvoirs Locaux: Version 'Douce' et Version 'Dure', les Nouvelles Relations État-Collectivités Locales – Colloque de Rennes, April 1990* (La Documentation Française 1991) pp.17–21.

18. Developed by companies such as the 'Lyonnaise des eaux' or the 'compagnie générale des eaux', these strategies of normalisation – 'technisisation' – of the political intercommunal issues have already been illustrated in the field of the local management of water. See D. Lorrain, *Gestions urbaines de l'eau* (Paris: Economica 1995) .

19. P. Le Galès, 'Du Gouvernement des Villes à la Gouvernance Urbaine', *Revue Française de Science Politique* 1 (April 1995).

20. P. Le Galès, J. Caillosse and P. Loncle-Moriceau, *SEML et la Gouvernance Urbaine, Rapport de Synthèse, Programme PIR-Villes* (1995) pp.4–5.

21. O. Borraz, 'Le Changement dans le Mode de Gouvernement des Villes', in J-Y. Nevers and S. Biarez, *Gouvernement local et politiques urbaines* (Grenoble: CERAT 1993).

22. D. Lorrain, 'Gouvernement et Villes', *Sociologie du Travail* 2 (Feb. 1995) p.123.

23. P. Mocquay asserts the hypothesis of a rural governance. See P. Mocquay, *Co-operation intercommunale et societé locale*, Doctoral thesis (U. of Bordeaux IV 1996) pp.463–6.

24. A. Mabileau, *Le Système Local* (Paris: Montchretien 1991) pp.37–8.

25. On the contrary, during the same period, sectorial policies (agriculture, health, education, defence, industry) were modernised due to the convergence of administritive and professional leadership. B. Jobert and P. Müller, *l'Etat en action, politiques, publiques et corporatismes* (Paris: PUF 1987). For a synthesis of this, see P. Müller, *Les politiques publiques* (ibid. 1990).

26. This capacity for neutralisation of the local political system has been widely demonstrated: Y. Mény, *Centralisation et Décentralisation dans le Débat Politique Français (1945–69)* (LGDJ, 1974); P. Grémion, *Le Pouvoir Périphérique* (Paris: Seuil 1976); J. Kervasdoué *et al.*, 'La Loi et le Changement Social: un Diagnostic, la Loi du 16 juillet 1971 sur les Fusions et les Regroupements de Communes', *Revue française de sociologie* 17 (1976). F. Dupuy and J.C Thoenig, *Sociologie de l'Administration Française* (Paris: Colin 1983).

27. D. Lorrain, 'La Montée en Puissance des Villes', *Economie et Humanisme* 305 (1989).

28. Idem 'De l'Administration Républicaine au Gouvernement Urbain', *Sociologie du Travail* 4 (1991).
29. M. Crozier and J.C Thoenig, 'La Régulation des Systèmes Organisés Complexes, le cas du Système de Décision Politico-Administratif Local en France', *Revue Française de Sociologie* 16 (1975); Dupuy and Thoenig (note 26).
30. A. Mabileau, 'Les Héritiers des Notables', *Pouvoirs* 49 (1989).
31. F. Gerbaux and P. Müller, 'Les Interventions Economiques Locales', *Pouvoirs* 60 (1992).
32. Grémion (note 6).
33. Ibid. pp.220–1.
34. J.C. Thoenig, 'La Décentralisation, Dix Ans Après', *Pouvoirs* 60 (1992).
35. P. Le Galès, 'Villes en Competiton?' in J.Y Nevers and Biarez, *Gouvernement Local et Politiques Orbaines* (Grenoble: CERAT 1993). P. Le Galès and M. Oberti, 'Les stratégies des Villes', in J.C Némery and S. Wachter, *Entre l'Europe et la Décentralisation, les Institutions Territoriales Françaises* (Datar: Editions de l'Aube 1993).
36. Grémion (note 6) p.428.
37. The example of Ille-et-Vilaine illustrates this situation. Forming a unified interommunal organisation, the district of Rennes has started early to plan its development at a departmental scale. This urban strategy destabilised the departmental council which decided from 1986 to counter, by a territorial strategy of resistance, the metropolitan expansion. In Ille-et-Vilaine, there is real competition between the departmental council and the major city to control the local territory. Between 1989 and 1993, the district was completely renewed in terms of its fiscal power, functions and territorial dimension. At the same time, the departmental council used the ATR law to resist the metropolitan expansion. In 1993, 24 of the 26 existing *communautés de communes* had already been created.
38. The *département* of Loire-Atlantique can illustrate this situation. Until 1995, the priority of the mayor of Nantes was to federate the communes of its conurbation. He did not try to develop its intercomunal territory; he tried to organise the transformation of the metropolitan multi-purpose *syndicat* into an integrated intercommunal organisation. Under these conditions, the conurbation of Nantes did not endanger the institutional territorial leadership of the departmental council. The departmental élite was not pushed to contain the urban development by intercommunality. It did not actively encourage intercommunal renewal which intervened progressively. In 1996, only 18 new intercommunal organisations had been created, covering two-thirds of the departmental territory.
39. For example, in Picardie, the regional council and the departmental council of the Oise have successively multiplied their own intercommunal devices in order to rally the rural communes. Finally, the regional council now seems to be the main partner of the local elected representatives. It has an increasing relationship with the 40 intercommunal organisations that extend over the whole regional territory.
40. D. Gaxie, 'Structures et Contradictions de l'Edifice Institutionnel', in idem (ed.) *Luttes d'Institutions* (Paris: l'Harmattan 1997) pp.4–5.
41. On this subject, refer to the studies of Le Galés, Lorrain, Balme.
42. D. Lorrain and G. Stocker, *La Privatisation des Services Urbain en Europe* (Documentation Française 1995).
43. A. Faure, 'Des Maires Ruraux Saisis par l'Esprit d'Entreprise', *Economie et Humanisme* 300 (1988). See also by the same author, 'Pouvoir Local en France: le Management Mayoral à l'Assaut du Clientélisme', *Revue Politique et Management Public* 3 (1991).

New Social Movement Politics in France: The Rise of Civic Forms of Mobilisation

SARAH WATERS

The term 'new social movement' (NSM) tends to be broadly used by scholars to denote all recently formed non-traditional types of social movement. Yet, the forms of social movement which have emerged in France over the past decade (anti-racist movement, solidarity movement, Aids advocacy groups) differ from earlier NSMs in important ways. The most salient feature of these movements is their strong civic dimension. Their principal role is to defend and advance the social and political rights of certain groups in society. This article examines key social movements in contemporary France and suggests that 'new citizenship' may be a more accurate concept for describing the role which these movements play within the French political system.

On 22 February 1997, over 100,000 people marched through Paris in protest against a government bill which sought to tighten controls on illegal immigration. Opposition to the Debré bill, seen by many as an attack on basic human rights, began as a petition movement and culminated in a mass demonstration bringing together scores of associations, voluntary groups and individual citizens in a spontaneous movement of public defiance. Faced with this overwhelming reaction, the government was forced to step down and retract the more controversial aspects of the bill. This demonstration has affirmed once again the importance of social protest within French politics. In France, more than any other Western European country it seems, protest constitutes a fundamental mechanism of political change and renewal. It is often through a mobilisation of social forces against the state that real and lasting political change is effectuated. Rather than signalling a breakdown of order, social protest seems to form part of the regular workings of the system. In the words of Stanley Hoffmann: 'There are few other nations where protest movements have been so frequent and so diverse in their origins, channels, and purposes, and so similar in their manifestations, as France.'[1]

West European Politics, Vol.21, No.3 (July 1998), pp.170–186
PUBLISHED BY FRANK CASS, LONDON

If France has witnessed a renewal of social protest in recent years, the forms of movement which now operate within its political system differ significantly from earlier movements. Over the past decade, France has experienced a rise of new types of social movement (anti-racist movement, solidarity movement, Aids advocacy groups) which have come to play a dominant role in mobilising protest and articulating changing demands. The rise of so-called 'new social movements' (NSMs) has attracted considerable interest within the social sciences.[2] These movements are seen to embody new 'post-materialist' issues and themes (eg. feminism, ecology, pacifism). They express new issues which are absent from or inadequately represented within the mainstream political agenda, seeking to 'communicate new claims into the political process of authoritative decision making'.[3] Often this involves co-operating with political parties. In the French case for example, NSMs clustered around the Socialist party (PS) during the early 1980s, in the hope of obtaining a policy response from this party. Within existing literature, the 'new social movement' approach remains the dominant paradigm for understanding the role of contemporary social movements. As such, this approach is often used in a broad way to describe all newly-formed non-traditional types of movement.

Yet, if we look at recent forms of social movement in France, they appear to differ from earlier NSMs in fundamental ways. Contemporary movements do not act as instruments of 'post-materialist issues and demands'. They do not seek to advance new issues within the political system. Nor do they explicitly seek political access as a means of furthering their aims. The key feature of contemporary movements is their strong civic dimension. What unites organisations as diverse as *SOS Racisme*, Amnesty International or Act-up is that they embody a civic conception of political action. Their role is to support and defend the basic rights and freedoms of groups in society. In the face of public policies which are seen to threaten or infringe the rights of these groups, social movements mobilise widespread support, forming a 'civic front' against government.

This article examines the new forms of social movement which have emerged in France since the mid-1980s. It draws partly on information gathered during interviews with representatives of key associations during April/May 1997. Looking in turn at the political values, strategies and forms of organisation of these movements, it argues that they are qualitatively different from those which prevailed during the previous decade. It suggests therefore, that a NSM approach may no longer be an accurate way of describing these movements. Indeed, the notion of 'new citizenship', recently developed by French social scientists, may provide a more appropriate framework for defining the role which these movements assume within the political system.

A NEW CYCLE OF PROTEST

Over the past decade, France has experienced a resurgence of new social movement protest after a period of relative absence from French political life. It began with the student movement of 1986, peaked in key demonstations (anti-racist rallies, peace movement) and culminated recently in the anti-government demonstrations of February 1997. Observers during the first half of the 1980s had commented on the disappearance of social protest from French politics: 'the major political event of the *septennat* is the demobilisation of political activists'.[4] France had entered what, according to some, was an 'era of individualism' marked by a growing indifference and disaffectation towards traditional forms of political participation: 'It is the search for individual identity and not collective interests which motivates social and individual action.'[5] Yet by the mid-1980s, France had experienced what some described as a 'democratic rebirth'.[6] A 'new civic generation' had emerged, informed by democratic values and ideals and characterised by 'a commitment to liberal democracy, a desire to extend the rights and freedoms of individuals (...) Far from being apathetic or indifferent, this generation formed a great democratic movement.'[7]

If this period was marked by a resurgence of social protest, this did not simply involve a revival of past movements and struggles. By the mid-1980s, most of the key movements of the preceding decade had disappeared. Some, like the feminist movement had succeeded in obtaining a political response from government: 'the feminist movement had practically disappeared by the mid-1980s, at least before the arrival of Mitterrand, and this was not due to the failure of the movement, but the fact that it had obtained its objectives'.[8] The creation of a Ministry for Women's Rights in 1981 and the nomination of several women ministers to government seemed to reduce the impetus towards social protest. Key organisations within the gay-rights movement (FHAR, CUARH)[9] were dissolved for similar reasons around this time. These had acquired recognition and support from the PS during the late 1970s. Indeed, PS activists had set up *Homosexualités et Socialisme* in 1983, to act as a liaison between the gay-rights movement and this party.

Other movements, like ecology were largely transferred from the social to the political arena. The creation of a new green party, *Les Verts* in 1984 meant that environmental issues were increasingly addressed and tackled within the parliamentary domain. This significantly undermined the role and importance of environmental protest groups. One study points out that whilst the mobilising capacity of the environmental movement in 1986 was 16 per cent in Germany, 10 per cent in The Netherlands and 7 per cent in

Britain, during the same year in France, it was only 4 per cent.[10] If organisations like Greenpeace and *Les Amis de la Terre* have survived, they nevertheless have limited influence over the direction of public policy and tend to have a weak capacity for mobilisation. This was highlighted recently by the comparatively small number of activists in France who demonstrated against the resumption of French nuclear testing in 1995.[11]

While the early issue-based movements had all but vanished by the mid-1980s, a range of new movements emerged at this time which would assume a dominant role in mobilising social protest. Undoubtedly, the major force to coalesce during this period, was the anti-racist movement: '*SOS Racisme* was before [...] 1986, the only important political force to have understood and subsequently mobilised the new generation'.[12] The formation of a mass-based anti-racist movement during the 1980s, was closely linked to political events and in particular, the surge of the *Front national* (FN) within the French political system. The spectacular rise of the anti-racist movement mirrored that of the FN and its progressive integration into the domain of mainstream politics. Some 500,000 people responded to the appeal of *SOS Racisme*, the largest anti-racist organisation, for a demonstration at the Place de la Concorde in 1985, 200,000 in 1986 at Place de la Bastille, 250,000 in 1987 and 300,000 in 1988 at Esplanade de Vincennes.[13] The success of *SOS Racisme* was linked in part to its use of popular cultural themes to attract a mass youth following. However, the anti-racist movement also encompasses other more militant groups such as, SCALP formed in Toulouse in 1984 and *Ras l'Front*, established by a group of left-wing intellectuals in 1990.[14] These associations focus more directly on creating a militant counter-movement to the FN, disrupting FN meetings and organising counter-demonstrations during local elections involving FN candidates. Some like SCALP advocate political violence as a means of achieving their ends. Beyond specific groups and associations, the anti-racist movement tends to act as a broad-based forum for anti-system opposition, gaining support from those disillusioned with the mainstream Left: 'Fighting against the extreme Right provides a just and moral cause of engagement for those whom the Left disappointed. It functions as a substitute ideology. In addition, the decentralized structures of the anti-FN movements and their concrete plans of action attract the young in search of a new kind of political involvement.'[15] Anti-racist rallies tend to bring together a vast array of associations and *ad hoc* structures which are not always directly involved in the movement.

Another important formation which emerged at this time was the 'solidarity' movement. This term has been used to designate the range of associations and groups concerned with civic or humanitarian issues (civil rights, political asylum, the Third World).[16] They constitute a solidarity movement in that they are concerned not with advancing political issues and themes, but with reinforcing civic and social rights. Their role is to defend and protect the rights of groups which are perceived to be disadvantaged or subject to discrimination. Ion[17] notes that if traditional types of political participation (union and party membership) have declined, newer forms of mobilisation and principally, the solidarity movement have undergone a considerable expansion. Indeed, the rise of such a movement is a powerful argument against those who presaged trends towards individualism within French society. According to Duyvendak, these associations 'share an altruistic outlook and for this reason have been neglected or misunderstood by sociologists who are concerned primarily with manifestations of self-interest'.[18] The solidarity movement encompasses traditional organisations (*Ligue des droits de l'Homme* (LDH), MRAP,[19] *Terre des Hommes*), some of which have undergone expansion in recent years. The LDH increased its membership during the early 1990s, partly as a result of broadening its scope of intervention to include issues such as, gay rights, anti-racism and homelessness. In 1986, this otherwise traditional organisation rallied behind the gay rights movement in opposition to Chirac's decision to ban the gay newspaper, *Gai-pied*. The solidarity movement also includes more recently-founded organisations concerned with international issues (Amnesty International, *Médecins sans frontières*), charitable concerns (*Restaurants du Coeur*), as well as *ad hoc* structures formed in order to generate support for a specific social issue (*Les sans-papiers*). Recent studies have emphasised the importance of international issues and concerns in the formation of social movements.[20] A growing number of movements are concerned with global issues and problems which transcend national political boundaries. At the same time, processes of European integration and the increased importance of the European Union as a centre of political decision making has led many movements to reorganise their activities along international lines.

A third key movement which emerged at this time was the network of Aids advocacy groups. Between 1981 and 1989, over 40 associations were created to mobilise support for victims of Aids and confront what was perceived to be governmental indifference to the Aids crisis. The failure of government to recognise and respond to this epedemic was a primary factor in the rapid expansion of this movement: 'it is clear that the absence of intervention by the state triggered the formation of a vast associative movement.'[21] Whilst not openly affiliated with the gay community, many of these associations were created by former gay rights activists. The first associations such as Aides, created in 1984 by the sociologist Daniel Defert and Arcat-SIDA set up the following year, were essentially non-confrontational, seeking a co-operative stance in relation to government for purposes of acquiring public legitimacy and support. However, a continued intransigence on the part of government, triggered a new radicalism within the movement. In 1989, Act-up was formed, based on its American counterpart established two years earlier. Act-up (Aids Coalition to Unleash Power) assumed a militant stance in relation to the authorities, using direct political methods (civil disobedience, occupations, demonstations, sporadic acts of violence) in order to provoke a policy response to their demands. Fillieule argues that 'political opportunity structure' was an important factor in provoking this new radicalism. The failure of government to open up to earlier groups, providing them with 'political opportunities' is seen by this author as an important catalyst in the emergence of Act-up.[22] This association expanded rapidly in the initial years, using an agressive modern image to attract widespread support. Indeed, in terms of its methods and strategies, Act-up remains among the most dynamic and innovative of recently formed associations.

The new types of movement which emerged during the mid-1980s, shared some distinctive characteristics, the most notable of which was their civic dimension. Their primary role was to defend and advance the rights of specific groups in society (immigrants, political refugees, Aids victims). In the face of an often hostile political system, contemporary movements mobilised support for these groups, furthering their social and political rights. Compared with earlier NSMs, they were concerned more with social groups than political issues. Yet according to the 'new social movement approach', as it became known in the 1980s, new social movements are formed in order to express changing social issues and demands. Their role is to advance these issues, seeking a policy response from the mainstream political domain. Whilst the NSM approach may have provided important insights into the role and function of earlier movements, it does not take account of the specific features of contemporary movements. We must, therefore, ask whether a NSM approach is an appropriate perspective for describing these movements.

NEW CITIZENSHIP

The notion of 'new citizenship' has been developed by several French social scientists to account for the rise of new forms of mobilisation in contemporary France.[23] New citizenship refers to a conception of the citizen as an active participant in the political process. Whereas the traditional idea of citizenship is essentially passive – the citizen is a member of a political community, involved in political life only indirectly through electoral processes – new citizenship involves 'a direct participation of citizens in processes of democratic decision making'. By acting collectively within associations, individuals affirm their right to participate fully in civic and political life. New citizenship is 'participatory and collective and is characterised by a direct involvement of individual citizens in civic and political affairs'.[24] The idea of new citizenship has been used to explain the rise, in recent years, of new forms of mobilisation which have flourished outside formal political structures and may include local community associations (*Maisons des potes*) or wider solidarity movements at national level (*Restaurants du Coeur*, Amnesty International). The rise of these new movements is seen to express a new and active form of citizenship: 'These new social and political movements form part of what is often referred to now as the new citizenship: movements that mobilise not simply through the institutional political channels but also within social and economic spheres in the attempt to redefine and repoliticise those spaces.'[25]

The term new citizenship denotes the civic and associative character of many of these movements. Formed within the civic community, they tend to use informal, participatory forms of organisation which facilitate the involvement of individuals in the political process. Avoiding formal structures, they place precedence on individuals and groups over structure and organisation: 'Citizenship in the civic community entails equal rights and obligations for all. Such a community is bound together by horizontal relations of reciprocity and co-operation, not by vertical relations of authority and dependency. Citizens interact as equals, not as patrons and clients nor as governors and petitioners.'[26] These are civic forms of mobilisation in that they aim to give responsibilities back to the individual citizen. They seek to 'restore meaning, form and dynamism to the notion of citizenship, giving individuals a right to decide in all domains, from the local to the national and the European to the global'.[27]

New citizenship is used to refer to the rise of democratic values among new social and political movements. Many of these movements are involved in varying ways in advancing social and political rights. Themes such as equality, freedom and solidarity are increasingly used in order to confront new social issues and struggles such as those of anti-racism, gay rights, political asylum, etc. This represents what some idealists have referred to as 'a great democratic revival' or yet still 'a discovery and celebration of civic humanism'.[28] It expresses a new form of citizenship in that civic values and ideals are recovered and used for new social purposes. These themes are invoked and 'applied to the needs of post-modern society'.[29]

Existing studies of new citizenship are limited to specific movements and associations. Some consider local associational practices, looking at the proliferation of new structures and associations at local level. As the first level of political participation 'new citizenship is especially evident within local communities'.[30] Others focus on particular social movements at national level, looking for example at the anti-racist movement as a form of new citizenship.[31] This movement is seen to embody the values of new citizenship in that it seeks to reinforce the rights of a particular social group, by way of collective action. Yet, it seems that new citizenship should have a wider relevance for the social movement sector as a whole. Indeed, this may be a useful way of accounting for the distinctive qualities of recently formed movements. Instead of categorising these as NSMs, similar to those which prevailed during the 1960s and 1970s, new citizenship may be a more valid notion for describing the role which these movements assume within the political system.

Whilst no unified theory or model has been developed, it is assumed for present purposes that new citizenship refers to movements which share at least three distinctive features: (i) they espouse civic and democratic values; (ii) they use informal, associative forms of organisation; and (iii) they favour, through their actions, citizen participation in the political process. We will go on to examine the political values, strategies and forms of organisation of contemporary social movements in the light of a new citizenship perspective.

CHANGING POLITICAL VALUES

If we look at the political values of contemporary social movements, the most striking feature is their strong civic basis. We have seen that the main role of these movements is to reinforce social and political rights and freedoms, extending these rights to new or disadvantaged social groups. They act with civic purpose, challenging 'all traditional forms of discrimination, all authoritarian forms of power'.[32] Social movements mobilise support for these groups in the face of policies which threaten or infringe their fundamental rights. In performing this role, they draw on democratic values and themes. The more traditional associations have incorporated these themes into their founding statutes. The role of MRAP, for example, is to 'confront all forms of racism, defending the rights to freedom and equality of all citizens', whilst that of LDH is to 'advance democratic rights and freedoms'. Both organisations refer to the Declaration of Human Rights and the Declaration of the Rights of Man, as key ideological references underpinning their social and political role. In the same way, more recently-formed organisations espouse a democratic and civic conception of political action. In describing the role of *SOS Racisme*, its founder Harlem Désir stated: 'Our only ideological reference is the rights of man. We have neither motions, programmes, nor platforms, at most, a basic charter. This would be a waste of time and a source of division. Our philosophy is humanism'.[33] Democratic references are used as a way of emphasising the rights of different social groups and highlighting discriminatory policies or practices.

Many of the movements which emerged during the mid-1980s mobilised around demands for equality. The anti-racist movement was launched through 'equality marches' during 1983 and 1984 which called for equal rights for immigrants. Indeed, the issue of equality has been central to the development of this movement, being as much a source of unity as division amongst the various associations within the movement. In a similar way, the 1986 student movement had a strong egalitarian focus. Faced with a bill proposing greater selection in universities, students affirmed the principle of equality in education, demanding 'equal rights for all'. Various observers have noted the importance of egalitarian themes during the 1986 demonstrations. Indeed, traditional Marxist-based political slogans seemed to have been abandoned in favour of references to equality and freedom:

> But these hundreds and thousands of students [...] marched without red or black flags, without portraits of great leaders, without raised fists or the *Internationale*[...] Instead, here and there, they marched behind enormous tricolour flags, bearing before all the old Republican slogan, Freedom, Equality, Fraternity.[34]

These egalitarian themes have become the dominant references through which social protest is articulated and expressed.

The theme of solidarity has also become an important rallying point for social movements. Many of the key demonstrations during this period were mobilised in order to express solidarity for a particular social group. Activists during the 1997 demonstrations appealed for mass civil disobedience in reaction to the Debré bill which sought to criminalise anyone giving residence to an illegal immigrant. This appeal was intended to demonstrate support for the basic democratic rights of all citizens irrespective of their political or civil status. Contemporary movements often forge new symbols and slogans used to convey solidarity for a disadvantaged social group. The slogan 'Hands off my mate' was popularised by *SOS Racisme* during the 1980s, in support of the political and social rights of immigrants. Aids advocacy groups introduced the red ribbon, signifying support for victims of Aids, while gay-rights groups used the pink triangle as a symbol of the struggle against sexual discrimination. These emblems tend to be used as much as a gesture of solidarity with marginalised groups, as a symbol of defiance against institutionalised values and policies which exclude or threaten these groups. They highlight the profoundly democratic nature of contemporary movements and their attempt to further the rights of all social groups rather than the narrow concerns of a particular movement or social category.

ALTERNATIVE STRATEGIES AND METHODS

Recent studies have highlighted the decline of traditional forms of protest amongst French social movements. Fontanaud and Matonti in *Que reste-t-il de nos manifs?*[35] point to the disappearance of the key political demonstrations of the 1970s. Events such as those at Larzac (1974) or Malville (1977) seemed to have little or not equivalent in the decade which followed. Fillieule highlights a decline of more militant types of protest in recent years.[36] Looking at demonstrations which occurred in three French towns during 1989 and 1990, he demonstrates that less than three per cent of these, involved some measure of political violence. He concludes that incidents of direct political violence (such as the death of Malik Oussekine in 1986) have become increasingly rare. If traditional forms of social protest have declined, these have given way to new and alternative forms of intervention. Contemporary movements draw on a vast range of innovative strategies (symbolic actions, festivals, media-directed events, petition movements, civil disobedience) in order to further their aims. Compared with earlier forms of protest, these might be described as directly democratic. They avoid traditional forms of militancy and instead, emphasise a wide and direct participation of individuals and groups in political action.

Contemporary movements tend to favour participatory forms of mass mobilisation which bring together a wide range of associations, groups and individuals. Emphasis is placed on a broad and direct involvement of individuals in political activity. Demonstrations are treated as an expression of collective demands and interests rather than narrowly representing the views of a particular association or movement. The 1997 demonstrations began as a petition movement which coalesced into a mass 'civil march' providing an informal and direct way for individuals and groups to participate in social action. Participation in demonstrations is often determined by cultural affinities and identification rather than political loyalties or affiliations. Social movements tend to draw on cultural symbols to encourage mass participation in political events. *SOS Racisme*, for example, excelled at a strategy which involved using the themes and symbols of popular culture in order to generate a mass youth following. This association launched rock concerts and youth rallies throughout the second part of the 1980s, as a means of popularising anti-racist themes. Demonstrations seem to act as much as a form of cultural participation as an expression of social protest. This confirms Alain Touraine's analysis of the role of social movements: 'a social movement, in my definition, is a collective action aiming at the implementation of central cultural values against the interest and influence of an enemy which is defined in terms of power relations. A social movement is a combination of social conflict and cultural participation'.[37] This perspective is reflected by the recent revival of gay- pride marches in France, during which activists affirm a shared cultural identity. These demonstrations act more as a celebration of cultural values than as an expression of discontent.

Social movements increasingly use direct forms of political intervention. One of the key innovations within the social movement sector during this period, was the increased use of the media for strategic purposes.[38] If earlier NSMs relied on party channels to communicate their aims, contemporary movements tend to favour the media which gives them a direct and immediate form of access to centres of political decision making. The success of a number of movements has been closely linked to their effective manipulation of media channels. *SOS Racisme* was publicly launched in 1985 with the appearance of its leader, Harlem Désir on the television programme, *Droit de réponse*. The subsequent spectacular rise of this association was the result of a highly-orchestrated media campaign, involving regular press conferences, television appearances and sponsorship by celebrities. According to one account: 'The media played a crucial role in the rise of the anti-racist association. The rules of the game were quickly mastered by the leaders of *SOS Racisme* particularly with regard to television, the first media form targeted.'[39] Other associations have made similar use of the media. The success of Act-up was based partly on its ability to construct, through the media, a modern and aggressive image. Marc Nectar, current president of Act-up confirmed during interviews,[40] that the media plays a central role in Act-up's strategy. Before undertaking a particular initiative, Act-up usually notifies the media in advance, so that most of their actions are directly televised. In 1994, Act-up launched a massive televised campaign (*Sidaction*), sponsored by several television companies in order to generate public support and provoke greater government involvement in Aids research and funding. Use of the media has allowed this otherwise small and marginalised organisation to acquire a strong presence within the social movement sector.

Another important development during this period was the increased use of symbolic forms of action. These may range from acts of civil disobedience to occupations or media-directed events which differ from more traditional or conventional types of protest. Symbolic forms of intervention are generally designed to highlight or represent a particular social issue or problem. Act-up has evolved a vast repertoire of symbolic actions which include 'die-ins' where activists lie on the ground, usually occupying a public space, in order to represent those who have died of Aids. The most recent and notorious action undertaken by Act-up involved sheathing the obelisk statute in the Place de la Concorde with a giant condom, intended to highlight the need for greater Aids awareness.

Elsewhere, acts of civil disobedience have become increasingly common. These have an important symbolic quality in that they appeal to participants as citizens with certain rights and duties. Civil disobedience is used widely by Greenpeace, to obstruct road development or the expansion of nuclear sites and by anti-racist organisations, to oppose aspects of immigration policy. Civil disobedience is used to express opposition to public policies which are deemed to infringe fundamental rights. Other examples include the use of symbolic forms of political language. The anti-racist organisation, SCALP uses political symbolism to mount its opposition against the FN. Drawing on the context of American Indians, it launched newspapers called 'Tomahawk' and 'Apaches', held 'Geronimo' concerts and used anti-FN slogans such as, 'Let's scalp them'.[41] Symbolic forms of political activity and expression have become increasingly widespread taking precedence over more traditional forms of protest. Indeed, given the importance of the media for social movements, the development of symbolic actions has tended to become a central part of their political strategy.

FORMS OF ORGANISATION

A key feature of contemporary movements is that they generally seek a position of independence in relation to formal political structures, favouring associative and informal types of organisation. Many of the demonstrations mobilised by these movements were marked by an absence of formal political representation or structure. Dray notes that during the 1986 student demonstrations, participants 'showed a genuine mistrust with regard to any form of political organisation or structure. What some would identify as the 'apoliticism' of the movement was, in fact a profound desire for independence not in relation to ideas but formal structures'.[42] Shunning formal or permanent types of organisation, these demonstrations were organised through *ad hoc* co-ordinating committees which were dissolved once the demonstrations had ended. Likewise, some of the recent anti-racist demonstrations were directed as much against the extreme right, as against the mainstream political parties. During the large anti-racist demonstration in Paris on 25 January 1992, political slogans targeted the former political ally of this movement, the PS. More recently, party activists were excluded from participating in the preparatory meetings which preceded the February 1997 demonstrations. This demonstration was described in one national newspaper as 'a large civil march, entirely free of formal structure'.[43] From Act-up to *SOS Racisme*, social movements increasingly tend to assert their autonomy in relation to the political parties. This situation clearly differs from that of earlier NSMs which actively sought political alliances as a means of furthering their goals. If these earlier groups moved towards the parties, clustering around the PS and its entry to government, later movements would follow an opposite trajectory, moving away from formal structures and alliances.

Contemporary movements tend to operate within a fragmented and heterogenous system of alliances lacking clear or dominant influences. They draw support from the whole spectrum of the Left, ranging from the extreme left (*Fédération anarchiste, Lutte ouvrière, Ligue communiste révolutionnaire*), to the Communist, Socialist and Green parties and their unions (CGT, CFDT, FO, UNEF), to associative and voluntary structures. During the late 1980s, a selected number of associations continued to receive support from the PS. *SOS Racisme* and LDH benefited from massive financial aid from the PS, via the governmental agency, FAS.[44] Indeed, this support was crucial to the successes of these associations during this period. Relations between *SOS Racisme* and the PS were particularly close, confirmed for some by the nomination of several of the association's former leaders (Julien Dray, Isabelle Thomas) as PS deputies: 'Behind the official history of *SOS Racisme*, one finds a story of political manipulation at the hands of Francois Mitterrand and the Socialist Party.'[45] Yet, by the close of the decade, *SOS Racisme* was already distancing itself from this party. Discredited by the relevations of a 'secret history', published by one of the association's former members, together with the impact of an increasingly repressive immigration policy, at the hands of the Socialists, *SOS Racisme* could no longer continue its relationship with this party.

Other key associations (Act-up, Greenpeace) are independent structures which refuse any form of collaboration with the parties. In the past, this has allowed them to assume a radical, openly critical stance in relation to government policy. Another group of associations has links with the extreme left. The anti-racist organisation, SCALP emerged from the anarchist libertarian left, whilst *Ras l'Front*, was founded by members of the Trotskyist LCR.[46] The overall picture which emerges is one of a horizontal cross-cutting set of alliances, with social movements retaining a measure of independence from the parties. This marks an important departure in relation to the earlier PS-dominated configuration which prevailed during the 1970s and early 1980s.

In describing the forms of organisation used by contemporary movements, at least two observers have referred to 'political spaces' rather than political structures.[47] Social movements are seen to operate through an informal network of associations, committees and voluntary groupings which lacks clear structural demarcations or political tendencies. They favour individuals and groups over structure and organisation, rejecting 'the authority of private or public bureaucracies to regulate individual and collective conduct'.[48] They occupy a 'new political space' which challenges the monopoly of centralised institutions and structures over political decision making: 'Rather than movements, one should speak about spaces or aggregations of interest: amongst youth and women's groups, ecology and counter-cultural movements, we find a diffused network of links and circuits of interaction which differs profoundly from traditional forms of politically organised collective action.'[49] Social movements provide their members with an alternative form of political participation, a way of 'doing politics differently' which avoids formal political structures. Often associations come together to form a temporary alliance or 'civic front' for purposes of presenting a strong united front on a particular issue. This was the case during the 1997 demonstrations when organisations as seemingly diverse as LDH, Act-up, MRAP, LCR and gay rights groups came together to establish a unified position in relation to the Debré bill. This strategy allows an otherwise fragmented network of organisations to create a strong alliance whilst avoiding permanent or formal ties.

CONCLUSION

With over 10,000 demonstrations a year and 1,000 in Paris alone,[50] social protest continues to play a fundamental role within French political life, shaping the process of political change and renewal. This article looked at recent forms of social movement in France, examining their changed role within the political system. Over the past decade, France has witnessed a rise of new forms of social movement (anti-racist movement, solidarity movement, Aids advocacy groups) which have been responsible for the bulk of demonstrations which took place during this period. Few studies have considered the distinctive qualities of these movements. Within existing literature, the 'new social movement approach' remains the dominant paradigm for understanding the role of contemporary movements. This perspective is invariably used to describe all recently formed non-traditional types of movement irrespective of their specific features or tendencies. New movements are treated as part of a more general trend towards 'post-materialist values and themes' which began as a result of 'structural transformations' within society during the 1960s and 1970s.

Yet we have seen that contemporary movements differ from earlier NSMs in fundamental ways. They are not vehicles of new political issues and themes. Indeed, they seem to prefer traditional democratic values and references such as, equality and solidarity. Nor do these movements seek political access as a way of furthering their goals. Instead they favour a position of autonomy in relation to institutionalised politics. In terms of their political values, forms of organisation and dominant strategies, contemporary movements appear qualitatively different from earlier NMSs. Given that this is the case, it seems inappropriate to continue defining these movements as NSMs.

This article suggests that 'new citizenship' may be a valid notion for understanding contemporary movements. So far, use of this concept has been limited to a number of specific movements and associations (local community associations and the anti-racist movement). Yet it seems that it might have wider relevance for other social movements in contemporary France. New citizenship refers to at least three important features of recently-formed movements.

First, they espouse civic values and ideals. We have seen that contemporary movements share a profoundly democratic outlook using themes such as, equality, freedom and solidarity to confront new forms of discrimination in society. Traditional civic values are recovered and applied to contemporary social problems and struggles.

Second, they emphasise the role of individuals and groups within the political process. We have seen that contemporary movements use strategies which place individuals at the forefront of political action. Demonstrations are typically mass participatory events, bringing together large numbers of organisations and individual citizens within a broad 'civic front'. From civil disobedience to direct action or media-directed events, social movements use methods which give individuals and groups a primary political role.

Finally, they favour informal associative types of organisation. It has been shown that social movements draw support from a network of organisations and structures which operate outside formal political institutions. Unlike earlier movements, they tend to avoid formal alliances, favouring instead a position of independence in relation to mainstream political structures. Given the distinctive attributes of contemporary movements, it seems that new citizenship may be an appropriate way of defining their role within the political system. Indeed, it may be more accurate to describe these as new citizenship movements rather than new social movements.

NOTES

Thanks are extended to Nonna Mayer, Michel Wieviorka and Daniel Boy for their kind help and support during my research in Paris. I would also like to thank Max Silverman and Jim House for their comments on an earlier draft of this article.

1. Stanley Hoffmann, *Decline or Renewal: France since the 1930s* (NY: Viking Press 1974) p.111.
2. Recent important studies include J.W. Duyvendak, *Le Poids du Politique. Nouveaux*

mouvements sociaux en France (Paris: L'Harmattan 1994); Hanspeter Kriesi *et al.*, *New Social Movements in Western Europe* (London: UCL Press 1995); and J.C. Jenkins and B. Klandermans (eds.) *The Politics of Social Protest* (ibid. 1995).

3. Herbert Kitschelt, 'Social Movements, Political Parties, and Democratic Theory', *The Annals of the American Academy of Political and Social Science* 528 (July 1993) p.14.

4. G. Mendel, *54 millions d'individus sans appartenance. L'obstacle invisible du septennat* (Paris: Laffont 1983). My translation.

5. Gilles Lipovetsky, *L'ère du vide. Essais sur l'individualisme contemporain* (Paris: Gallimard 1983) p.14. My translation.

6. Henri Weber, *Vingt ans après. Que reste-t-il de 68?* (Paris: Seuil 1988). See also Laurent Joffrin, *Un coup de jeune. Portrait d'une génération morale* (Paris: Arléa 1987).

7. Weber (note 6) p.210. My translation.

8. Duyvendak (note 2) p.259. My translation.

9. *Front homosexuel d'action révolutionnaire* and *Comité d'Urgence Anti-Répression Homosexuelle.*

10. Duyvendak (note 2) pp.242–3.

11. See Jolyon Howorth 'HiroChirac and the French Nuclear Conundrum: A Testing Time for the Pursuit of Grandeur', *French Politics and Society* 13/3 (Summer 1995) pp.1–17.

12. Joffrin (note 6) p.13.

13. Kriesi (note 2) p.77.

14. SCALP stands for *Sections Carrément anti-Le Pen*. For a detailed study of these organisations, see Nonna Mayer, 'The Dynamics of the Anti-National Front Counter Movement', *French Politics and Society* 13/4 (1995).

15. Mayer (note 14) p.24.

16. See Duyvendak (note 2) pp.224–39 and also, Jacques Ion, *La fin des militants* (Paris: Editions de l'Atelier 1997).

17. Ion (note 16).

18. Duyvendak (note 2) p.225. My translation.

19. MRAP stands for *Mouvement contre le racisme et pour l'amitié entre les peuples*.

20. See for example, Sidney Tarrow, *Power in Movement* (Cambridge and NY: CUP 1994); Alberto Melucci *Challenging Codes. Collective Action in the Information Age* (Cambridge: CUP1996); Philip Cerny 'Globalisation and the Changing Logic of Collective Action', University of York – Working Papers, No.5 (U. of York 1995); and Gary Marks and Doug McAdam, 'Social Movements and the Changing Structure of Political Opportunity in the European Union', *West European Politics* 19/2 (April 1996) pp.249–78.

21. Fabienne Dulac, 'Du refus de la maladie à une prise en charge exigeante. Le rôle des associations issues des milieux homosexuels' in Pierre Favre (ed.) *Sida et politique – les premiers affrontements* (Paris: L'Harmattan 1992) p.67. My translation.

22. Olivier Fillieule, *Sociologie de la protestation* (Paris: L'Harmattan 1993).

23. C. Wihtol de Wenden, 'La Nouvelle Citoyenneté' and Albano Cordeiro, 'Pratiques associatives, Pratiques citoyennes' *Hommes et Migrations* 1196 (March 1996); Bertrand Badie, 'Quelles citoyennes à l'heure de la mondialisation?', ibid. 1206 (March–April1997).

24. Wihtol de Wenden (note 23) pp.14–15. My translation.

25. Max Silverman, *Deconstructing the Nation. Immigration, Racism and Citizenship in Modern France* (London and NY: Routledge 1992) p.126.

26. Robert Putnam *et al.*, *Making Democracy Work – Civic Traditions in Modern Italy* (Princeton UP 1993) p.88.

27. Georges Labica (ed.), *Les Nouveaux Espaces Politiques* (Paris: L'Harmattan 1995) p.8. My translation.

28. Weber (note 6) and Don Herzog, cited by Putnam (note 26) p.87.

29. Joffrin (note 6) p.161.

30. Wihtol de Wenden (note 23) p.15.

31. See for example, Wihtol de Wenden, 'Que sont devenues les associations civiques issues de l'immigration?' *Hommes et Migrations* 1206 (March–April 1997).

32. Weber (note 6) p.30. My translation.

33. Cited by Joffrin (note 6) p.66. My translation.

34. Weber (note 6) p.198. My translation.
35. H. Fontanaud and F. Matonti, *Que reste-t-il de nos manifs?* (Paris: Grasset 1990).
36. Olivier Fillieule, *Stratégies de la rue. Les manifestations en France* (Paris: Presses de Sciences Po 1997).
37. Alain Touraine, 'Commentary on Dieter Rucht's Critique' in D. Rucht (ed.) *Research on Social Movements* (Boulder, CO: Westview Press 1991) p.389. See also A. Touraine, *Pourrons-nous vivre ensemble? Egaux et différents* (Paris: Fayard 1997).
38. See Fillieule (note 36).
39. Serge Malik *Histoire secrète de SOS Racisme* (Paris: Albin Michel 1990) p.77. My translation.
40. Interview with Marc Nectar, 24 April 1997.
41. See Mayer (note 14).
42. Julien Dray, *SOS Génération* (Paris 1987) p.70. My translation.
43. See *Libération* 24 Feb. 1997.
44. Duyvendak (note 2) observes that the FAS (*Fonds d'Action Sociale pour les Travailleurs Immigrés et leurs Familles*) supported 1,700 associations during the early 1980s.
45. Malik (note 36).
46. Mayer (note 14).
47. See Labica (note 27) and Ion (note 16).
48. Kriesi (note 2) p.xx.
49. A. Melucci, 'Mouvements sociaux, mouvements postpolitiques' *Revue internationale d'action communautaire* 10 (1983) p.14. My translation.
50. These figures are taken from Fillieule (note 36).

The Relationship between Government and Opposition in the Bundestag and House of Commons in the Run-Up to the Maastricht Treaty

MOSHE MAOR

This article analyses modes of interaction between government and opposition in the German Bundestag and the British House of Commons in the run-up to the Maastricht Treaty, and the implications of co-operation or a lack thereof for the parties involved. The article is based on the premise that the government–opposition relationship is not derived solely from power relationships and institutional factors, but is also a matter of democratic legitimacy. Three indicators are used to ascertain the level of government–opposition co-operation: the creation of parliamentary committees, information exchange and incentive management. Based on an institutional analysis and interviews with legislators, the finding is that although parties in Germany and the UK have created parliamentary committees dealing with European affairs, only in the former did the government utilise the new tool for co-operation with the opposition, in terms of information exchange and incentive management. Consequently, informal co-operation in Germany brought about an outcome compatible with the interests of the parties involved. By contrast, the lack of co-operation with opposition parties in Britain led to an extreme parliamentary crisis.

In domestic matters, virtually any policy implemented by a government is reversible by a subsequent administration. In foreign policy, this is not so. Negotiations over an international treaty which touches upon a country's sovereignty highlights the sense of urgency and the importance of national consensus when the weightiest of issues are at stake. Such cases, therefore, far exceed the government–opposition game of everyday political life.

Specifically, scholars of parliamentary politics correctly argue that the relationship between government and opposition is based on, and derived from, a power relationship (i.e., the relative size of the parliamentary parties

West European Politics, Vol.21, No.3 (July 1998), pp.187–207
PUBLISHED BY FRANK CASS, LONDON

and the composition of the coalition). Institutional imperatives, such as government structure, constitutional arrangements and voting procedures are additional factors affecting the relationship between government and opposition. Beyond these considerations, however, lies the basic premise that democratic decision making demands broad public support. 'To achieve democratic legitimacy, decisions in parliament must have the support of the members of the parliamentary party groups, the party members and the electorate. Consequently, not only decision-making efficiency, but also achieving public support through a sometimes time-consuming and complex democratic process are values which parliaments must consider.'[1]

Two case studies are analysed here, namely, interaction between government and opposition in the German Bundestag and the British House of Commons in the run-up to the Treaty on European Union (Maastricht Treaty) on 7 February 1992 and its ratification by the legislatures of Germany (December 1992) and Britain (July 1993). The methodology employed combines an institutional analysis with interviews of 50 members of the Bundestag and 26 members of the House of Commons. The interviews were conducted in English during late 1992 and early 1993.

Three indicators are used to ascertain the level of government–opposition co-operation: (i) the establishment of sites for government–opposition co-operation, such as parliamentary committees; (ii) information exchange, that is, government – opposition negotiations within committees and advance notice by government of policy initiatives; and (iii) incentive management, namely, formal or informal incorporation of opposition members into the governmental mechanism.[2]

The rationale for the selection of countries under examination is based on the premise that interaction between government and opposition takes place within a given institutional arena and that this arena significantly influences the character and extent of co-operation subsequently observed. The countries examined show considerable variation over five dimensions: government structure, constitutional arrangements, voting procedures, separation of powers and electoral system (see Table 1). In Germany, lines of political accountability connecting government and opposition parties are clearly defined whereas in Britain, the linkage between public policy, incumbents and opposition parties is much more fractured, ambiguous and weak. This discrepancy implies that in Germany there are greater restrictions on the government's use of institutional manipulation and agenda setting, because opposition parties may control some *Länder* governments and a majority in the Bundesrat. Further constraining factors are the highly codified constitution, which is hard to amend and embodies extensive judicial review and well-specified citizenship rights; strong separation of powers; effective bicameralism; and a system of proportional

TABLE 1
CONSTITUTIONAL AND INSTITUTIONAL INFLUENCES ON THE CHOICE OF
TACIT GOVERNMENT–OPPOSITION CO-ORDINATION

	Germany	The UK
Structure of government	Federal state	Centralised unitary state with weak sub-national governments
Constitutional arrangements	Codified constitution/ strong judicial review	Uncodified constitution/ no judicial review
Voting procedures in legislature	absolute majority and two-thirds majority rules	Simple majorities
	Veto powers by Bundesrat on bills subject to an affirmative vote	The House of Lords can only delay legislation by one year
Separation of powers	Strong separation	Weak separation
Electoral system	Proportional representation	Plurality rule

representation. These constitutional conditions, which are non-existent in the UK, significantly handicap the ability of the government to exploit its state power, unless it does so in tandem with opposition parties.[3]

The article begins with a brief review of studies which have addressed government–opposition relationships, followed by a description of the German and British policy contexts in the run-up to the Maastricht Treaty. Subsequently, government–opposition interaction is analysed over the three dimensions. Finally, the implications of varying levels of co-operation for the parties involved are discussed and lessons drawn.

THE PATTERNING OF GOVERNMENT AND OPPOSITION

Despite the growing interest in inter-party interaction, scant attention has been devoted to the government–opposition relationship. There is a considerable descriptive literature on opposition parties.[4] Much of this material, however, has no direct bearing on government–opposition relationship. Notable exceptions are several discussions of variables that encompass the character and behaviour of an opposition,[5] as well as studies which introduce the strategic interaction between government and opposition as a central property of the party system.[6]

A refreshing development was proposed by Strøm who advanced a rational choice theory of minority government formation based on two explanatory variables, the potential influence of parliamentary opposition and the decisiveness of elections.[7] Opposition influence, according to Strøm 'measures the benefits of governing (or, more precisely, the policy costs of being in opposition), [and] represents the opportunities for legislative influence open to parliamentary oppositions'.[8] The opposition predicament depends on the internal structure and procedure of parliament. Accordingly, the index which represents the potential influence of the opposition aggregates the following five indicators: the number of standing committees, areas of specialisation, correspondence to ministerial departments, number of committee assignments, and the method of committee-chair distribution.[9] 'A strong and decentralized committee structure offers much better prospects for oppositional influence than the more centralized and less deliberative mode of decision making traditionally found in such parliaments as the British House of Commons'.[10]

Another contribution took into account the institutional development of the European Union.[11] The concept advanced by Maor is that of 'interlinked political markets' which – like the European Parliament and the parliaments of member states – are multiparty systems in which the structure of party competition in one system affects the structure of party competition in another. Maor has argued that parties competing in interlinked political markets are likely to face mounting incentives for government–opposition co-operation.[12] The rationale for this assessment is that, in interlinked markets, party competition in one market may impose significant constraints on party competition in another. One reason for this is that party competition over the dominant dimension is often geared to encompass issues which emerge within society without disrupting the party system. Issues which are generated by an interlinked market (i.e., outside the society) may threaten to disrupt the existing institutional system, destabilise the electorate, or threaten the internal unity of the major parties. These issues, when emerging from an interlinked market, are less susceptible to accommodation by the recipient parties. This constraint shapes the motivation of party leaders in the parliamentary and electoral arenas towards growing co-operation or collusion over impending issues of importance.

The discussion so far indicates that what today defines the research agenda for the topic at hand is the lack of empirical examination of the costs and benefits associated with different modes of government–opposition interaction. To fill this gap, an attempt will be made to account for the variability in government–opposition co-operation in Britain and Germany in the run-up to the Maastricht Treaty. Before turning to this analysis, a few preliminary remarks are in order regarding the policy contexts in these countries during the period under study.

THE POLICY CONTEXT

The policy contexts in Germany and the UK prior to the Maastricht Treaty do not indicate fundamental differences in terms of government and opposition views over European affairs. Differences were recorded, however, within the Conservative Party. In Germany, negotiations between the different parties over the Maastricht Treaty were undertaken shortly after the first all-German elections since 1932. In the 1990 election, the CDU-CSU and the FDP gained 54.8 per cent of the votes (CDU-CSU, 43.8 per cent; FDP, 11 per cent); the SPD, 33.5 per cent (35.7 per cent in western Germany; 24.3 per cent in eastern Germany); the PDS/Left list, 2.4 per cent nationwide but 11.1 per cent in eastern Germany; and the Alliance 90/Greens, 6.1 per cent in eastern Germany. Thus, the number of parties in the new Bundestag increased from four to five following the PDS's success in crossing the electoral threshold. In addition, the merger of the western and eastern branches of the three 'old' parties and, later, the Greens, meant that significant organisational changes had to be made, and eastern leaders had to be allotted positions in the enlarged policy-making units of each party.

Despite the changes produced by these new circumstances, in the early 1990s, 'Bonn's stated objective, which it pursued persistently in the course of the Intergovernmental Conference (IGC) on political union in 1990–91, was the creation of a federal structure in the EC, capable [...] of accommodating a more powerful united Germany and strong enough to cope with the new daunting demands of the continent in the post-Cold War era'.[13] Generally speaking, the realisation of this dual objective has received considerable support from almost all major collective political actors in Germany, with the exception of half-hearted support from the German *Länder* and criticism on specific details by the SPD. Although the *Länder* supported the move towards European integration, they have attempted to draw the line at further expansion of political integration. According to Schmidt, 'This mirrors the apprehension of the state governments, and most politicians at the state level, that continued European political integration undermines federalism and, thus, destroys the raison d'être of the *Länder*.'[14] Regarding the SPD, criticism was focused on specific details, such as 'regulation of political union and democratization of the European formation',[15] and not on general attitudes to the treaty.[16]

In Britain, when the Maastricht Treaty was debated in the House of Commons in early 1992, the Labour Party opposed it only on the grounds that the Conservative government had demanded that the Social Chapter would be taken out of the draft treaty and placed in a separate protocol to which Britain would not be a signatory. Labour officially supported the treaty on condition that it include the Social Chapter. Near-unanimous support for the treaty was also forthcoming from the Liberals.

However, within the Conservative Party a vocal minority expressed strong opposition to the continuation of European integration. Margaret Thatcher's increasingly strident attacks on European integration's manner of development led in November 1990 to her replacement as leader of the Conservative Party by John Major, but not before she had effectively split the party on the issue.

To contain the havoc in Conservative ranks during the early 1990s, Major was forced to propose policies contradicting those advocated by the Labour Party. Opposing stances were taken, for example, over the convergence criteria, the independence of an European central bank, the primary objective of a central bank, the level of economic policy co-operation, the level of fiscal harmonisation, the question of EC citizenship, the Social Chapter and the powers of the European Parliament.[17] These differences, however, should not be overemphasised; the ratification of the Maastricht Treaty did not feature prominently in the general election of April 1992,[18] and all three main parties supported the Maastricht Bill with Labour criticising the social opt-out.

In the Labour Party, opposition towards integration never totally disappeared within the parliamentary party, with Tony Benn, Peter Shore, Dennis Skinner and Austin Mitchell, among others, remaining unconvinced of the merits of Britain's integration with the rest of Europe. However, 'no one with any real influence in the party's leadership took up the mantle of Euro-opposition throughout the late 1980s and early 1990s'.[19]

To sum up, the policy contexts in Germany and the UK prior to the Maastricht Treaty do not indicate great disparity between government and opposition views. Whereas the German political system saw considerable support by the main political actors for the view taken by Chancellor Kohl's government, the British polity experienced a bitter internal conflict in the Conservative Party which highlighted differences between the government and the opposition over some aspects of the Treaty. These differences should not be overemphasised. The fact that the three main British parties supported the Maastricht Bill (with Labour criticising the social opt-out) would seem to undermine any assertion of fundamental policy differences. However, the policy differences between the British government and the opposition can not be considered secondary to the internal conflicts within the Conservative Party.

DIMENSION I: ESTABLISHMENT OF SITES FOR GOVERNMENT–
OPPOSITION INTERACTION

In the parliamentary democracies of the EU member states it is a condition of governance and scrutiny that national parliaments should be able to debate Union legislative proposals or Treaty amendments before final approval in the EU Council or the IGC. Given that national parliaments themselves have no formal relationship with the Commission and thus no locus for seeking information, government declarations and reports of scrutiny committees together with the vigilance of pressure groups and other affected organisations are the main sources by which MPs can keep abreast of proposals emanating from Brussels. The question is whether these channels alone can ensure that national parliaments in the EU will not be caught unaware of the existence of a particular item of Union legislation.[20]

Five reasons can be advanced to support the claim that, during the period investigated and beforehand, national parliaments were likely to be uninformed about Community legislation. First, the number of documents which move rapidly through the EU Council has been accelerated by the more frequent use of majority voting under the Single European Act. Second, the growing desire on the part of presidencies to secure the passage of as many proposals as possible during their tenure has led to hasty consideration and cramming as the six months expire. Third, proposals re-examined by the Commission (following amendments by the European Parliament) within the deadline imposed by the co-operation procedure has not left sufficient time for response by national parliaments. Fourth, the implications of changes in proposal, whether initiated by the Commission or made by the Council in the course of negotiations, created obstacles for assessment of their importance by scrutiny committees. And fifth, governments have avoided arranging prompt debates in order to prevent the embarrassment of appearing highly divided in public. A classic example is the failure of the British government to arrange a debate in the House of Commons on matters known to be on the Madrid summit agenda. Another case was the lack of a single oral statement by the British government following meetings of the Foreign Affairs Council from June 1988 to June 1989.

In the UK, there were three additional factors which boosted the likelihood that the House of Commons would be kept in the dark regarding a particular item of Community legislation:

(1) British MEPs were hardly incorporated into decision-making processes
   (e.g., as witnesses and specialist advisers) in the House of Commons. By
   the late 1980s and early 1990s British MEPs had no special status at

Westminster and, for almost all practical purposes, they were considered 'strangers'.[21] No Select Committee had ever invited an MEP to become a specialist adviser, nor was it ever reported that an MEP with expert knowledge was asked to give evidence, formally or informally, to a Select Committee. With no cultivation of informal contacts between the House of Commons and the European Parliament, British MPs were deprived of early warnings about proposals still in their formative stage and of the possibility to launch inquiries before the relevant legislation was published in draft form.[22]

(2) British MEPs were also marginalised in the decision-making processes within British parties.[23] Since the European Parliament works largely through party groupings rather than national delegations, the party structures in Westminster would seem to offer the most appropriate conduit for exchanges between members of the House of Commons and MEPs. This potential in the UK has remained largely untapped during the period examined.

(3) Practical difficulties created obstacles in promoting a closer relationship between MPs and MEPs. During the study period, MEPs were facing problems of access to the House of Commons and its facilities due to security reasons. In addition, British MPs wishing to telephone or write to Community institutions had to do so out of their office expense allowance. Furthermore, whereas MEPs calling the House of Commons could do so on an internal government line, the reverse was not possible, the only such line being the office of the United Kingdom Permanent Representative. These difficulties indicate that during the period investigated neither the House of Commons nor the main parties were genuinely committed to the promotion of a closer relationship between themselves and Community institutions as a contribution towards more effective discussion of European matters.

The aforementioned stumbling blocks (i.e., those found in parliaments in EU member states and those relevant to the UK) exacerbate two trade-offs. First, there is trade-off between the need of the national parliament to express its views on Union legislative proposals or amendments of a treaty before they are finally approved, and the risk that it may eventually be approved in a substantially different form. In other words, the earlier in its life a proposal is debated in a national parliament, the greater the risk that eventually it may be approved in substantially different forms. The second trade-off is faced by national governments between, on one hand, conducting a debate too early in the life of a proposal which may lead to concentration on controversial features, which in turn, may be dealt with by negotiation and, on the other, conducting a debate too late, which means that the scope for seeking to accommodate points made by the House may be very limited.

These trade-offs call for heavier use of current parliamentary committee system or the establishment of such committees. By utilising and expanding the committee system, a government could keep members of parliament abreast of developments in the EU bargaining arena and on the policy stance of the government without undermining its bargaining power in the European bargaining arena.

Indeed, calls for a greater use of parliamentary committees or their invocation were voiced both in the UK and Germany. In the UK, the Select Committee on Procedure received two main proposals designed to provide an alternative to the House as a forum for expressing MPs' views on individual items of Community legislation. These ideas entailed the expansion and development of the existing Standing Committee system and the creation of a European Grand Committee.[24]

The official Opposition spokesmen argued for the latter. In their written evidence to the Select Committee on Procedure, they summarised the purpose of a Grand Committee as providing a forum 'which might combine the day to day questioning of Ministers which occurred when we had regular oral statements, the flexibility of the House of Lords Select Committee on European Legislation ... and the necessity of debates on issues which are yet to go to Councils of Ministers'.[25] They hoped that, by meeting monthly, such a committee could fulfil a threefold function of considering specific items of European legislation, hearing ministerial statements, and holding debates on general Communiy issues. An alternative proposal – making greater use of Standing Committees – was presented by a few Conservative MPs. Underlying the case for doing so was the contention that many debates on European documents were held late at night, after ten o'clock, on the floor of the House. It was argued that if these debates were transferred to a Standing Committee, where two-and-a-half hours are available, and if any MP were allowed to attend, debates would be better attended, more serious, and more widely covered by the media.[26]

Additional proposals designed to provide alternatives to the House as the forum for expressing MPs' views on individual items of Community legislation by expanding the role of Select Committees were presented to the Select Committee on Procedure.[27] The first proposal advocated the establishment of a Select Committee on European Affairs whereas the second envisaged the creation of a European Business Sub-Committee for departmentally related Select Committees.[28] The aim of the first proposal was holding ministers to account (by debate and vote) for their actions in the EU Council. These actions grew rapidly due to the evolution and increased use of majority voting. The central concept was that, drawing upon the 'consensual tradition' of the Select Committee system, a Select Committee on European Affairs would be equipped with the power to send for persons, documents and records, thereby becoming the main forum for the consideration of EC business. The second proposal for developing the role of Select Committees in the scrutiny of European legislation was that any departmentally related Select Committee wishing to undertake more systematic examination of European legislation should have the power to appoint a sub-committee of not more than six members for that purpose. The sub-committee would enjoy the usual powers of a Select Committee to summon persons, documents and records, yet the departmentally related committee would determine the priority to be assigned to European business within its overall programme and the extent to which this justified the creation of a sub-committee.

The centerpiece of *the Procedure Committee's Report on The Scrutiny of European Legislation*, published in November 1989, was the recommendation to create five European Standing Committees of ten members each.[29] Their role, according to the report, should have been 'to provide a more structured and effective forum than the floor of the House offers for the *questioning* of Ministers on a particular European document.'[30] The committees were thus conceived as part of the House of Commons legislative function, that is separate from the investigative activities of Select Committees. Consequently, they have not been equipped with powers to summon persons, documents or records. The British government accepted the main thrust of these recommendations but chose to implement them in a form which differed materially from the recommendation. In particular, whereas the committee had suggested five European Standing Committees of ten members each, the government first opted for three committees of ten because of difficulties in finding enough members of parliament to serve on these committees; several weeks later it reduced the number further from three committees to two, with 13 members each. This was, of course, in apparent contradiction to the purported shortage of members. Although the number of committees originally proposed by the government had been cut by a third, the number of members required to fill them had fallen only by four, from 30 to 26.

In the author's opinion, the British government's reluctance to create five European Standing Committees is due to the risk of being defeated in a committee, and because much committee work is concerned with details which cut across party lines, rather than with principles. This implies that its majority in the committee might be smaller than its majority on the floor of the House. Although the fate of the government is not threatened by defeat in a standing committee, the opposition can embarrass the government and force it to use harsh parliamentary measures (e.g., the 'Guillotine') to block attempts by the opposition to delay the government legislative programme at the committee stage.

A similar strategy was followed in Germany by the main government and opposition parties with the formation of a few sites for co-operation. At the outset, before the ratification of the Maastricht Treaty, article 2 of the law of affirmation of the treaties regarding EEC and EURATOM provided the legal basis for the participation of the Bundestag in the formulation process for European laws.[31] According to this clause, the federal government must 'inform the Bundestag and the Bundesrat – on a regular basis – about developments in the Councils of the EEC and EURATOM ... If a decision by one of these councils necessitates a change of German law, or if present laws are affected, the Bundestag and the Bundesrat shall be informed about the actual decision making of the Council.'[32] This requirement, imposed on German governments, stands in stark contrast to the British case wherein the government is only required to inform Parliament about its legislative initiatives and is not obliged to update it on events in the European bargaining arena.

An additional contrast with the British practice is that the Bundestag offers full membership in its European Committee to MEPs. Its *Europa Kommission* was established in 1984 as an independent committee, half of its members being from the Bundestag and half German MEPs. The Kommission was replaced in 1987 by the Sub-Committee for EC Affairs of the Committee on Foreign Affairs which was comprised of 13 members of the Bundestag and 13 members of the European Parliament. German MEPs were also allowed to participate (only in individual cases) in the Committee for EC Affairs which had been established in the Bundesrat in 1957.

In the run-up to the Maastricht Treaty, the Committee on European Affairs was set up. It comprised 44 regular and 44 substitute members, including 11 MEPs in each category. Members of other Bundestag committees were included in this committee, and MEPs were given the right to speak in this committee, but not to vote or to present motions.[33] In addition:

> The European Affairs Committee had competence on European questions for which no other committee was clearly competent, such as: (a) to discuss all proposed amendments to the Treaties; (b) to discuss the institutional affairs of the EC; (c) to act on its right to be informed by the federal government of all government proposals with a European dimension, and in particular to scrutinise government activity closely in the period preceding a meeting of the European Council. Alongside the European Affairs Committee, the Committee

on Budgets and the Committee on Legal and Economic Affairs constituted sub-committees on EC affairs.[34]

Another parliamentary forum which was established in the run-up to the Maastricht Treaty was a special committee, namely, the *Sonderausschuss Europaeische Union/Vertrag von Maastricht*. This forum provided Bundestag members with the opportunity to obtain information regarding developments in the European bargaining plane in the run-up to the Maastricht Treaty. However, its mandate was restricted to matters related to the treaty; indeed, it expired after ratification. Although the committee has not operated on a permanent basis, 'in form and procedure [it did] not differ from the permanent committees [...] as it is usually legislation that is referred to [it]'.[35] The Committee consisted of 39 members of the Bundestag who represented all parties on the basis of proportional representation. The creation of this committee, according to its chairman, Renate Hellwig, took 'nearly one year, from January to September [1991],[because] the FDP did not want it. It was the common opinion of the two big parties to have such a committee'.[36] A key reason underlying the FDP's rejection was stated as: 'we have the [Permanent] Committee for Foreign Affairs [so] we do not need a Special Committee'.[37] In the end, a compromise was achieved with the main parties supporting the creation of the committee. The FDP's support was acquired not without cost, as Gerhart R. Baum, a Liberal member of the Bundestag, explained: 'We demanded a Committee for Cultural Affairs, but neither of the big parties [CDU/CSU and SPD] wanted it, so we reached a compromise to have this committee.'[38]

This compromise reflected the general orientation of German governments, which is derived from their wish not to risk rejection of their proposals. Before submitting a proposal or a bill, the government will have secured majority support, either through majority discipline or because the *Fraktionen* (party groups) will have had the opportunity for amendments in the non-public committee system.[39] 'German politics places high priority on decision-making capacity and constructiveness, which accounts for the majority's emphasis on unity and the opposition's principal willingness to co-operate in lawmaking.'[40] A classic example is the creation of a new special committee, the *Sonderausschuss zum Ratifizierungsgesetz* after the signing of the Maastricht Treaty. Although the PDS/Linke (the Communists and other left-wing groups) categorically opposed the treaty, the final report of this committee was phrased in such a way that the respective points of view of the two sides appeared as if they were the views of the committee itself.[41]

DIMENSION II: INFORMATION EXCHANGE

Information exchange between government and opposition in Britain and Germany differs significantly. In Britain, there is no tradition of inter-party consultation and information exchange. The general view held by Conservatives is, as MP David Howell, the chairman of the Foreign Affairs Committee during 1987–97, notes, 'We inform the world through the Queen's Speech [...] but other than that, very little. When we are going to announce something we give the opposition spokesmen the papers an hour or two in advance. They are not the Government; we do not consult them and they would not consult us.' John Redwood, a Conservative MP and a junior minister at the Department of Trade and Industry from 1990–92 adds:

> An opposition spokesman would probably be given a statement on policy half an hour or an hour before it is made in the House of Commons, on a confidential basis. So they could have some preparation time. But considering their reply, they would not be given days in advance because then they would be informed before Parliament [is], which would not be right in our system.[42]

Given such views, it is hardly surprising that opposition MPs were informed about the Maastricht negotiations only through the regular channels, namely, the debates in Parliament and the Queen's Speech. The various parliamentary committees 'played a relatively unimportant part',[43] and did not discuss any of the drafts leading to the Treaty on European Union. As Graham Ellen, a Labour MP, explains:

> I was a member of the Procedure Committee, which was reviewing the way in which Parliament scrutinises European matters. [In the final document] I put a minority report which shows how irrelevant this process has been; that none of these committees had discussed the Luxembourg draft, the Dutch draft, and the British government positions prior to Maastricht. No one knew the details. No one was allowed to see [Britain's] negotiating position. Even the original documents were not analysed by the committees in charge of European affairs. So, in a sense, all Labour MPs were in ignorance of what was happening in Maastricht in terms of its details. [Consequently], the Conservative and the Labour Party responded on a political basis, on a point-scoring basis. It was political football.[44]

Donald Anderson, a Labour MP, adds:

> There was little or no briefing by the Conservatives. We obviously learned from some of our friends in governments elsewhere, but the scene was changing so rapidly, for example, in terms of the draft

treaties. The drafts put forward by the Dutch had not been translated before they were obsolete and another draft put forward. My clear impression was that we were obtaining information from secondary sources such as our socialist friends [in other member countries]. Our sources of information as an opposition were largely those we created for ourselves.[45]

Faced with similar difficulties, the Liberal Party has utilised its contacts abroad to obtain relevant information. Russell Johnston, the Liberal's European spokesman, explains: 'We had very little information out of the British government. We were able to establish some of the things that were going on via our German contacts, particularly our contacts with the FDP.'[46]

Indeed, the 'German contacts' were highly informed about the position of the German government during the Maastricht negotiations, as well as on the bargaining position of other member-state governments. In the Bundestag, the main forum for information exchange was the Foreign Affairs Committee and the new special committee dealing with the Maastricht negotiations. Although the main discussions and votes took place in the former, the importance of the special committee should not be underestimated. Foreign Minister, Hans-Dietrich Genscher attended many of the Committee's meetings, and his junior minister, Ursula Seiler-Albring, all of them.[47] It can be argued, therefore, that this committee served as an arena wherein opposition parties were informed in detail on the negotiations, including the bargaining positions of all member states.

Given that there were no fundamental differences among the main German parties during the Maastricht negotiations, it is important to examine the role of the Joint Mediation Committee, which is a joint body of the Bundestag and the Bundesrat, as prescribed by the German constitution. In the run-up to the Maastricht Treaty, the increasing transfer of *Länder* competences to the EC level led the *Länder* to demand more formal involvement in the information, negotiations and legislative aspects of the EC policy process and a more institutionalised procedure for their participation in EC matters.[48] The *Länder* also complained that the extension of Community authority to areas which, under the German constitution, were exercised by them, eroded their independence and legislative powers.[49] As the *Länder* were not represented in the Council of Ministers, the main policy-making body of the Community, the federal government was making decisions in the Council which extended beyond its internal powers under the Basic Law. Consequently, the *Länder* demanded the right to participate in internal discussions and the decision-making process related to EC matters.[50]

Through the Bundesrat, the governments of the Länder were able to press for involvement in defining Germany's position *vis-à-vis* those areas of EU competence that touch upon the *Länder*'s realm of authority. According to the SPD's Foreign Affairs Spokesman, Karsten Voigt, 'We had in-depth informal and formal talks with the government on the level of the Bundesrat, on the level of the Joint Mediation Committee, and on the level of government officials and ministerial departments'.[51] Subsequently, the German *Länder* obtained a constitutional amendment which obliges the federal government to consult the Bundesrat in all areas where the interests of the *Länder* are affected; in those areas which are the exclusive competence of the *Länder*, the government could delegate its right to sit in the Council to a representative of the Länder appointed by the Bundesrat.[52]

Additional non-public channels of information exchange utilised in the run-up to the Maastricht Treaty were the 'normal meetings between the chancellor and the opposition leader every four to five weeks without any press attending',[53] the meetings taking place two to four times a year between the minister presidents of the 16 *Länder* with the Chancellor and the Foreign Minister, which are commonly known as 'chimney talks' (*Kamingespräche*),[54] and the meetings every Wednesday in the Standing Committee of the Bundesrat between the minister presidents of the 16 *Länder* and the state minister in the chancellor's office (Anton Pfeifer) during which they are informed of the key cabinet decisions.[55]

DIMENSION III: INCENTIVE MANAGEMENT

The British state is highly centralised – there is a central governing authority located in the government, directed by the prime minister – and the government's parliamentary majority provides it with the power to enact laws. To achieve parliamentary majorities, parties must win general elections. The electoral arena wherein 'the winner takes all' is, therefore, a decisive arena for government–opposition interaction. Due to party discipline, the prime minister can often count upon his majority in the House of Commons to support the government's policies. Although absence of a written constitution puts great formal power in the hands of the incumbent government, the presence of a strong opposition party ensures that the government has to act cautiously – not because of any veto the opposition can impose in Parliament, but rather because of potential troubles at the next general election. The parliamentary arena is, therefore, not a decisive one for co-operation between government and opposition.[56] Not surprisingly, British opposition MPs or individuals associated with opposition parties are not incorporated into the activities of the executive branch.[57] This also occurred in the run-up to the Maastricht Treaty. None of the opposition MPs were involved, for example, in the explanation of the government's viewpoint in the European Parliament and national parliaments.

By contrast, the German state is a federal system in which opposition parties normally control *Länder* governments. *Länder* governments not only are accorded a measure of constitutional protection, they also play an important part in delivery of public services and structuring of policies in some areas. Efforts by the governing parties at the center to impose policies or change voters' views evoke strong reactions at the periphery. Not surprisingly, a tradition has developed whereby opposition MPs or party members are incorporated into the activities of the executive branch. Formal incorporation is well documented in the area of internal security whereas informal co-operation is evident in parliamentary committees. In addition, until 1985, former opposition MPs or those associated with the main opposition party were nominated by the German chancellor for one slot in the European Commission and another in the European Court of Justice (ECJ). In 1985, this tradition was modified; today only the latter position is available for the opposition.

In the run-up to the Maastricht Treaty, SPD Foreign Affairs Spokesman, Karsten Voigt, co-operated closely with the ministerial team at the Foreign Office: 'A fortnight ago, the CDU spokesman in the Foreign Affairs Committee and I made a one-day visit to the European Parliament to talk with the different parties ... and expressed the German view concerning specific points. I also visited the French and British parliaments.'[58]

Although the implications of such co-operation between government and opposition should not be overemphasised, it still provides an indication of the marginalisation of party voting in the Bundestag because party ties are overridden by opposition co-operation. The practice of filling one-half-minus-one of the committee chairs with members of the opposition creates incentives for the opposition to co-govern. Parliamentary committee chairmanship is not automatically a governmental task; in some countries which lack a consensual tradition (e.g., Italy, Israel), opposition committee chairmen usually play a strictly anti-government role. In consensual contexts, however, the role of opposition members, who either hold formal positions in parliamentary committees or take part in governmental tasks, reflects a basic congruence of interests between the majority and the main opposition party. The incorporation of opposition members into the governmental mechanism in the run-up to the Maastricht Treaty provides a classic example of such congruence of interests.

IMPLICATIONS FOR THE PARTIES INVOLVED

Formal co-operation between government and opposition is a rather rare phenomenon in modern politics. However, informal co-operation – as was recorded in Germany over the three dimensions examined – brought about an outcome which was compatible with the interests of the parties involved. The Treaty on European Union and the concomitant constitutional changes were adopted by an overwhelming majority in the Bundestag on 2 December 1992. There were 543 votes in favor of the Maastricht Treaty, eight opposed and 17 abstentions; only the PDS voted against it. The constitutional changes were approved by a vote of 547 to 18. The Bundestag also passed joint resolutions (*Entschliessungantrag*) supporting both a Europe close to the citizens and able to act (*handlungsfähig*), and European Monetary Union. On 18 December 1992, the Bundesrat unanimously approved the Treaty and the constitutional changes. Neither the votes nor the preceding debates have resulted in resignations among members of the party élite.

In the electoral arena, the CDU/CSU/FDP coalition was restored to power for a fourth term in the national elections of October 1994. The CDU/CSU lost 25 seats (from 319 in 1990 to 294) and the combined strength of the coalition was only ten seats more than the combined opposition parties. Despite losing, the SPD fared much better than it had in the 1990 elections, gaining 13 seats (from 239 in 1990 to 252 in 1994). During and after the campaign, none of the main opposition parties supported a referendum over the treaty; inasmuch as they were consulted in the process, they were considered sharing responsibility for its outcome.

By contrast, in Britain the lack of co-operation between government and opposition (among other factors) has produced damaging consequences for the Conservative Party as well as for Labour. At the outset of the period under consideration, Major's government had a tiny majority in the House of Commons over European affairs, due to a vocal minority of Eurosceptics.[59] Co-operation with a handful of opposition members, whether from the Labour Party or the Ulster Unionists, could have ensured a majority in the House sufficient to guarantee the passage of European-affairs legislation. This, in turn, could have convinced the Eurosceptics in the Conservative Party that their struggle was doomed, thereby marginalising their room for manoeuvre as well as their influence.

At the parliamentary level, an unprecedented crisis occurred on 4 November 1992, when the government depended on the votes of 19 Liberal Democrat MPs to usher the Maastricht 'paving bill' through the House of Commons. Twenty-one Tory backbenchers resisted all the whips' efforts and joined Labour in voting against the bill, with six other Tories abstaining.[60] This level of dissent is remarkable, given that the vote was clearly a 'confidence' issue for the government – had it been defeated, John Major's position as a prime minister would have been significantly undermined. Major's desperate attempt to delay the third reading of the Maastricht Bill until May 1993, in order to gain the necessary votes, undermined the cohesion of the Conservative Party, and caused immense political damage at the highest levels of the party and government.

The fiercely fought battles within the party over European integration prompt a comparison with historic Conservative battles over the repeal of the Corn Laws in the 1840s and over free trade versus imperial protection in the early 1900s. The reverberations of the Conservative Party's internal conflicts over European policy – like the two earlier struggles – stretched over many years, with the more recent conflict leading to a decline in the party's image as a 'united and loyal organisation whose defence of the British state and of British interests abroad is not destabilised by intra-party fractures'.[61] This, in turn, contributed to the decline of its electoral strength from 57.8 per cent in 1987 to 51.6 per cent in the 1992 general election.

The Labour Party suffered its fourth successive general election defeat on 9 April 1992, making a change in the party's leadership inevitable.[62] In addition, the party experienced a rebellion led by traditional anti-marketeers such as Peter Shore and Brian Gould, who were joined by those critical of the EMU provisions. The Labour revolt faded at the annual party conference in September 1992, the one casualty being the resignation of Brian Gould from the shadow cabinet. Subsequently, the Labour Party conference overwhelmingly endorsed Maastricht as 'the best agreement that can currently be achieved'.[63]

To conclude, the analysis has clearly demonstrated that the creation of parliamentary committees *per se* is not sufficient to influence legislative policy output. Although committees are commonly one locus of power in legislatures, the other is typically government and opposition. Attempts to comprehend government–opposition interaction in legislatures should, therefore, take into account the ways these actors utilise parliamentary committees as sites for co-ordination of activities. In Germany, when a newly created committee was utilised in this way alongside the operation of the relevant permanent committees, the government successfully avoided embarrassing decisions by plenary majorities.

NOTES

This research was supported by the Konard Adenauer Stiftung. An earler version was delivered as a paper to the conference, 'Developments in Europe in the Aftermath of the Cold War' (Jerusalem, Nov. 1997) which was sponsored by the Konard Adenauer Stiftung and organised by the Helmut Kohl Institute for European Studies. For useful suggestions I thank Emanuel Gutmann, Gabi Sheffer Reuven Hazan, and Antje Naujoks.

1. H. Hegeland and I. Mattson, 'The Swedish Riksdag and the EU: Influence and Openess', in M. Wiberg (ed.) *Trying to Make Democracy Work: The Nordic Parliaments and the European Union* (Södertlje: Bank of Sweden Tercentenary Fdn and Gidlunds Förlag 1997) p.74.
2. The combined analysis of institutional and behavioural dimensions indicates the presumption

concerning the compatibility of neo-institutionalism and behaviouralism. See M. Maor 'Party Competition in Interlinked Political Markets: The European Union and Its Member States', in K. Dowding and D. King (eds.) *Preferences, Institutions and Rational Choice* (Oxford: Clarendon Press 1995) pp.114–34.

3. P. Dunleavy, *Democracy, Bureaucracy and Public Choice* (Hemel Hempstead: Harvester Wheatsheaf 1991).

4. See the following papers delivered at the conference entitled 'The Repositioning of Opposition', University of Reading, England (April 1997): J. Boyd, 'Opposition in Japan'; C. Clapham, 'Opposition in Tropical Africa'; N. Johnson, 'Opposition in the British Political System'; P.G. Lewis, 'The Repositioning of Opposition in East-Central Europe'; A. Pizzorno, 'Opposition in Italy'; N.W. Polsby, 'Political Opposition in the United States'; J.E. Spence, 'Opposition in South Africa'. See also G. Ionescu and I. de Madariaga, *Opposition* (London: Watts 1968); E. Kolinsky (ed.) *Political Oppositions in Western Europe* (London: Croom Helm 1988); G. Rodan (ed.) *Political Oppositions in Industrializing States* (Sidney: Routledge 1996); L. Shapiro (ed.) *Political Oppositions in One-Party States* (London: Macmillan 1972); R.L. Tokes (ed.) *Opposition in Eastern Europe* (Oxford: OUP 1979).

5. R.A. Dahl (ed.) *Political Opposition in Western Democracies* (New Haven, CT: Yale UP 1966); O. Kirchheimer, 'The Waning of Opposition', in R.C. Macridis and B.E. Brown (eds.) *Comparative Politics* (Homewood: Dorsey 1964) pp.280–90; O. Kirchheimer, 'The Vanishing Opposition', in Dahl (*supra*) pp.237–59; idem. 'The Transformation of the Western European Party System', in J. LaPalombara and M. Weiner (eds.) *Political Parties and Political Development* (Princeton UP 1966) pp.177–200; K. von Beyme, 'Parliamentary Opposition in Europe', in E. Kolinsky (ed.) *Opposition in Western Europe* (London: Croom Helm 1987) pp.30–49; G. Smith, 'Party and Protest: The Two Faces of Opposition in Western Europe', in idem, pp.49–73; J. Blondel, 'Political Opposition in the Contemporary World', Paper delivered in a conference on The Repositioning of Opposition (note 4).

6. M. Maor and G. Smith, 'On the Structure of Party Competition: The Impact of Maverick Issues,', in T. Bryder (ed.) *Party Systems, Party Behaviour and Democracy* (Copenhagen Political Studies Press 1993) pp.40–51; M. Maor and G. Smith, 'Government–Opposition Relationships as a Systemic Property: A Theoretical Framework', Paper presented at the annual ECPR Joint Session, Leiden, April 1993.

7. K. Strøm, *Minority Government and Majority Rule* (Cambridge: CUP 1990).

8. Ibid. p.70.

9. Ibid. p.71.

10. Ibid. p.70.

11. M. Maor, 'Party Competition in Interlinked Political Markets: The European Union and Its Member States', in K. Dowding and D. King (eds.) *Preferences, Institutions and Rational Choice* (Oxford: Clarendon Press 1995) pp.114–34.

12. Ibid. p.124.

13. R. Beuter, 'Germany and the Ratification of the Maastricht Treaty', in F. Laursen (ed.) *The Ratification of the Maastricht Treaty: Issues, Debates and Future Implications* (Dordrecht: M. Nijhoff 1994) p.87.

14. M.N. Schmidt, 'The Grand Coalition State', in J. Colomer (ed.) *Political Institutions in Europe* (London: Routledge 1996) p.89. In the parliamentary debate on the Maastricht Treaty, and in concomitant legislation, the *Länder* gained substantial concessions from the federal government.

15. 'SPD auf Distanz zu Maastricht', *Die Welt*, 6 March 1992.

16. R. Moeller, 'The German Social Democrats', in J. Gaffney (ed.) *Political Parties and the European Union* (London: Routledge 1996) pp.44–5.

17. M. Maor, *Political Parties and Party Systems: Comparative Approaches and the British Experience* (London: Routledge 1997).

18. A. Duff, 'Ratification', in A. Duff, J. Pinder and R. Pryce (eds.) *Maastricht and Beyond: Building the European Union* (London; Routldge 1994) p.54.

19. S. George and D. Haythorne, 'The British Labour Party', in Gaffney (note 16) p.118.

20. For the link between national parliaments and decision making in the EU, see T. Bergman, 'National Parliaments and EU Affairs Committees: Notes on Empirical Variation and

Competing Explanations', *Journal of European Public Policy* 4/3 (1997) pp.373–87.

21. House of Commons, *The Scrutiny of European Legislation*, Fourth Report from the Select Committee on Procedure, Vol.I (London: HMSO 1989) p.xxxv.
22. By contrast, the House of Lords during that period maintained close links with various Community institutions. From time to time, evidence was taken from *Rapporteurs* of European Parliament Committees, from Commissioners, and from heads of Commission directorates. See House of Commons (note 21) p.xxviii.
23. P.D. Webb, 'The United Kingdom', in R.S. Katz and P. Mair (eds.) *Party Organisations: A Data Handbook on Party Organisations in Western Democracies 1960–90* (London: Sage 1992) pp.837–70.
24. Standing Committees exist to consider legislation. Each committee is normally made up of 16 to 50 members, chosen roughly in proportion to party strength in the House of Commons, and in accordance with their knowledge of the piece of legislation to be considered.
25. Cited in House of Commons (note 21) p.xxii.
26. Ibid.
27. Select Committees are appointed to inquire into aspects of executive activity. Departmentally-related Select Committees, for example, are charged with examining expenditure, administration and policy of government departments.
28. House of Commons (note 21) p.xxvii
29. P. Bains, 'The Evolution of the Scrutiny System in the House of Commons', in P. Giddings and G. Drewry (eds.) *Westminster and Europe: The Impact of the European Union on the Westminster Parliament* (Houndmills: Macmillan 1996) pp.49–90.
30. House of Commons, *Review of European Standing Committees*, First Report from the Select Committee on Procedure (London: HMSO 1991) p.vii.
31. Vom 27.7.1957 (BGBI II S. 753).
32. Cited in S. Hölscheidt, ''Parlamentarische Mitwirkung bei der europäischen Rechtssetzung', *Kritische Vierteljahresschrift für Gesetzgebung und Rechtswissenschaft* 77/4 (1995) p.416 (my translation).
33. Ibid. pp.405–29.
34. D. Millar, 'Scrutiny of European Community Affairs by National Parliaments', in Giddings and Drewry (note 29) p.343.
35. N. Johnson, 'Committees in the German Bundestag', in J.D. Lees and M. Shaw (eds.) *Committees in Legislatures: A Comparative Analysis* (Oxford: Martin Robertson 1979) p.113.
36. Renate Hellwig, interview with the author, Bonn, Dec.1992.
37. Gerhart R. Baum, interview with the author, Bonn, Dec. 1992.
38. Ibid.
39. W. Steffani, 'Parties (Parliamentary Groups) and Committees in the Bundestag', in U. Thaysen, R.H. Davidson and R.G. Livingston (eds.) *The US Congress and German Bundestag* (Boulder, CO: Westview Press 1990) pp.273–96; W. Steffani and J.-P. Gabriel, 'Bundesrepublik Deutschland', in *Regierungsmehrheit und Opposition in den Staaten der EG* (Opladen: Leske + Budrich 1991) pp.127–55.
40. S.S. Schüttemeyer, 'Hierarchy and Efficiency in the Bundestag: The German Answer for Institutionalizing Parliament', in G.W. Copeland and S.C. Patterson (eds.) *Parliaments in the Modern World: Changing Institutions* (Ann Arbor, MI: U. of Michigan Press 1994) p.44.
41. G. Verheugen, 'Die Arbeit des Sonderausschusses "Europäische Union"', *Zeitschrift für Gesetzgebung* 8 (1993) pp.164–7.
42. John Redwood, interview with the author, London, Feb. 1993.
43. R. Ware, 'The Road to Maastricht: Parliament and the Intergovernmental Conferences of 1991', in Giddings and Drewry (note 29) p.245.
44. Graham Ellen, interview with the author, London, Feb. 1993.
45. Donald Anderson, interview with the author, London, Feb. 1993.
46. Russell Johnston, interview with the author, London, Feb. 1993.
47. Hellwig (note 36).
48. S. Bulmer and W. Patterson, 'West Germany's Role in Europe: "Man-Mountain" or "Semi-Gulliver"?', *Journal of Common Market Studies* 28/1 (1989) pp.95–117.

49. R. Hrbek, 'The German Länder and EC Integration', *Journal of European Integration*, 15/2–3 (1992) pp.173–93.
50. R. Beuter, 'Germany and the Ratification of the Maastricht Treaty', in Laursen (note 13) pp.87–112.
51. Karsten Voigt, interview with the author, Bonn, Dec. 1992.
52. R. Corbett, *The Treaty of Maastricht* (London: Longman 1993).
53. Klaus Francke, interview with the author, Bonn, Dec.1992.
54. Florian Gerster, interview with the author, Bonn, Dec. 1992.
55. Ibid.
56. On co-operation between government and opposition in the electoral arena, see Maor (note 17) pp.56–62.
57. However, former Labour MPs have been nominated by Conservative prime ministers to positions in the European Commission (e.g., Bruce Millan, Neil Kinnock).
58. Voigt (note 51).
59. D. Baker, A. Gamble and S. Ludlam, 'Whips or Scorpions? The Maastricht Vote and the Conservative Party', *Parliamentary Affairs* 45 (1993) pp.151–66.
60. Ibid.
61. Baker *et al.* (note 59) p.164.
62. R.K. Alderman and N. Carter, 'The Labour Party Leadership and Deputy Leadership Elections of 1992', *Parliamentary Affairs* 46/1 (1993) pp.49–65.
62. Cited in Corbett (note 52) p.68.

Socialism in France: An Appraisal

JOHN GAFFNEY*

The Mitterrand Era. Edited by A. DALEY. Basingstoke: Macmillan, 1996. Pp.xiv + 285, index, £45.00 (cloth). ISBN 0-333-63265-6.

France during the Socialist Years. Edited by G. RAYMOND. Aldershot: Dartmouth, 1994. Pp.xi + 278, £41.50 (cloth). ISBN I85521-5187.

The Politics of Fun: Cultural Policy and Debate in Contemporarv France. Edited by D. LOOSELEY. Oxford: Berg, 1997. Pp.xv + 279, biblio, index. £34.95 (cloth); £14.95 (paper). ISBN 1-85973013-2 and -153-8.

Throughout the 1980s and into the 1990s, the French Left's tenure of the presidency and government were rather like the Conservative years in the UK: they seemed endless. Now, as the years fall away, is, perhaps, the time properly to assess the Socialist years, for on this subject the passions, even of political scientists, ran high when analysing events as they happened. Two important things to retain, however, from the immediacy of lived experience are how unexpected and how overwhelming was the Left's victory in 1981, and how, therefore, a bizarre combination of the unexpected and a stampede of expectations (by the public, by the party, and by observers) dominated the first years of Socialist rule, and so shaped the period as a whole. Even as late as 1980, it was still the received view that the Fifth Republic had, as it were, been designed to keep the Right in power and the Left, especially a radical left, in the wings. The mechanism was seen as being so sophisticated, with its complex interplay of legislative and executive imperatives and the consequences of these for both political organisation and political mobilisation, that even when the Left *almost* took power within the Republic, as in 1978, the pressures upon its component elements would be too great, and disperse its resolve. All the Right needed

* Keele University

West European Politics, Vol.21, No.3 (July 1998), pp.208–213
PUBLISHED BY FRANK CASS, LONDON

to do was update itself and modernise from time to time. Perhaps if the Left also became 'modern' under the still young, and darling of the opinion polls, Michel Rocard; but then the Communists with their 20 per cent of the electorate would not buy it, and the Socialist Party leader, François Mitterrand, still held the reins of power in the party: it looked as if President Giscard d'Estaing would lead France through the 1980s, alongside his international colleagues Margaret Thatcher and Helmut Kohl. Then, in 1981, the unexpected happened, and Socialism – radical, utopian, Marxian, if not in some areas revolutionary – swept into and throughout the corridors of presidential and then parliamentary power.

It was not of course completely accidental. In fact, to the extent that contingency is part of politics it was not accidental at all; what Mitterrand had called the Left's 'sociological majority' had been building up for a generation, but the nature of the radical rhetorical supply was – in order to hold the faction-ridden Left together throughout the years of opposition – far greater than either public demand or, more importantly in the long run, the ability to deliver. One should see the 1981–83 period when the Socialists began to implement, then reverse, policy initiatives (for nationalisations, wage rises, and increased public spending; read: rocketing unemployment and rocketing inflation) as akin to the period it takes an ocean liner to slow down, turn and change direction..

The notion that there was an alternative to what happened next: pinning the franc to the deutschmark, and French fortunes to Germany, and then to Europe, gradually diminishing state intervention and subsidies, modernising industry, responding to the internationalisation, then globalisation of national economies and, therefore, hastening the end of the 'French exception' in a range of areas, as well as, of course, the hopeless idea of 'socialism in one country', was perhaps to be expected on the part of some of the French Socialist Party (PS) factions and its politicised trade-union support. That researchers should share the same view is more surprising, and obscures the true and lasting significance of the Left's coming to power in the Fifth Republic, along with the interesting questions this raises.

Anthony Daley's *The Mitterrand Era,* is divided into three main parts: governance, the economy, and political mobilisation. It brings together French specialists and some of the leading American scholars on French politics. The essays are informed and provide detail and interpretation that now, nearly two decades later, are useful to the student of the period (the main thrust of the book being on the early years of the Socialist government). The book suffers, however, from a series of defects which relate essentially to how the editor and authors (some went willingly, some were pushed) see politics in general, or rather these politics, once so full of promise for the leftist imagination: governance means only constraint upon, rather than opportunity for, governance; the economy means the overwhelming imperatives of capitalism; mobilisation, how it was neutered. In spite of real quality – the essay by Ross on the role of the presidency is good; the detailed illustrative discussion by Rand Smith informative – the volume is a classic case of a scholarly élite of political science being cross with political actors for not fulfilling their own expectations. The essential disappointment centres upon the idea that the Socialist government abandoned its mission and broke its promises, and underlying why it did so lies a kind of handwringing sense of affront at the right roads forsaken, strait gates missed, and temptations leading off into the thickets of opportunism and betrayal. Not all the authors see it this way. Schmidt on the new managers keeps her head while many about her fail to keep theirs: Groux and Mouriaux are preoccupied with the question of significant trade-union influence in a country where the unions, even then, were extremely weak.

There is little editorial and authorial doubt generally, however, that within two years, by 1983, the experiment was over, the true path lost, the bright shining moment gone; whereas, in reality, the interesting part had just begun. In spite of some analyses of the later period, the real emphasis in the book is on the victory and subsequent loss of potential, rather than on the 'era' as a whole. The book, and especially the editor's contribution, abounds in clichés, especially those of the Left: true reality is *behind* the politics, while façades and *trompe l'oeil* must be torn down; if only the government had done this or that, because 'everything seemed possible': imaginations were captured, radical programmes promised, dramatic shifts occurred, then crises erupted, hopes were dashed, with the 'wily' manipulative Mitterrand always there in the background like a master puppeteer pulling strings. The book also, Cassandra-like and without evidence, claims that the subsequent misfortunes of the Left in the 1990s (the book was published before the 1997 victory) were the consequences of this lack of faith and resolve back in 1981–83.

The preoccupation with the 'U-turn' of 1983 echoes the historians who have searched for when the Revolution of 1789 (or 1917) began to deviate from the true path. Mercifully, in the 1980s no one was guillotined; in fact, Socialist path or not, the list of the Left's achievements is long indeed. And, thanks to many people, not least François Mitterrand who, among other things, abolished the death penalty, the Left in power should not be seen as an experiment which went wrong, but as the first time in French history (really) that the Left held and exercised power for a period of time beyond a couple of weeks. The problem, however, with the approach of Daley's book, like so many dealing with the Left's tenure of power, runs deeper than questions of leftist disappointment: the approach is simply misplaced. For the interesting question is not what the Fifth Republic did to the Left, but the opposite, what the Left did to the Republic, and what the consequences of this were upon political choices and subsequent political organisation. Such an approach would enable us to see the politics of the Fifth Republic as through a prism: in this way several of the chapters would have been cast in a more illuminating manner, and environmentalism, women's issues, the Communists, immigration, factionalism within the presidential Socialist Party would then be seen in terms of their interdependence with the institutions and highly-sophisticated political culture of the Fifth Republic, rather than as the tattered casualties of a failed Socialist experiment.

Indeed, as regards the PS, such a view was always misplaced. It is more helpful to see 1981 in comparison and contrast with 1958 (rather than, say, as yet another failed Popular Front): the coming to power of another section of the French political élite, and its influence upon political institutions and mores, and its relation to the party system. Instead, the final chapters point to, and mourn, the passing of leftist political mobilisation (it is assumed that we know what mobilisation is) and wonder what might be the condition of its renewal. The Left's tenure of power for 14 years from 1981 is a highly complex historical, political, institutional and cultural phenomenon where personnel, policy, discourse, ideas and contingency interacted with the ambivalent institutional structure of the Fifth Republic. In spite of the scholars and the scholarship which inform many of the essays in this volume, the organising principle underlying this book limits their value.

If Daley's book is driven by a concern with what the Socialists did not do, Raymond is concerned with what they did. *France during the Socialist Years* is organised into three parts, politics, culture, and society. In the first part, the contributors deal with the interactive responses of politics and political institutions over time: Gaffney (the same!) on the shifts in presidential language; Drake on foreign-policy shifts; Cole on shifts within the party; Raymond on shifts within the party system. The following two sections, on culture and on society, are wide-ranging, from the workmanlike survey of Socialist social policy (Hantrais) to the status of intellectuals (Flower), the blasphemy laws, in particular as they pertain to cinema (Harrison), the education issue as portrayed in the press (Collier), cultural policy (Looseley, see below), and immigration policy (Shields). Such a wide range also means an incomplete range, of course, and the relative tightness of the first part of the book gives way to a not entirely successful interdisciplinary experiment as the book progresses.

One wonders today whether some of the topics discussed would have been better replaced with some of the more substantive issues discussed in Daley's volume. It is true that Raymond's volume is more attentive than Daley's to the sweep of the whole decade than to the early upheavals. In fact, these two books could well be read in conjunction, because if Daley concentrates too exclusively on considerations of political economy, Raymond does not concentrate enough on the hard economic realities. Taken together these two books cover much of the experience of the Socialists in government. By design, however, neither can address other pertinent issues, an understanding of which is crucial for an overall view of the decade. If one were to identify the three main developments of the period 1981–95, they would be the rise of the extreme right, the impact of Europe on domestic policy and the internal dynamics of French socialism. The first is referred to only obliquely because the books have taken government as their focus. The irony is the greater in that Shields, one of the UK's specialists on the extreme right, is a contributor to Raymond's volume. The second two get some good treatment but not nearly enough. Overall, neither of these books are appropriate texts for a course on France in the 1980s; both serve, however, as interesting additions to a reading list on French politics, particularly when read together as differing interpretations of how to comprehend the Left's long tenure of power.

Looseley's book, *The Politics of Fun* , should be on everybody's shelf. It covers the same period as the other two books, but looks at one ministry, Culture, and the career of, essentially, one person, the colourful Jack Lang. Looseley does everything a good book should: his discussion of culture as a theoretical concept (rather, dilemma), as a history, and as an endeavour, is illuminating of French cultural policy from the 1930s, through the war years, the Liberation, the Malraux years, and the coming to power of the Left (i.e. the 1968 generation) in 1981. His evocation of the underlying similarities and differences between different phases, the tortuous unfolding of the dilemmas of culture as high art versus culture as the artistic expression of a people, of the state as a facilitator of culture (from providing mobile libraries to encouraging local initiatives) versus the state as the guardian of the patrimony, of the relation of Paris to the provinces, and where all the money is going to come from, as well as his analysis of politics as planning versus politics as a series of 'cock-ups', is excellent.

The bulk of the book covers Lang's ministry (even when the Left was out of government, though not the presidency, between 1986 and 1988, he was still regarded as the 'true' minister of culture). In many ways, a study of the Socialists' tenure of power is incomplete without a study of Lang and his ministry. His style, his outspoken interventionism, his highly personal profile and his ringing poetry (sometimes inspiring, sometimes excruciating, especially to the more reserved Anglo-Saxon ear) in many ways reflect the overall Socialist experience of government: crusading, personalised, adaptive, and locked into both the populism and élitism of a modern democracy.

Lang's culture, moreover, was not 'cut off' from the rest of government and the real world of economic policy but was, in part, deliberately driven, for better or for worse, by economic and technological change; across the range of audio-visual innovation for example, France became an inspiration. Even its pop music became finally worth listening to, in part because of the French state's contradictory and fascinating relationship to French culture – which is at its best when it is open to other cultures. In many ways, 'culture' was the Socialist experience that went unquestionably right. As both an analogy of the fortunes of the Left in the 1980s, and as a riveting story of the interrelationships of policy, vision, personality, change, continuity and opportunity within one aspect of the Mitterrand era, Looseley's book illuminates the period as a whole. It is good news that it is available in paperback.

Book Reviews

Bicameralism. By GEORGE TSEBELIS and JEANNETTE MONEY. Cambridge: Cambridge University Press, 1997. Pp.xiv + 250, biblio, index. £14.95 (paper). ISBN 0-521-58972-X.

Bicameralism matters. Existing studies of legislative instructions have substantially underestimated or totally neglected the importance of second chambers even when dealing with truly bicameral systems. Therefore, the majority of such studies are neither useful nor reliable for the formulation of satisfactory generalisations. Tsebelis and Money ground their analysis on an excellent, extensive review of the historical and geographical dimension of bicameralism. They indicate that the justification of bicameralism is not solely based on federalism, on territorial representation, but on different criteria having to do with the nature and the desired quality of legislation. Next they provide a lot of material necessary to grasp the many differences existing in the composition, role, functions, and power of second chambers. Especially useful is their dense and complex table containing all the relevant information on the mode of selection of the upper house, the way final decisions are made on non-financial and financial legislation and on who makes the final decision in case of unsolved disagreements. Their goal consists in identifying and describing the different methods utilised to reconcile the diversity of opinions and votes between the lower and the upper houses. Who breaks the mediation system between the houses and how this rupture is produced remain major questions and major issues for bicameral systems. Because, usually, the mediation system comes to an end and the differences are reconciled through a conference committee, the authors explore the way conference committees are created, the type of power they have, the voting rules they employ and the consequences they entail. In order to do this, they shape their predictive theory around three concepts: the *core*, that is 'the set of points that cannot be defeated by the application of the decision-making rules'; the *uncovered set*, that is 'the set of points that cannot be defeated directly and indirectly by any other point'; and the *tournament equilibrium set*, defined as the smallest set within which legislators resort to a 'co-operative recontracting process'.

Their major contention is that 'bicameralism promotes stability by making changes from the status quo more difficult'. If and when changes occur, they attribute it to a process of 'both co-operation and conflict between the two chambers'. Here one finds the two dimensions of bicameralism: the efficient and the political, or redistributive. 'The *efficient* dimension recognises that the two legislative houses have common interests', while the *political* dimension recognises that 'different interests or preferences may be expressed in the two legislative bodies'. Then, intercameral bargaining becomes indispensable to avoid the stalemate of the political system.

The outcome is, of course, affected by several rules governing the process. However, Tsebelis and Money argue that most outcomes are predictable not only on the basis of the knowledge of those rules, but also more precisely when impatience and uncertainty are correctly evaluated. *Impatience* refers to the urgency manifested by one chamber to come to a decision; *uncertainty* refers to the lack of knowledge by one chamber of the other chamber's degree of impatience and/or position. Their intermediate conclusion is that 'second chambers alter legislative outcomes even if they do not have the power to veto legislation and even if they have the same composition as the first chamber'.

They test their model at some length comparing its predictive strength with that of other available models. The testing ground is offered by several bills in the case of the semi-presidential regime of the Fifth French Republic and less systematically by some selected bills in such diversified political and bicameral systems as Germany, Japan, Switzerland, the USA and the European Parliament.

In their formal analysis and concrete testing, Tsebelis and Money offer many important insights into the way bicameral systems work and why. They are able convincingly to reject a famous quotation from the Abbé Sièyes who maintained that 'if the second chamber agrees with the first, it is useless, and if not, it is bad': neither is the case. They also show that second chambers do make an impact on the legislative process that does not simply consist in slowing it down. It seems less clear whether they would go so far as to claim that the existence of second chambers significantly improves the quality of legislation. In my opinion, one question remains outstanding. Do second chambers succeed, through their existence and their activities, in taking legislation closer to the preferences of the voters than if only one chamber had proceeded to the passage of that legislation? It is one of the many merits of this excellent book, densely documented, carefully crafted and intelligently argued, that it raises this important democratic question.

GIANFRANCO PASQUINO
University of Bologna
Bologna Center of the Johns Hopkins

The New Challenge of Direct Democracy. By IAN BUDGE. Cambridge: Polity Press, 1996. Pp.viii + 198, biblio, index. £12.95 (paper). ISBN 0-7456-1765-4.

The Referendum Experience in Europe. Edited by MICHAEL GALLAGHER and PIER VINCENZO ULERI. Basingstoke: Macmillan, 1996. Pp.x + 254, index. £14.99 (paper). ISBN 0-333-67018-3.

Ian Budge seeks to defend direct democracy by showing both that it is technically feasible and that it is a threat neither to representative and party institutions nor to good government. Many of the attacks on it, Budge believes, criticise a straw man, direct democracy as a continuous and unmediated mass meeting of citizens. In fact, even in ancient Athens, there were primitive political parties, while Pericles, a professional politician if ever there was one, built an organisation not unlike that of a modern political party. In the modern world, direct democracy, just like representative democracy, would be regulated by parties, interest groups and single-issue groups.

Thus the contrast between direct and representative democracy is too sharply drawn. It makes far more sense to see them, not as two distinct alternatives, but as points on a continuum, from a party-based direct democracy, the Athens of reality rather than the Athens of myth, to a pure representative system, such as that, for example, of The Netherlands. The real issue is not whether one or other of two extreme forms should be adopted, but the precise balance between representative and direct elements in the political system.

Budge analyses findings showing that a greater element of direct democracy would not lead to the evils feared by its critics. Moreover, direct popular voting has become more feasible in the world of electronic technology of the late twentieth and twenty-first centuries than it was in the world of print and postal technology of the early twentieth century, for the essence of the new technology is that physical proximity is no longer required for participation. 'Mass participation', as Budge points out, 'can be carried on interactively even when individuals are widely separated'. We no longer have to meet together in the *agora* if we wish to participate.

The New Challenge of Direct Democracy is the first work to analyse the effect of direct democracy on political parties, and Budge is particularly good at undermining the thesis of the 'decline of parties'. Sweeping generalisations about party decline, Budge believes, find no support from the evidence. For parties are 'in rude health, active everywhere, endlessly adapting to new political circumstances, and hence monopolising government office and electoral competition. Fears for their survival simply fly in the face of the facts or base themselves on unsubstantial speculation about the long-term effects of the media.' It is a magisterial verdict, and one difficult to controvert.

There is, therefore, much that is original in the book. It is, however, badly organised and very repetitious. The theoretical analysis of democracy and participation is weak, while the discussion of countries using referendums frequently, such as Switzerland and Italy, is over-simplified. The student needing to gain a more accurate picture of the complexities should consult the chapters on those countries in *The Referendum Experience in Europe*. Moreover, the analysis of the relationship between modern technological advance and democracy is less sophisticated than that in F. Christopher Arterton's *Teledemocracy*, published in 1987. Nevertheless, *The New Challenge of Direct Democracy* constitutes a genuine addition to the literature. It clears up many misconceptions, and makes a powerful case.

The Referendum Experience in Europe derives from an ECPR conference in Madrid in 1994. It contains highly detailed chapters by country experts, including a short chapter on Russia, the former Soviet Union and eastern Europe, by Stephen White, together with an introduction and conclusion by the editors. The editors and contributors face the problem of competition from Butler and Ranney's *Referendums Around the World*, published in 1994, in which the present reviewer contributed a long comparative chapter on the western European experience of referendums. The editors modestly state that their work 'sets out to build on, that of Butler and Ranney, not to supersede it'. This in fact underestimates the value of the book. The individual chapters are uniformly of very high quality, and serve to combat some misconceptions, including one or two factual errors in the present reviewer's chapter in the Butler/Ranney volume.

No small part of the value of the essays in *The Referendum Experience in Europe* is that they conform to a common framework of analysis, each chapter containing sections on the constitutional provisions, the historical experience and the nature of voting behaviour in referendums. The concluding chapter by Gallagher is of particular value in undermining many preconceptions. It is, for example, widely believed that the use of referendums is increasing in western Europe. This, however, is largely because of the massive increase in referendums in Switzerland and Italy and the upsurge in Ireland. For the other 15 states in western Europe, there were 22 referendums between 1969 and 1995, and 24 from 1945 to 1969. Thus, 'Far from being addictive – the appeal of the referendum appears to pall with use.' This is partly because many of the immediate post-war referendums were concerned with regime change, and we would 'expect the number of contests to decline as west European states have adopted a common form of political organisation'.

However, Gallagher's argument that the referendum is not intrinsically a conservative weapon is fallacious. Admittedly, 50 per cent of the referendums between

1945 and 1995 in Europe were for change, with only 39 per cent being for retention of the status quo. However, a referendum, where it is constitutionally required, cannot be a 'vote for change'. It can only *endorse* a change already decided upon by government. The referendum, like an effective second chamber, must, therefore, as a matter of logic, be a conservative institution.

The editors are, rightly, careful about drawing any general conclusions. They seem to share the view of Butler and Ranney that the historical experience of referendums fails 'to fit any universal pattern'. Gallagher's puzzled conclusion is that 'Perhaps in the end we simply cannot avoid treating each country as *sui generis*. Even after every quantifiable fact has been taken into account, the use or non-use of the referendum is to some extent the product of specific historical experiences and traditions.' Political science is unlikely to find laws on the model of those in physics, economics or even psychology. Instead, political science takes its place as a new way of looking at history, as part of an essentially historical discipline.

The Referendum Experience in Europe is an important addition to the literature in an area which now looks as if it will be subject to the law of diminishing returns in so far as further research is concerned.

VERNON BOGDANOR
Brasenose College, Oxford

Territorial Competition in an Integrating Europe. Edited by P. CHESIRE and I. GORDON. Aldershot: Gower, 1995. Pp.xv + 317, index. £40. ISBN 1-85972-112-5.

The European Union and the Regions. Edited by BARRY JONES and MICHAEL KEATING. Oxford: Clarendon Press, 1995. Pp.xiii + 306, 14 tables, index. £35. ISBN 0-19-827999-X.

The Regions and the New Europe: Patterns in Core and Periphery Development. Edited by MARTIN RHODES. Manchester and New York: Manchester University Press, 1995. Pp.xiv + 359, 11 figures, 36 tables, index. £45. ISBN 0-7190-4251-8.

It has become fashionable in academic circles, at least in Anglo-Saxon countries, to express scepticism about the notion of a 'Europe of the Regions'. Yet, books continue to appear with increasing regularity about this very phenomenon or, at least, about 'Regions in Europe'. It is true that we should express scepticism about the notion of a 'Europe of the Regions' in a strong sense whereby the phrase means a federalist Europe in which regions have somehow replaced nation-states as the key political units in an integrated Europe. This was indeed the goal of European federalists such as Alexandre Marc and Denis de Rougement who were active in the European Federalist Movement, but there is little sign either that the nation-state is about to disappear or that we are on the verge of a fully federalist Europe. However, a 'Europe of the Regions' has been developing in a rather different sense. In this scenario, because of 'windows of opportunity' opened up by both increasing European integration and changes in the role and functions of nation-states, regions of various kinds are emerging as key players in a new political game which embraces the entire European Union.

The three books under review, each written from a different disciplinary perspective, offer interesting case studies, mostly within member-state perspectives, outlining some of these developments. *The European Union and the Regions* is an updated and revised version of an earlier work by Keating and Jones published in 1985 with the title *Regions in the European Community*. However, the current work is much more than a revamp of the original. Only some of the original chapter authors have contributed to the present volume. The most important difference, as the editors point out, is the dramatic change in the contexts within which the two books have been written. In 1985, regions in the then EC were regarded as peripheral both geographically and academically. In 1995, the 'regional question', now including developed regions, has moved to centre stage and is producing a burgeoning academic literature.

The European Union and the Regions is still based on a country case-study approach with two chapters of a broader nature – 'Europeanism and Regionalism', Michael Keating and 'The Role and Evolution of European Community Regional Policy' by Harvey W. Armstrong – and a general conclusion by Barry Jones. Keating's introductory chapter examines the link between European integration and different kinds of regionalism – 'top-down' and 'bottom-up' – as well as some of the main factors that have led to the current upsurge of regionalism, such as globalisation and the changing nature of the state. Some of the country chapters are also very valuable as surveys of the 'regional question' in those countries. The country chapters almost all confirm the phenomenon of regional mobilisation as a result of both internal pressures toward decentalisation and pressures and opportunities which result from increasing European integration.

Some of these are already well-known such as the cases of Belgium (L. Hooghe), Spain (F. Morata), France (R. Balme) and Italy (C. Desideri) but readers may also be intrigued to learn of regionalisation occurring in The Netherlands (F. Hendriks, J. Raadschelders and T. Toonen) and the United Kingdom (M. Keating and B. Jones). Of course, countries such as Ireland (M. Holmes and N. Reece) and Greece (K. Featherstone and G. Yannopolous) are still resisting internal regionalisation while Portugal (A. Pereira) has not yet implemented the regional dimension of its 1974 Constitution, with the exception of its islands, the Azores and Madeira. Nevertheless, even in these countries there are pressures to set up some form of regional administration if not government.

It is interesting to read the work edited by Martin Rhodes immediately after the Jones/Keating volume. Its analytical approach and economics orientation usefully complements the more descriptive nature of the latter. Rhodes and his team accept that there is a debate about *the significance* of the upsurge of the 'regional question' in Europe and whether regions are important political actors or whether the EU is strengthening the nation-state. The basic assumption of the authors in this book is that subnational policy makers across Europe may influence the forces that shape their futures. However, the authors use the word 'region' in different senses. The first two chapters by Paul Chesire (European Integration and Regional Responses) and by Michael Parkinson and Alan Harding (European Cities toward 2000: Entrepreneurialism, Competition and Social Exclusion) mean city-regions or metropolitan regions. The rest of the book uses the term region in the traditional sense of a territory with or without a regional government between the central state and the province. Sonia Mazey, a political scientist, contributes a valuable chapter on regional lobbying.

Other chapters have an approach based in economics. Philip Cooke, Adam Price and Kevin Morgan write on regulating regional economies such as Wales and Baden-Württemberg. Mick Dunford has an excellent analysis of Rhônes-Alpes. Chris Moore provides a useful analytical framework for discussing the Scottish Development Agency. Adam Tickell, Jamie Peck and Peter Dicken look at the North-West of England as a fragmented region. All of these chapters contribute valuable insights into the nature of contemporary European regionalism but it is probably a mistake to treat city-regions as basically the same kind of phenomenon as the traditional sub-state region. In fact, it is a moot point which scenario, if any, is the more relevant for the future development of Europe. Nevertheless, the book hangs together well and pushes forward the debate about the significance of regions in Europe.

The final book, *Territorial Competition in an Integrating Europe*, is edited by Paul Chesire and Ian Gordon. Chesire wrote the chapter on this theme in the Rhodes book and is here again concerned with the role of cities. This book is the most focused of the three as it provides the first results of a research project called TeCSEM (Territorial Competition in the Single European Market) funded in part by the Economic and Social Research Council. The book is divided into three parts. Part I provides the context and attempts to raise broader questions related to territorial competition although the three chapters are, in fact, case studies of Mälardalen, Germany and the Randstad respectively. The chapter on the Randstad by Bramezza, van den Berg and van der Borg is particularly good. Part II deals with the 'demand side', that is, what companies look for before making the decision to invest in particular cities. It too consists of a series of case studies: the South-East of England; Milan and central Veneto; another chapter on Milan, Stockholm and Zurich. Part III deals with the 'supply side', that is what localities have to offer. These chapters are more general and less based on case studies although Milan and London figure again. This division is rather artificial as it is difficult in most of the chapters to speak of one side without at the same time referring to the other. Decisions to invest are in fact the result of protracted negotiations between several different sets of actors. However, the book is very useful as it gives us a large amount of empirical data related to these decisions as well as much information about the relative position of cities in a Europe where these geographical entities are forced to compete with each other in order to be economically viable and provide a good standard of living for their inhabitants.

We have thus, in these three books, moved from the traditional understanding of regions as territories and levels of government and administration between the central state and the provincial to an understanding of regions as cities in competition with each other. What is needed is further analysis which brings out the connections, if any, between the two kinds of region. Does a successful region in the first sense also need a successful city-region? Does competition between these two levels harm or benefit them? A good example would be Catalonia and Barcelona. Perhaps we will see another edited book on this topic.

JOHN LOUGHLIN
Cardiff University, Wales

Divided Nations: Class, Politics, and Nationalism in the Basque Country and Catalonia. By JUAN DIEZ MEDRANO. Ithaca, New York, and London: Cornell University Press, 1995. Pp.xvii + 236, 27 tables, an appendix on sources, biblio, index. Cdn $38.66. ISBN 0-8014-3092-5.

The prevalent political tendencies in Quebec, Scotland, Belgium and Spain attest to the importance of substate nationalist movements in the industrialised West. Therefore, it is not surprising that substate nationalism has increasingly become a topic of scholarly attention. In this respect, Diez Medrano's book is a welcome contribution that moves beyond a historical description and aims to discern generalisable attributes of the Basque and Catalan nationalisms through a comparative approach. Diez Medrano's main focus is on the differences between these two nationalist movements despite their almost identical backgrounds. Both regions are ethno-linguistically different from the larger polity; they have both faced Francoist repression; they both constitute the most industrialised and prosperous regions of Spain; and both have attracted large immigrant populations from the rest of Spain.

Despite these similarities, Basque nationalism is separatist and radical, whereas Catalan nationalism has been federalist and moderate. According to Diez Medrano, existing theories on nationalism can help explain the emergence of these nationalisms, however these theories are incapable of accounting for the differences between them. Therefore, he devises his own model for explaining the persistent contrast. His model is based on the divisions within these sub-state nations, which explains the title of the book. Diez Medrano places emphasis on the differences in socio-economic structures. While a capital goods-based Basque production pattern firmly entrenched that region within Spain and thus led to the dependence of the middle classes on the rest of Spain, Catalan specialisation in consumer goods gave the middle classes relative political autonomy. Anti-Francoist Catalan nationalism was thus a middle-class phenomenon in contrast with its radical Basque counterpart. As a consequence, in the Basque country, revolutionary separatists monopolised the anti-Franco movement, while in Catalonia the opposition consisted of various groups across the political spectrum.

Divided Nations is strongest when Diez Medrano tells the history of both nationalisms. It is a well-researched and comprehensive work, and he is able to capture the complexity of each case while retaining the comparative angle. However, when he tries to generalise from his findings, his open-ended plausibility probes make the arguments rather hesitant. The concoction of theories that Diez Medrano uses captures the idiosyncratic elements of the two cases, yet such tailor-made frameworks of analysis rarely have applicability elsewhere. The book provides a comprehensive account of the Basque and Catalan sub-state nationalist movements, however the *post-hoc* explanatory model smacks of retrospective determinism and is probably of limited transportable quality.

Diez Medrano concludes by stating that the findings of his study reveal that 'except in explaining the emergence of the *idea* of nationalism, no special theory of nationalism is required' (p.197). Maybe this is precisely why a separate theory about nationalism is required: what makes nationalism such a forceful idea that can surpass and encompass all other social bases of collective action? At the end of the day, *Divided Nations* is a good book on Basque and Catalan nationalisms, and would be useful not only for Iberian specialists but also for students of sub-state nationalism.

CAN ERK
McGill University, Montreal

Catalan Nationalism: Past and Present. By ALBERT BALCELLS, edited by GEOFFREY WALKER. London: Macmillan, 1996. Pp.xv + 226, further reading, index. NP (cloth); £12.99 (paper). ISBN 0-333-62260-X and -62261-8

The translation of Albert Balcells's seminal work *Catalan Nationalism* is a welcome addition to the field of Iberian Studies and, more generally, to the study of national movements in Europe. First published in Spanish in 1991, the book was a resounding success. It has now been expertly translated by Jacqueline Hall and edited by Geoffrey

Walker. It provides a readable and comprehensive historical analysis of the development of Catalan identity from the ninth century to the present day. It will also be useful for anybody interested in the politics of modern-day Catalonia as it traces the ideologies that have influenced the development of political Catalanism. The final chapter offers an up-to-date summary of the first years of political autonomy.

There is little doubt as to Balcells's position on Catalan identity. His is an essentialist vision, based on a collective personality that develops from a shared language. His utopian vision of Europe is one where the nation-states will be replaced by 'the reconstruction of the historical territories of nations, based on their languages'. Indeed, throughout his book, Balcells is eager to emphasise the relationship between Catalonia and Europe.

An excellent translation and helpful footnotes will guide the reader not so familiar with details of Catalan culture and history. It is a pity that in the introduction it is suggested that there are only 'two' kinds of nationalism: 'overbearing' (the example given being Germany in the 1930s) and 'defensive' (used to describe Catalonia, although according to the editor, it has now transformed itself into something 'positive'). This over-simplification is incongrous in a book concerned with furthering our understanding of the complexity of human identity.

SIÂN JONES
University of Wales, Swansea

The Autonomous Elections in Catalonia (1980-1992). By FRANCESC PALLARÉS and JOAN FONT. Barcelona: Institut de Ciències Polítiques i Socials (ICPS), 1995. Pp.71, biblio. ISBN 18118-95.

Public Administration and the Recruitment of Political Elites: Formal and Material Politicization in Catalonia. By JORDI MATAS. Barcelona: ICPS, 1995. Pp.29, biblio. ISSN 1133-8962

There is little up-to-date material published in English on political research in Catalonia so the translation of these working papers from the institute of political and social science at the Autònoma university is very welcome. Established by the Autònoma and the Barcelona Diputació in 1988, the papers reflect research in progress.

The Autonomous Elections in Catalonia describes the structure of the Catalan parliament and outlines the main political forces and the party system before moving on to examining the elections and electoral behaviour. In many ways, this study is already out of date because of recent changes in the Catalan political scene. But this is forseen by the authors, who regard the period as a particular stage in the development of Catalan politics. The main features of Catalan electoral behaviour are (i) abstentionism, (ii) the 'dual vote' phenomenon and (iii) vote orientation. Although the abstention rate is similar to the Spanish average, it increases in the autonomous elections, reaching 45 per cent in 1992. Both structural and attitudinal data imply that increased abstention has nothing to do with any anti-Catalan feeling. Conversely, the authors conclude that it has been more difficult to mobilise leftist social bases, especially the less politicised sectors of the community, and the party that suffers most is the Catalan Socialist Party (PSC). It is a pity that these conclusions are not developed further, since this is an important factor in Catalan politics.

The issue of the dual vote seems to be particular to Catalan political elections. It means that in the general elections, a sector of the Catalan electorate (around a sixth) will vote for a state-wide Spanish party, whereas in the autonomous elections they will switch allegiance and vote for a Catalan nationalist party. The fluctuations mainly involve the Socialist party and Convergència i Unió. One suggestion put forward for this alteration is that the choice in the autonomous elections is more limited, but the authors of this paper propose that the voters involved feel that this is how their interests are best met. Finally, as far as vote orientation is concerned, the results of regression analysis suggest that this is determined by identification with the party, evaluation of the leader, the Left-Right scale as well as by national issues. The overall conclusion reached is that the Catalan party system was stable, and electorally stable as well, during the first ten years of autonomy. But in many ways this is a stage which has come to an end. As the authors themselves point out, in 1992 the situation was already displaying 'obvious symptoms of exhaustion'.

Jordi Matas has examined the degree of politicisation in the Catalan administration. In contrast to the 'Whitehall model', the Catalan administration is formally politicised but the author is particularly interested in determining the degree of 'material politicisation', and especially, the criteria used to recruit candidates. He has focussed on the higher levels of the administration, namely the Secretaries General and the General Directors, politically designated positions proposed by ministers and approved by the President's executive council. Roughly 95 per cent, that is 77 of the 81 officials, were questioned. An analysis of their political affiliation confirms that two-thirds of these positions are assigned to members of the governing coalition parties, CDC (70 per cent) and UDC (30 per cent). To understand the extent of the politicisation during the period of autonomy it is worth bearing in mind that a study carried out in 1981 found that around 18 per cent of the Catalan administration were politically affiliated. There is also a high percentage of officials who come from a background in the private sector (48 per cent), showing a dramatic increase since 1981 when there were only 26 per cent. This link with the private sector has been explained as the result of the strong, often personal ties between CiU and the local banking sector and private businesses.

The report suggests that since the present governing coalition has enjoyed a majority in the parliament over a long period, the role of the administration has been strengthened. The weakness of parliament, combined with the absence of a public service body, and a coalition government, are the basic reasons for this politicisation. Matas concludes that, compared to other autonomous communities, the Catalan administration is one of the most politicized in Spain: 'two out of three high officials are affiliated to one of the parties that together form the governing coalition; almost half of them come from the private sector; one out of five has held an elective public position; and only about 40 per cent are actually employed in the public service' (pp.15–16).

SIÂN JONES
University of Wales, Swansea

Politics of Identity: Ethnicity, Territories, and the Political Opportunity Structure in Modern Italian Society. By O. SCHMIDTKE. Sinzheim: Pro Universitate Verlag, 1996. Pp.366, 17 tables, biblio. DM 89 (paper). ISBN 3-930747-56-1.

The aim of Schmidtke's work is to provide a theoretical framework for the appraisal of 'territorial politics', rather than the traditional methods of analysing 'regionalism'.

The distinction between these two terms is fundamental to the book – yet it is never explicitly outlined. 'Territorial politics' is described as utilising a spatial reference as the basis of identity but – in contrast to regionalism (or nationalism) – it does not rely on specific boundaries to delineate the territory in question (p.20). The description could have been expanded to include the presence of a pre-existing cultural identity as an essential element of regionalism. In territorial politics, this element, although it may be present, is largely superseded in favour of the economic relevance of territory. The tendency to use conceptions of regionalism to understand territorial politics – and the consequent *mis*understanding – provides the *raison d'être* for *Politics of Identity*. In relation to his principal case study, Schmidtke states that the characterisation of the Northern League 'on the basis of prefabricated labels' indicates that 'the applied interpretative tools were inadequate to come to terms with the new type of territorial movement' (p.13).

The book is broadly divided into three parts. The first outlines the growth of territorial politics and its contemporary political relevance. Specific attention is paid to the connection between territory and populism, and the resulting form of 'communitarian populism'. This utilises territory as a source of identity which, in turn, is used as a focus for protest against the national political establishment.

The second section deals with methodological and theoretical considerations. The established methods employed in the analysis of regional and ethnic mobilisation are examined and found to be wanting. Schmidtke rejects the 'individual-based microsocial approach' and 'research operating with broad macro-structural variables' and presents a 'meso-level' approach which focuses on the interaction between the construction of collective identity and political opportunities.

The final, empirical, section of the book centres around two case studies from Italy. The first, the Northern League, represents the new form of territorial politics, while the second, the Sudtiroler Volkspartei, is more in keeping with 'traditional' regionalism. A comparison is made between the two in order to demonstrate how political opportunities helped shape the parties' collective identities, which in turn affected their respective political mobilisation. Schmidtke justifies the choice of two unequal case studies from the same country by the fact that both will be subject to the same external challenges and opportunities. It could be argued, however, that the choice of another form of new territorial movement in a different national setting would have helped to reinforce the validity of his theoretical approach.

Overall, Schmidtke has produced a book which effectively combines theory with empirical work and which is conceptually very rich – possibly too rich, as the focus of the book threatens to become obscured in places. The book is also marred by occasional errors in the use of English and infelicitous phraseology, and contains some factual errors. For example, the date of the formation of the Northern League is given as 1987, rather than 1989 (p.12). None the less, as the case of the Northern League shows, traditional conceptions of regionalism are inadequate to understand territorial politics. *Politics of Identity*, therefore, provides a theoretical framework and a methodology with which an accurate assessment can be made and, as such, should be regarded as a valuable contribution to the understanding of contemporary territorial politics.

RICHARD BARRACLOUGH
University of Wales, Cardiff

European Security. An Introduction to Security Issues in Post-Cold War Europe.
A. M. DORMAN and A. TREACHER. Aldershot: Dartmouth, 1995. Pp.xiii+207, 3
maps, glossary, appendices, index. £40 (cloth); £15 (paper) ISBN 1-85521-604-3 and
611-6.

As the flagship of Darmouth's new series of introductory texts on *Issues in
International Security*, Dorman and Treacher present their readers the dominant
European security themes in European policy-making circles. These themes are
addressed regionally – Western Europe, Central and Eastern Europe, and former
Soviet Union and, last, from a pan-European perspective. The theoretical and
historical contexts are set in chapter 1. Looking at the various definitions currently
ascribed to *Europe*, the authors assess that because none of them is entirely
satisfactory, *Europe*, in security terms, has now become an *essentially contested
concept* (p.3). *Security*, they explain, is now generally seen as a complex phenomenon,
encompassing several dimensions – political, military, economic, social, and
environmental. Although the authors' unit of analysis is the state, they include
transnational issues affecting security on multiple levels.

Chapter 2, on Western Europe, concerns itself with the post-Cold War institutional
rivalries that have plagued the European continent, the national responses of Western
countries to the end of the Cold War, and the impact of American policy changes on
Western European security concerns. The following chapter on Central and Eastern
Europe observes the various movements towards cooperation and competition
between the states of the region. The authors discuss the new general security themes
in the region (such as democratisation, nationalism, and migration) and assess the
impact of the Yugoslav conflict and the emergence of sub-regional groups of states in
the region. In Chapter 4, the authors review Russia's economic, political and foreign
policy problems and conclude that developments on the territory of the former Soviet
Union represent the principal European security risks. The last chapter goes beyond
the state to address pan-European issues, including arms control, terrorism, religion,
minority rights, and the environment.

In a concise manner, the authors have done a good job. However, it is obvious that
their book was written with British students in mind. Many of the examples selected
and the suggested readings testify to that. It would thus have been useful that the
authors provide a more diversified list of readings, drawing on the rich North
American, French and German literature on the subject. With the exception of three
typographical errors, the book is well edited and is recommended to British students
as a basic introductory text on European security issues.

STÉPHANE LEFEBVRE
Ottawa, Canada

The Council of Ministers. By F. HAYES-RENSHAW and H. WALLACE.
Basingstoke and London: Macmillan, 1997. Pp.xii + 340, 34 boxes, figures + tables,
biblio, index. £45.50 (cloth); £14.99 (paper). ISBN 0-312-16410-6 and -16411-4.

Given the paucity of focused studies of the Council – the EU's most pivotal institution
– this book would be welcome almost regardless of its quality. As it happens, the
authors have written an extraordinarily lucid and perceptive study, based on exhaustive
research and close observation.

Hayes-Renshaw and Wallace stick to their remit, but also do an excellent job of placing the Council in the context of the EU's wider institutional system and consensual norms. The book is particularly strong on the Council's fascinating and fast-changing relationship with the European Parliament (Chapter 8). Its general argument is that the Council works remarkably well given the powerful constraints under which it operates, particularly new ones which arise from the Union's enlargement and its post-Maastricht crisis of legitimacy. The authors are not complacent: they offer thoughtful proposals for reforming the Council (p.289) and are unafraid to suggest that qualified majority voting might be desirable at the level of the European Council (p.171). They accept no excuses for the poor records of the Maastricht Treaty's new 'pillars' for the Common Foreign and Security Policy and justice and home affairs.

The book is not perfect. The quite significant differences in attitude, outlook and output between different Councils (i.e. for agriculture, industry, the internal market, etc.), and especially between the General Affairs Council (of Foreign Ministers) and the sectoral Councils, are never really treated in sufficient detail. Some readers may get lost in the middle part of the book. Chapter 4 on the Council's General Secretariat seems longer and more detailed than it needs to be, even given its central (and underestimated) role in EU decision making. Chapter 5 on the Council presidency contains far too many lists, which break the book's narrative and are a poor strategy for stressing the importance of what appear to be 'dull procedural precisions' (p.139). The authors' somewhat bald conclusion (p.296) that not much more can be done to make the workings of the Council more transparent seems at odds with their otherwise detached, critical analysis.

These criticisms should be viewed in the context of what this book achieves. It is certain to be essential reading for students of the EU for many years to come. An instant classic.

JOHN PETERSON
University of Glasgow

Euro-Corporatism? Interest Intermediation in the European Community. By MICHAEL J. GORGES. Lanham, MD: University Press of America, 1996. Pp.xii + 251, biblio, index. $53 (cloth); $34 (paper). ISBN 0-71618-0274-6 and -275-4.

The European Union and National Industrial Policy. Edited by HUSSEIN KASSIM and ANAND MENON. London: Routledge, 1996. Pp.xii + 300, 17 tables, biblio, index. £50 (cloth); £15.99 (paper). ISBN 0-415-14177-X and -14178-8.

Orchestrating Europe: The Informal Politics of the European Union 1973–1995. By KEITH MIDDLEMAS. London: Fontana Press, 1995. Pp.xlii + 821, 10 tables, 20 figures, biblio, index. £27.50 (cloth); £12.99 (paper). ISBN 0-00-686263-2.

Lobbying the European Union: Companies, Trade Associations and Issue Groups. Edited by R.H. PEDLAR and M.P.C.M. VAN SCHENDELEN. Aldershot: Dartmouth, 1994. Pp.xii + 311, 11 tables, 8 figures. £37.50 (cloth). ISBN 1-85521-609-4.

In recent years scholars of the European Union have become increasingly concerned with questions of governance rather than with international integration as traditionally understood. From the vantage point of much contemporary work, the EU should be read not only as an experiment in international relations where the core dilemma is about the surrender of sovereignty by states, but also as a living (proto-) polity riddled with an assemblage of formal and informal actors playing nested games at several levels of action. In the Euro-polity the *telos* of integration is less important than the complex, multi-level interaction of interested actors within an array of institutional forms. The literature is becoming rich, both theoretically and empirically and these four volumes all contribute in a positive sense, albeit in quite distinct ways.

The book by Michael Gorges – a revised version of his doctoral dissertation – explores a somewhat old-fashioned and reasonably well-trodden theme: the dilemmas faced by organised interests when confronted with a new layer of authoritative institutions at the European level whose decision rules present challenges as well as strategic opportunities. As suggested by the title, the empirical focus concerns the peak associations of business and labour, particularly in their transnational ('Euro-group') form and the institutional configuration that fosters quasi-tripartism in the EU. The book is well-organised and the argument is made with coherence and clarity. Its claim to originality and, as suggested on p.190, superiority over other studies resides in the use of a 'modified neo-institutionalist' theoretical framework. The unsurprising conclusion is that 'institutions matter' and an unkind critic might suggest that such reasoning is inevitable in the light of the way in which the study has been set up theoretically. The bigger difficulty with the book rests with the rather underdone theoretical exposition which runs to a few pages in the introduction. This does not really do justice to the multi-faceted nature of contemporary institutionalist political science as exemplified by the recent flow of institutionalist contributions to EU studies. The consequence is that the book already looks a little dated, but that should not detract from Gorges's useful empirical work.

Lobbying the European Union is much less theoretical, but may prove to be a more useful and enduring reference point. The book brings together academics and practitioners in an exercise of what might be called dense description of 14 very specific case studies of lobbying in the EU context. At first sight the cases may seem impossibly recondite to all but the dedicated specialist on lobbying, but the authors are careful to lay out the issues very clearly. Additionally, more often than not the general lessons for lobbying (as an object of study as well as in a practical sense) in the EU context are identified and discussed. The collection is prefaced by a very intelligent essay by Marinus van Schendelen about organisations, institutions and political interventions in general and the peculiarities of EU 'public affairs' as distinct from national policy systems. This chapter in particular would be more than useful to give to all students of EU policy making.

What makes reflection upon lobbying so important is that it is an instance of 'informality' in policy making which is a potentially decisive shaper of policy outcomes. One of the important side-effects of the 'governance turn' in EU studies is that informal policy dynamics are being investigated seriously. Which brings us to the massively ambitious, sporadically brilliant and often infuriating book by Keith Middlemas. Middlemas is rightly revered for his extraordinary body of work on twentieth-century British political economy, notably in works such *as Politics in Industrial Society* and the three-volume masterpiece of *Power, Competition and the State: Orchestrating Europe*, which is beguilingly billed as 'the book that reveals how to get the most out of Europe' in the accompanying publisher's blurb, is an attempt to apply the techniques of contemporary history to the EU. The book is an exercise in so-called 'élite oral history' and relies on a mass of interview data accumulated by

Middlemas and his team. It commences with a historical account of post-war integration, including two solid chapters by Richard Griffiths which cover the period between 1945 and 1973. This is followed with substantial chapters on the supranational institutions, the member states, the regions and various other 'players' of the EU game ranging from individual companies to central banks. The product is a major contribution to chronicling the complexity of the multi-level EU polity. It is a dense read and its sheer size may stop it from becoming a 'must buy' for undergraduates. Having said that, the book should be used to supplement existing texts, particularly given its emphasis on informal policy dynamics.

The book deliberately raises an important debate about how best to study the EU. For Middlemas, historians can offer much because by standing aloof from 'often highly theoretical and unempirical debates' (p.671), they can provide a detailed cartography of actors, their interests and the games they play over time. This is not the place for a detailed rebuttal, but it is worth pointing out that the most sophisticated work on the EU has to be theoretical for two reasons. First, there is the argument that it is impossible to abdicate from theory in the way suggested by this book. Second, it is the recognition of the sheer complexity of the Euro-polity that has led scholars to develop increasingly sophisticated *theoretical* schema to manage and interpret their empirical data. Even 800 pages cannot do justice to the intricacy of the EU as a whole, although Middlemas's 800 pages are worth engaging with more than most.

Also of manifest importance, but emerging from the EU studies mainstream, is the volume edited by Kassim and Menon. This takes a serious look at the interplay between EU action and state autonomy, which the editors note has been rather neglected in the EU policy literature. This work can also be located in the move away from the analysis of 'history-making moments' in the study of the EU towards the everyday and the regulatory. The book is well integrated and each of the chapters has something to offer to students of the EU from the advanced undergraduate upwards. Jeremy Richardson offers a significant essay on actor-based models in EU policy making, which should be immediately consulted by anyone emerging from reading Middlemas. There are empirical chapters on steel, aerospace, energy policy, water, high technology, TV, R & D, and banking and financial services. The virtue of these contributions is that they point out clearly why 'high politics' is not everything in the EU and the circumspect conclusion by Menon and Jack Hayward points helpfully to the way ahead for future research. There is evidently still much to be done, and in spite of the important contributions made by these books, we are only still examining the tip of the iceberg that is EU governance.

BEN ROSAMOND
University of Warwick

Racism and Society. By J. SOLOMOS and L. BACK. London: Macmillan, 1996. Pp.xii + 252, 7 figures, biblio, index. £40 (cloth); £12.50 (paper). ISBN 0-333-58438-4 and -58439-2.

Racism and Society is much more than a wide-ranging survey of the issues and debates surrounding race and racism in contemporary Western societies. Along with a comprehensive coverage of aspects as diverse as the theoretical perspectives used to analyse race and racism, the practical public policies adopted to counter racial discrimination and the representation of 'race' in popular culture, Solomos and Back provide their own challenging critique of the various ways in which the phenomena of race and racism have been both understood and addressed. For example, having clearly traced the way in which the theoretical analysis of race and racism has developed from the sociology of race relations, to Marxist and neo-Marxist approaches and, more recently, to feminist and post-modern positions, the authors go on to suggest that any such attempts to present a general theory of race and racism should now be abandoned for a much more historically specific and contextualised approach. The idea of race, they argue, is neither rigid nor fixed. Likewise, there is no single, monolithic definition of racism to be found. Because of this they favour an approach in which the meanings of race and racism are always 'located within particular fields of discourse and articulated to the social relations found within that context' (p.28).

This approach informs their subsequent analysis of the politics of anti-racism and the politics of difference. While a crucial force in contemporary society, they argue that anti-racism still has some way to go with regard to shedding a fixed, essentialised notion of race and embracing, instead, more fluid and transforming notions of race and ethnicity. On the other side of the coin, they argue that care must be taken by those who endorse the politics of difference not to end up simply celebrating cultural hybridity as something that is good in itself – Nazism (not to mention contemporary neo-fascism) was, they point out, also a cultural hybrid.

The authors readily admit that they do not have all the answers to the questions raised by their critical analysis of such issues – they see *Racism and Society* as 'a beginning rather than an end' (p.203). It is, I would argue, a very stimulating beginning, prompting us not only to think more carefully about what we mean when we talk of anti-racism and multi-culturalism but also to reconsider the very way in which we seek to analyse contemporary racisms.

ROSE GANN
University of Central Lancashire

Die Politiker. Edited by H. DACHS. Vienna: Manz, 1995. Pp.632. 780 Austrian schillings. ISBN 3-214-05964-5.

This book provides useful information on individuals in Austria who have played a part in shaping contemporary politics. The politicians selected come from a variety of different parties and their contributions and impact vary considerably. Inevitably in a work of this kind some omissions seem unaccountable such as Jörg Haider of the Freedom Party and former chancellor, Franz Vranitzky.

The book attempts to classify types of politicians which include the polarisers, conciliators, the professional types, the managers, the movers and stars (some fallen). The individual contributions provide photographs, short biographies and further literature as well as a study of the politicians' lives and careers. Many politicians have become legends in their own time such as the trade unionist Anton Benya, fervent advocate of Austria's social partnership. The former 'crown princes' of Bruno Kreisky, such as Hannes Androsch, Leopold Gratz and Karl Blecha, are also included. None of these succeeded Kreisky, the great communicator, who is discussed in masterly fashion by Wolfgang Müller. Kreisky addicts are still thick on the ground in Austria and Müller helps to explain some of the fascination with the cult. As chancellor, Kreisky was an aristocratic-style politician with a popular touch. He could joke with journalists and his telephone number could be found in the book. He was approachable, stylish, entertaining and showed leadership. In retrospect he got many things wrong, but this kind of politician seems an endangered species.

Other contributions in the book deal with politicians who have since become more famous, such as the provincial governor of Salzburg, Franz Schausberger. Thomas Barmüller, former Freedom Party politician, turned Liberal is now also better known than when the book was written.

An interesting study by Anton Pelinka is made of former president, Kurt Waldheim, seen as a typical career for the Austrian Second Republic. In all, this compendium provides concise information on personalities in Austrian politics.

MELANIE A. SULLY
Diplomatic Academy, Vienna

Secrets of Life and Death, Women and the Mafia. By R. SIEBERT (English translation by L. HERON). London: Verso, 1996. Pp.xiii + 333, 1 map, biblio. £45 (cloth); £14 (paper). ISBN 1-85984-903-2 and -023-X.

Mafia Women. By C. LONGRIGG. London: Chatto & Windus, 1997. Pp.xxii + 266, 1 map, biblio. £16 (cloth). ISBN 0-7011-6509-X.

Since the early 1990s, the Italian state's fight against organised crime has been greatly intensified, encouraging an important number of criminals to become state-witnesses. Consequently, it is now possible to scrutinise more closely the different Italian Mafias and some of their more unfamiliar aspects such as the role played by women. English readers now have the opportunity to learn about this complex subject with these two studies. They present an overview of the role of women, but also distinguish between the different Mafias and how, for instance, the Camorra [Neapolitan Mafia] in contrast to the Sicilian Mafia does allow women to have prominent roles.

Both Siebert and Longrigg have attempted to understand the role of women in organised crime, but they have ended up writing very different books. Whereas Siebert, a German scholar, produces a personal analysis of the Sicilian Mafia and the 'Ndrangheta (Calabrian Mafia), Longrigg, a *Guardian* reporter, produces a journalistic account of women in organised crime – their lives, loves and losses.

Siebert divides her book into three sections: Mafia through the prism of gender, women with the Mafia and women against the Mafia. It is her examination of the concept of gender in the Mafia which is particularly innovative, compared with the other two sections which cover familiar ground. In this first section, she uses a vast amount of documentation with great subtlety to show how these Mafias have ambivalent attitudes towards the 'feminine': they are 'male-only societies', dealing daily in 'masculine' activities: death, money and power, with the consent and support of mothers, wives, daughters and sisters, while nevertheless keeping them ruthlessly subordinate. She analyses their different characteristics such as the use of the family within which mothers are revered, the resort to violence, the glorification of hunting and the tradition of murderous vendettas to show how they construct a contradictory ideology, the Mafia ideology, based on misogynist popular cultural codes, yet deeply rooted in the strong matriarchal system which exists in southern Europe. In this way, Siebert challenges the notion that women are silent victims, suggesting that it is their complicity, as transmitters of cultural values and name-lenders which, in addition to their domestic tasks, form the solid foundations of these violent organisations.

Women, she argues, are responsible participants, profiteers and are ultimately guilty of Mafia conspiracy.

Siebert's discussion takes place within a theoretical framework based on a comparison between the Mafias and German Nazism. She argues, by looking at the literature on Hitler's regime, that they are very similar in terms of objectives and methods with the key aim of destroying human rights. This may be taking the analysis a bit far, but it does transmit that overwhelming feeling of powerlessness and imprisonment that law-abiding Italians must have when confronted with these pervasive Mafias in their everyday lives. This book is well worth reading. It is elegantly written and well-documented, presenting a new exciting analysis of the Sicilian and Calabrian Mafias as seen through the perspective of gender.

Longrigg undertakes a similar type of study using much the same material. She, too, attempts to understand the role of women in the different American and Italian Mafias because she also believes that they are just as guilty as men. Indeed, this book was undertaken by her in response to a 1983 Palermo judgment which declared women incapable of Mafia crimes because of their sex.

Her book has two sections: (1) Mafia women and (2) how changes in the law have revealed the role of women. She uses original first hand material (interviews with important protagonists such as Pupetta Maresca, whom she has met) to discuss the issues. This is a refreshing aspect of the book especially for a more academic reader. However, because it does not have a theoretical framework or clear definitions, the subject matter at times appears confused, comprising the usual stereotypes with some surprising factual errors. For example, she quotes a Calabrian judge who suggested that the only way to stop the transmission of criminal culture was to 'sterilise' people. Either she does not understand the concept of culture or she has no sense of humour! Ultimately, Longrigg's is an entertaining and ambitious book which tackles interesting questions, but raises issues which may be beyond the scope of the subject.

These two books are important as they introduce English readers to the enigmatic lives of women in the Mafia: their plight, their contradictions and their courage such as that of Rita Atria, daughter and sister of Mafiosi, who became a state-witness and committed suicide out of desperation when the public prosecutor, Paolo Borsellino, was murdered. Through these books it is hoped that her words will be better understood: 'the only thing that scares me is that the Mafia State will win' (19 July 1992).

FELIA ALLUM
Brunel University

Civil Society and State Relations in Sweden. By M. MICHELETTI. Aldershot: Avebury, 1995. Pp.xi + 200, 9 figures, biblio. £35. ISBN 1-85972-037-4.

Foreigners have often either lauded Sweden as the 'prototype of modern society' or lambasted its rulers as 'the new totalitarians'. (These phrases were in titles of books written in 1970 and 1971 respectively.) Similarly, cursory examination of the literature on the 'Swedish model' depicts its interest organisations as large, centralised monoliths, while the visitor to the country is struck rather by the ubiquity of smaller groups and clubs. Micheletti's excellent book describes a tremendously pluralistic society, with centralised corporatism confined to particular eras.

Although it is surprising to find no mention of Mancur Olson, Micheletti's theoretical approach is nevertheless rigorous. She envisages distinct 'waves' of collective action in Sweden. For example, the first, up to the mid-1880s, involved struggle for political freedom, which spawned (*inter alia*) free churches and temperance societies. The second, from which the powerful trade unions sprang, was animated more by aspirations for economic rights. More recently Sweden has undergone 'repluralisation'. Some groups, such as the trade-union and employers' confederations, had become entrenched in public policy making. Others had become almost absorbed by an 'expanding state' (p.80). The boundary between state and civil society had blurred; questions began to be asked about democracy and accountability. Amid a new individualist *Zeitgeist* (a much used term), such groups lost members to newer social movements, green and feminist ones especially. Indeed, the author also examines the 'life cycles' – genesis, institutionalisation, maturity, stagnation and possibly self-renewal – that groups appear to undergo.

Micheletti takes a swipe at scholars who have glorified the 'golden ages' of Swedish collective action organisations, or exaggerated the consensualism of the corporatist system (it was, she claims, a precariously balanced 'cold war' between labour and capital). Most importantly, she recognises explicitly that much collective action has been based on social-democratic political hegemony, which in turn depended largely on a growing economy. Corporatism was underpinned by non-zero-sum deals on sharing an ever-growing cake. When, from the 1970s, growth slowed, increased conflict was the consequence.

An abridged and translated version of earlier work, this is written in generally clear American English. An index would have been welcome, as might more thorough proof-reading of the English draft (I doubt whether the plural of NIMBY can be NIMBIES). But the book could usefully be added to reading lists for courses at any level on interest groups or European politics – although its price might make it one for the library rather than the private bookshelf.

NICHOLAS AYLOTT
Keele University

Party, Parliament and Personality: Essays Presented to Hugh Berrington. Edited by PETER JONES. London: Routledge, 1995. Pp.xi + 229, index. £37.50 (cloth). ISBN 0-415-11526-4.

Written in honour of Professor Hugh Berrington on the occasion of his retirement from the Chair of Politics at the University of Newcastle-upon-Tyne, *Party, Parliament and Personality* is a stimulating collection of specially commissioned essays addressing many of the themes that Hugh Berrington was most interested in during his distinguished career.

The often overlooked or underestimated importance of individual circumstances and characteristics in influencing the behaviour and decisions of MPs is clearly illustrated by Ivor Crewe and Anthony King in their study of the formation of the Social Democratic Party (SDP) in 1981. Challenging the common assumption that the MPs who formed the SDP were merely right-wing revisionists who had grown disillusioned with the leftward drift of the Labour Party, Crewe and King suggest that a crucial yet neglected variable was the relationship between individual MPs and the Labour movement, via Constituency Labour Parties, local government service and trade unionism. Those Labour MPs who left to form the SDP were those who tended to have the weakest relationship with the labour movement, while those with stronger more enduring links, were inclined to stay and 'fight, fight, and fight again to save the Party' they loved. Thus, personal characteristics and circumstances influenced political behaviour at least as much as disagreements over policies and ideology did.

The 'unwisdom' of explaining intra-party disagreements over policy primarily in terms of a left–right ideological division is endorsed by Philip Daniels and Ella Ritchie in their essay on the impact of the European issue on Britain's two main political parties. For example, while acknowledging that Conservative hostility towards the European Union (particularly further integration) is strongest among MPs on the right of the party, Daniels and Ritchie emphasise that 'contemporary divisions within the Conservative Party over Europe are complex, and cut across the traditional left–right cleavages … of domestic policy' (p.94). Thus, we are reminded that while prominent Conservatives like Lord (Geoffrey) Howe and Lord (Norman) Tebbit are undoubtedly on the right of the Conservative Party with regard to domestic economic policies, the latter has always been much more hostile towards the EU than the former; Lord Howe believing in the inevitability of closer European integration, whereas Lord Tebbit insists that parliamentary sovereignty is inviolate and indivisible.

The role and significance of parliament itself provides the basis of three chapters, with Iain Mclean, for example, providing a critical evaluation of Berrington's own ground-breaking work on backbench opinion in the House of Commons, and suggesting ways in which such studies might be developed further today on the basis of new knowledge and methodologies, coupled with the availability of computer databases and information technology. The outcome of applying these new methods and facilities, Mclean suggests, would yield much more sophisticated, yet accurate, explanations of backbench opinions and behaviour than traditional ideological classifications or typologies.

Meanwhile, Miller, Timpson and Lessnoff provide a fascinating study of the British electorate's own attitudes towards Parliament, from which the conclusion is drawn that 'public support for the doctrine of parliamentary sovereignty is … weak, and likely to weaken still further … It is a doctrine of lawyers, textbooks, and government propaganda, not a doctrine of the people' (p.178).

Party, Parliament and Personality is a worthy testimony to a distinguished career. Not only has Peter Jones assembled an esteemed list of contributors writing on topics which reflected the academic interests of Hugh Berrington himself, many of the chapters contained therein challenge some assumptions taken for granted in political science. In this respect, the book simultaneously looks back over Hugh Berrington's career whilst skilfully taking his ideas forward. A remarkable achievement in honour of a remarkable scholar.

PETER DOREY
University of Wales, Cardiff

INSTITUTE ON WESTERN EUROPE
Columbia University in the City of New York

A Call for Papers

The 16th Annual Graduate Student Conference

The Changing Face of Europe
March 25-27, 1999

The Organizing Committee of the 16th Annual Graduate Student Conference seeks papers addressing economic, political, cultural and historical perspectives of the new Europe as it approaches the millennium and proceeds toward greater integration. We seek submissions from all disciplines. Potential topics include, but are not limited to, immigration and labor issues, the changing role of the nation-state, gender and family issues, Economic and Monetary Union and other challenges of deepening and widening the European Union.

Submissions **must** adhere to the following guidelines for consideration:

- Papers must be written in English.
- Submission (only one will be considered per author) must be an original work which has not been previously published.
- Papers should be 20-50 pages in length, double-spaced with citations, and include a one-page abstract.
- Footnotes and bibliography must follow the Modern Language Association (MLA) guidelines documentation style.
- Papers must be submitted in hard copy AND in Microsoft Word format on a 3.5" diskette—faxes or e-mails will not be accepted.
- Please do not include any identifying information on any page other than the title page of the paper.

Eligibility Authors must be enrolled in a degree-granting graduate or professional school program.

Selection Papers are selected on a competitive basis in an anonymous referee process. All decisions made by the Selection Committee regarding eligibility and awards are final.

Travel & Accommodations The Conference will pay for presenters' travel and accommodations during the Conference. Please note only one author per paper will be accommodated in the case of co-authored submissions.

Awards Presenters will compete for three awards of $500 each.

Submission Deadline Papers **MUST BE RECEIVED** by December 31, 1998.

Please direct inquiries to   Ashley Gross or Stephen Tobey (e-mail: st237@columbia.edu)
at the Institute on Western Europe
Phone 212-854-4618, facsimile 212-854-8599 or on the Internet at
http://www.columbia.edu/cu/sipa/REGIONAL/WE/iwe.html

Send submissions to   Student Conference Organizing Committee
Institute on Western Europe
420 West 118th Street
Mail Code 3337
New York, NY 10027 USA

Notes for Contributors [1998]

West European Politics is a refereed journal.

Articles submitted to *West European Politics* should be original contributions and should **not** be under consideration for any other publication at the same time. If another version of the article is under consideration by another publication, or has been, or will be published elsewhere, authors should clearly indicate this at the time of submission.

Each manuscript should be submitted in duplicate. Articles should be typewritten on A4 paper, on one side only, **double-spaced** and with ample margins. All pages (including those containing only diagrams and tables) should be numbered consecutively.

The standard length for articles is 25–28 A4 pages (including about 40 endnotes). The article should begin with an indented and italicised summary of around 100 words, which should describe the main arguments and conclusions of the article.

Details of the author's institutional affiliation, full address and other contact information should be included on a separate cover sheet. Any acknowledgements should be included on the cover sheet as should a note of the exact length of the article.

All diagrams, charts and graphs should be referred to as figures and consecutively numbered. Tables should be kept to a minimum and contain only essential data. Each figure and table must be given an Arabic numeral, followed by a heading, and be referred to in the text.

Following acceptance for publication, articles should be submitted on high-density 3½ inch **virus-free** disks (IBM PC or Macintosh compatible) in rich text format (.RTF) together with a hard copy. To facilitate typesetting, notes should be grouped together at the end of the file. Tables should also be placed at the end of the file and prepared using tabs. Any diagrams or maps should be copied to a separate disk in uncompressed .TIF or .JPG formats in individual files. These should be prepared in black and white. Tints should be avoided, use open patterns instead. If maps and diagrams cannot be prepared electronically, they should be presented on good quality white paper. If mathematics are included 1/2 is preferred over ½.

Each disk should be labelled with the journal's name, article title, lead author's name and software used. It is the author's responsibility to ensure that where copyright materials are included within an article the permission of the copyright holder has been obtained. Confirmation of this should be included on a separate sheet included with the disk.

Authors are entitled to 25 free offprints and a copy of the issue in which their article appears.

Copyright in articles published in *West European Politics* rests with the publisher.

STYLE

Authors are responsible for ensuring that their manuscripts conform to the journal style. The Editors will not undertake retyping of manuscripts before publication. A guide to style and presentation is obtainable from the publisher.

Authors whose first language is not English should have their article read and corrected by a competent English linguist. Short sentences, short paragraphs, simple, clear phraseology, and direct tenses are distinct virtues. Foreign words should be underlined.

Quotations should be in single quotation marks, double within single. Quotations of five lines or more should be indented, without quotes. British spellings and punctuation (double quotes inside single quotes) to be used throughout, including the -ise ending in organise, politicise, etc., and per cent rather than percent or %. Dates in the form 5 September 1990; 1994–98; the 1990s.

Sub-headings should be in capitals, ranged left; sub-sub-headings in italics, also ranged left. They should not be numbered.

NOTES

Notes should be kept to a minimum, be double spaced and numbered consecutively through the article with a raised numeral corresponding to the list of notes placed at the end. In this list numbers should not be raised and should be followed by a full point, not a bracket. Harvard-style and bibliographical references are unacceptable.

(a) Books: Italicise all titles of books. Give author, title, place of publication, year and page reference.
e.g. Richard Scase (ed.) *The State in Western Europe* (London: Croom Helm 1980) p.87. [NB three commas are now deleted.]
(b) Articles: Place titles of articles within *single* inverted commas. Italicise the title of the book or journal in which the article appears. Cite journal volume, number and part, date of publication, and page reference.
e.g. F. Attiná, 'The Voting Behaviour of the European Parliament Members and the Problem of the Europarties', *European Journal of Political Research* 18/9 (Sept. 1990) p.557 [NB one comma deleted].

BOOK REVIEWS

Title (underlined), author (in capitals), place of publication, publisher, date, number of pages and illustrations, price and ISBN. The reviewer's name (in capitals) and affiliation (in italics) should be ranged right at the foot of the review.

Ecology and Democracy

edited by Freya Mathews

What is the optimal political framework for environmental reform - reform on a scale commensurate with the global ecological crisis? In particular, how adequate are liberal forms of parliamentary democracy to the challenge posed by this crisis?

These are the questions pondered by the contributors to this volume. Exploration of the possibilities of democracy gives rise to certain common themes. These are the relation between ecological morality and political structures or procedures and the question of the structure of decision-making and distribution of information in political systems. The idea of 'democracy without traditional boundaries' is discussed as a key both to environmentalism in an age of global ecology and to the revitalisation of democracy itself in a world of increasingly protean constituencies and mutable boundaries.

288 pages   0 7146 4252 5 paper £18.00/$22.50
1996

Frank Cass Publishers

Newbury House, 900 Eastern Avenue, Ilford, Essex, IG2 7HH
Tel: +44 (0)181 599 8866 Fax: +44 (0)181 599 0984
North America: c/o ISBS, 5804 NE Hassalo Street, Portland OR 97213 3644
Tel: (800) 944 6190 Fax: (503) 280 8832
Website: http://www.frankcass.com E-mail: sales@frankcass.com

THE KURDISH QUESTION AND TURKEY

An Example of a
Trans-state Ethnic Conflict

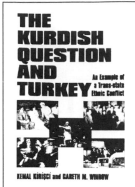

KEMAL KIRISCI and GARETH M WINROW

This book provides a comprehensive examination of the Kurdish question in Turkey, tracing its developments from the end of the Ottoman Empire to the present day.

The origins and evolution of the Kurdish question are discussed through a close examination of events immediately before and after the founding of the republic of Turkey, when Atatürk and his supporters were confronted with the dual task of building a nation and a modern state. The historical narrative and analysis runs up to the 1990s and focuses on the recent acknowledgement by certain key politicians in Turkey of a 'Kurdish reality'.

However, in order to acquire a better understanding of the Kurdish question in Turkey, the regional context must also be taken into account. It is a trans-state ethnic conflict and PKK forces, which are active in Turkey and aim to establish an independent Kurdish state through violent means, have been able to find sanctuary, especially in northern Iraq in Kurdish-populated areas.

256 pages	0 7146 4742 2	cloth	£32.50/$47.50
1997	0 7146 4304 1	paper	£17.50/$25.00

Frank Cass Publishers

Newbury House, 900 Eastern Avenue, Ilford, Essex, IG2 7HH
Tel: +44 (0)181 599 8866 Fax: +44 (0)181 599 0984
North America: c/o ISBS, 5804 NE Hassalo Street, Portland OR 97213 3644
Tel: 1 800 944 6190 Fax: 503 280 8832
Website: http://www.frankcass.com E-mail: sales@frankcass.com

PRIVATIZATION IN EASTERN GERMANY
A Neo-Institutional Analysis

Herbert Brücker, *German Institute for Economic Research*

This book gives the first comprehensive analysis of privatization and restructuring by the Treuhandanstalt in East Germany. It also addresses the theoretical and conceptual problems of large-scale privatization in the transformation process.

The study first discusses the effects of different privatization procedures in transition economies on the allocation and distribution of property rights, using the framework of the neo-institutionalist approach. Second it investigates the privatization strategy of the Treuhandanstalt under the specific macroeconomic and institutional conditions of German unification. Finally it analyses the problems of the agreement and enforcement of employment and investment objectives in privatization contracts under incomplete information, based on a game-theoretical model.

304 pages 1997
0 7146 4335 1 paper £24.50 / $37.50

GDI Book Series No 8

Frank Cass Publishers

Newbury House, 900 Eastern Avenue, Ilford, Essex, IG2 7HH
Tel: +44 (0)181 599 8866 Fax: +44 (0)181 599 0984
North America: c/o ISBS, 5804 NE Hassalo Street, Portland OR 97213 3644
Tel: 1 800 944 6190 Fax: 503 280 8832
Website: http://www.frankcass.com E-mail: sales@frankcass.com

Hungary 1956 - Forty Years On

Hungary 1956
– Forty
Years On

edited by
TERRY COX

edited by TERRY COX

This collection of new articles offers a retrospective view of the events of the 1956 revolution in Hungary, the consequences they have had for Hungary's political development since, and the significance of 1956 in current Hungarian politics. Different articles draw on the findings of various kinds of research, including work in documentary and archival collections that have only recently been opened up, sociological survey research and, in some cases, on personal reminiscences as well.

This volume provides new information on such questions as the nature of support for the revolution, the response of the Soviet army in Hungary, diplomatic politics concerning the events in Hungary, and the way the decision to intervene was taken within Soviet ruling circles. A further article reports on a sociological survey of the views of schoolchildren on the 1956 revolution and their views on its relevance to current Hungarian politics, and discusses the relation between the formal history of 1956 and private family histories of the period.

168 pages   1997
0 7146 4766 7   cloth   £30.00/$45.00
0 7146 4309 2   paper   £16.00/$24.00

Frank Cass Publishers

Newbury House, 900 Eastern Avenue, Ilford, Essex, IG2 7HH
Tel: +44 (0)181 599 8866 Fax: +44 (0)181 599 0984
North America: c/o ISBS, 5804 NE Hassalo Street, Portland OR 97213 3644
Tel: 1 800 944 6190 Fax: 503 280 8832
Website: http://www.frankcass.com E-mail: sales@frankcass.com

Subscription Order Form

To place a subscription order for this journal, please fill in the order form below (photocopying it if preferred) and return it to us.

Please enter my subscription to

WEST EUROPEAN POLITICS
Volume 21 1998

Quarterly: January, April, July, October

UK/Overseas   £40 (Individuals)   £170 (Institutions)
USA $65 (Individuals) $245 (Institutions)

(All individual subscriptions must be accompanied by cheques drawn on a personal bank account and may not be paid for by institutions or by organizations)

I enclose a cheque for £/US$ ———

Please charge my
☐ Visa   ☐ Mastercard   ☐ American Express

Card Number _____

Expiry date _____

Signature _____

Name _____

Address _____

_____

_____

Tel: _____ Fax: _____

FRANK CASS

UK/OVERSEAS:

**Newbury House,
900 Eastern Avenue,
Newbury Park, Ilford,
Essex, IG2 7HH
Tel: +44 (0)181 599
8866
Fax: +44 (0)181 599
0984**

NORTH AMERICA:

**c/o ISBS,
5804 NE Hassalo
Street, Portland,OR
97213 3644
Tel: (800) 944 6190
Fax: (503) 280 8832
E-mail: jnlsubs@
frankcass.com**

For more information on all of our publications please visit our website: http://www.frankcass.com